JEAN-PHILII
WITH LUKE SHULLENBERGER

DANCING

WITH

DEATH

REVISED EDITION

AN INSPIRING REAL-LIFE STORY OF EPIC TRAVEL ADVENTURE

Revised Edition 2021

ISBN: 978-0-9843448-4-0 Paperback
ISBN: 978-0-9843448-3-3 eBook

Published by Native Planet Adventures
www.jeanphilippesoule.com

DEDICATION

I dedicate both this book and the expedition to my grandfather, Pierre Soulé, who passed away on the last day of December 1999. Although he never understood the meaning of this expedition, he traveled with me until the last stroke. This book is also dedicated to two of my strongest supporters who also died during CASKE2000: my maternal grandfather, Floris Lentenois, and my close friend and soul mate, Gilles Lacouture, who died in a bicycle accident two months prior to our Baja launch. Finally, I also dedicate this book to Liz Farr, who became the vice-president of Native Planet and helped me edit this entire book. She passed away before having a chance to see it published.

DANCING WITH DEATH

BELIZE

HONDURAS

NICARAGUA

COSTA RICA

PANAMA

AN INSPIRING REAL-LIFE STORY OF EPIC TRAVEL ADVENTURE

CONTENTS

PROLOGUE

A Paddle into the Past with an Eye to the Future

Jean-Philippe

As this journey unfolded, it became an experience that we just couldn't keep to ourselves, so both Luke and I regularly wrote journal entries and stories that we posted on our website. To share the essence of this expedition and to better illustrate our different personalities, experiences and opinions, we've opted to weave Luke's best entries intermittently with mine in the order that the events unfolded. Here, the journals are presented to you in the present tense, while some special feature stories are written in the past tense. This co-authored approach represents our finishing this expedition together as partners—a critical challenge from the moment of our very first paddle strokes in Baja California.

↑

EMAIL SENT TO John "Caveman" Gray from Sapporo, Japan, November 20, 1997:

Dear Caveman,

I have been a silent member of the sea kayaking mailing list for
eight months and it is clear that you are one of the most

knowledgeable people on the list, as well as the one everybody turns to with seamanship questions. I'd like to seek your guidance.

For the last two years, I have been planning the Central American Sea Kayak Expedition 2000 (CASKE2000), a three-year, 3,000-mile paddle that will take us across seven countries from Baja California to Panama, alternating between the Atlantic and Pacific coasts.

It is a two-man expedition, and both Luke and I are world-class athletes who have competed at the highest levels—Luke in cross-country skiing and myself in mountaineering. We really need your help because I have never even sat in a kayak and Luke has only had a half-dozen experiences on the Great Lakes. Currently working in Japan, we cannot afford kayak lessons, but we need the skills and expertise to survive whatever the ocean might throw at us. You seem to be the most qualified experienced instructor and we are keen students. We hope to stay in Thailand for training from April 1st until the end of June, then launch on October 1st, 1998.

We have a marginal budget and would like to ask you to be our first sponsor. Because you are a leader in ecotourism and conservation, I know that you will find the mission behind our expedition compelling.

The CASKE2000 goal is to experience and write about the culture and lifestyle of the native peoples we will meet. We know that the lifestyles and skills of Indigenous peoples are one of the keys to the preservation of our earth's precious ecosystems so, as we learn how they live from the land and the sea, we'll become self-sufficient ourselves. We plan to document the way they live and the influence of development on their environments and lives, and then use a variety of media to make people aware of their humanitarian, environmental and cultural preservation issues.

We chose sea kayaking as a low-impact way to penetrate untouched jungles and their inhabitants without disturbing them. We won't meet Indigenous people as high-tech tourists, but as people like them, living from the land and sea.

I believe that our expedition would be a perfect way to promote your kayak ecotours while furthering a cause important to you. We realize all the dangers we will be facing, but are very determined and hope that you will provide us with the training and experience we need in kayaking and seamanship to lead this expedition safely and successfully.

Yours truly,

Jean-Philippe Soulé

Expedition Leader, CASKE2000

↑

I knew this letter was a long shot; I didn't expect John "Caveman" Gray to instantly lay down a red carpet all the way to Thailand. After spending eight months as a silent observer on the paddling mailing list, I knew of only two people who would be able to train us in the time frame we had: Caveman, nicknamed for his extensive kayak explorations and tour guiding through the numerous Hawaiian sea caves, and Ed Gillet, a living legend of sea kayaking. In 1985, Ed had paddled sixty-four days, solo and unassisted, from Monterey, California, to Hawaii, an exploit unmatched to this day. We were hoping that Ed, owner of a kayaking operation in San Diego, would help us fine-tune our skills just prior to our departure, but we couldn't afford to live six months in the U.S. prior to the expedition. Because we had a lot of gear to buy and our savings had to last the three years of the expedition, I hoped that we could do the bulk of our training with Caveman in Thailand, but I knew that I'd have to do some fast talking to get him to take us under his wing.

↑

My childhood fascination with the jungle cast a permanent spell over me, leading me on expeditions all over the world. The roots of this expedition lie in one such adventure on a remote Indonesian island in the early 1990s: I spent four months in an isolated Mentawai community, immersed in an environment and lifestyle I could not have imagined, even in my wildest dreams. Stories of Mentawai black magic first lured me to Siberut Island more than a decade ago. I was traveling on a cargo boat from the island of Nias to the port of Padang, the capital of West Sumatra, Indonesia, when the ship dropped anchor about eighty miles from Padang, off the coast of Siberut, the largest of the four main islands in the Mentawai archipelago. I was peering at the dense jungle across the water when dozens of dugout canoes suddenly appeared, racing toward our vessel. Had it not been for the women and children accompanying these strong tattooed men, and their cargo of coconuts, bananas, durian fruits and rattan, I would have thought they were pirates!

Over the frenzy of excited conversation and haggling on the deck below, the boat captain told me: "These wild Mentawai live inside the jungles of Siberut. They dress only in loincloths and are feared by all Indonesians for their practice of black magic and their use of deadly poisonous arrows." Although I was bound for the wilderness of Irian Jaya, this first encounter with the Mentawai would change my travel plans—and my life—forever.

I had faith in my physical ability and in the survival skills I had learned during my two years in the French Special Forces, but knew I needed experience in the jungle before heading back to Siberut, so I went to the rainforests of Irian Jaya (West Papua) to train with a local expert. I studied Indonesian there, although I knew that in the more remote villages, few if any people would speak the national language. There, outsiders must develop a keen instinct and perception of gestures and energy flow to communicate; I was confident that my experience in massage therapy, Chinese meridians and Thai healing techniques would serve me well. After months in Irian Jaya, I felt ready for the challenge of Siberut. I landed on the island, spent a few days acclimating in coastal communities and then headed for the interior. From there, I set off on a six-week expedition that ultimately lasted more than sixteen.

Two weeks into the trip, slogging through sticky, knee-deep mud, I was making slow progress through the dense jungle. I had to keep the river in sight at all times—it was the only guide that could lead me to the Mentawai village of Matotonan—since the village didn't appear on my map and had seldom been visited by white outsiders since an Italian missionary first set foot on the island in the 1950s.

In Matotonan, I hoped to find a Mentawai who could guide me to the settlement of the Sakudei people, made famous by Dutch anthropologist Reimar Schefold, who, only a few years earlier, had been the first westerner to live with a traditional Mentawai clan. During my first evening in Matotonan, the primal beating of drums rising above the cacophony of the jungle's nocturnal creatures caught my attention. I left my host and strolled along the dark trails, following the captivating music. I noticed the flickering orange blaze from a fire and I could hear deep, hypnotic chants accompanying the drums. A man came out to the trail to meet me, shook my hand and brought his hand to his heart. He was a young apprentice *sikeirei* (Mentawai shaman) named Martinus. A magical evening of fireside chanting followed and I thought I had found my guide to the Sakudei, but Martinus had other plans. "You don't need to go see the Sakudeis," Martinus told me. He invited me to move into his *uma* (communal long house) and live with his clan so they could teach me what I wanted to learn. I was struck as much by the incredible energy of his spirit as I was by his words. Later, Martinus told me that months ago I had appeared to him in a vision and two days earlier, knowing that the time was right, he had come to Matotonan to await my arrival. I tried to explain that I could not possibly be the man in his vision; I was just a tourist interested in the rainforest and its people and I had no special power to help the Mentawai. Martinus looked at me, paused for a few seconds and laughed. We never talked about it again. It was the beginning of a friendship that transcended all borders and a dream that would answer my childhood calling and fulfill my fantasies about jungle living and Indigenous peoples. For three and a half months

I shared Martinus' *sikeirei* training, experiencing a world I could never have imagined.

There, I had both time and occasion to reflect on the way we live in the "modern" world and about the people we call "primitive." Each successive day affected me so profoundly that I could not bring myself to leave. They even offered to build me a house so I could live with them permanently. I remained undecided for weeks, but finally realized that I must return to the developed world and lend myself to the struggles of Indigenous groups trying to preserve their lands and cultures. I gained a sense of the deep harmony with which the Mentawai live in their natural surroundings—it is not what I learned about the jungle there that made the most difference to me, it is what I learned about Mentawai wisdom, life and about myself. Their unique egalitarian society, combined with their tremendous knowledge and respect for their natural environment, make them ideal role models for balanced sustainable communities.

Upon returning to the States, I experienced severe culture shock. Although my dire financial straits forced me to look for a job, I still yearned to travel and experience foreign cultures. Going to Japan offered me an excellent compromise: I was able to earn good money while studying a new language and learning about the complex Japanese culture. While working there as an English teacher, I also had time to spend researching subjects dear to me: jungles and Indigenous people. I found that the Mentawai were not the only traditional people at risk; Indigenous communities worldwide have much in common, including the multiple threats of modernization. As developed countries became more aware of wildlife and natural preservation, people still seemed unaware of the life, culture and rights of native people. I soon realized that these unknown people never receive help. They vanish as silently as they have lived. For two years, I considered the best way to bring attention to their plight.

I realized that I could not help the Mentawai effectively by returning to live on Siberut. I was neither a talented writer nor an anthropologist and had no money or connections, so I had to find another way to educate and inspire people. I realized that I needed to break into popular media. To do it, I also had to find a place closer to the States that appeared on tourist maps, and I had to link it with a trendy sport. Adventure travel and extreme expeditions were hot topics and sea kayaking was one of the fastest growing outdoor activities in North America at the time. For my purposes, it would also become a way to travel long distances, carry loads of food and equipment, and access remote jungle villages. Although I had never been in a kayak, I decided in the winter of 1996 that it would be my craft of choice and I would travel the coast of Central America from Mexico to Panama.

Thus CASKE2000, the Central American Sea Kayak Expedition 2000, was born. I envisioned a journey that would take me into the next millennium as I passed through ancient lands and lifestyles: a paddle into the past with an eye to the future.

Although originally planned as a solo expedition, my friend Luke Shullenberger joined me in the preparations in November 1997. For years, many friends and travelers have asked us how we first met and later decided to venture on such a journey together—and how we have remained friends since we seem to bicker all the time. Tired of repeating the same tale many times over, Luke put it into words.

↑

The Genesis of a Friendship

Luke

The party line is that it was love at first sight and that, with a joint bank account, cohabitation and only another year to wait until our relationship becomes common law marriage, we squabble just like any other couple. A few people are left uncomfortably silent by this explanation but most pick up on the smirk and wink, then laugh. Whatever the reaction, it always works as a great prelude to the real story.

Prior to the expedition, until April 1998, we were both living in Japan. We each spent nearly four years there, with Jean-Philippe based out of Sapporo the entire time while I spent two years in a small town in Northern Hokkaido, followed by two more in Sapporo.

The short version is that we met on the starting line of a cross-country ski marathon. We both love winter and getting out into the mountains and woods to enjoy it. We share a love of nature and of physical challenges that both put us in the middle of it and pit us against it. However, as far as our respective involvements in cross-country skiing go, this is where the commonalities end.

The longer version starts on a clear, cold day in January of 1996. I was lined up on the starting line of the Sapporo International Cross-Country Ski Marathon and looked to my right to find two other foreigners on the front line among the thousands of Japanese entrants. It was a self-seeding start, where if you're fast you start at the front and if you're a weekend warrior you take your rightful place in the middle or the rear of the starting corral. I had raced at the national level in high school and college. Seeing those two on the front line, I figured they were a couple of ringers, hotshots working for a Japanese firm or something.

Bengt was from Sweden and had raced a bit as a youth, and then there was Jean-Philippe. He looked the part, with racing skis and a nice Lycra suit, but something wasn't quite right. I first felt it when he asked me questions about his equipment: "Is my wax okay? Is there a left or a right binding? How about pole straps?" After a few minutes I came to find out that he'd started cross-country skiing only two weeks before and had signed himself up for a ski marathon after being encouraged by Bengt and some friends. I was quite surprised and a bit amused, and commented about it being a self-seeding start and that the appropriate way to line up was according to ability. But it was too late and the race was about to begin.

Jean-Philippe finished eleventh place in a field of over 2,500 on that day and we have been great friends ever since. From backcountry skiing the highest peaks in Hokkaido to kayaking in Thailand, we continue to challenge and inspire each other. Jean-Philippe usually leads the way and I try to keep up. And even though I finished ahead of him, taking the silver medal that day, it was a humbling experience. And so, with mutual respect tempered by the heat of competition and the understanding that comes from true friendship, we set off together on this odyssey.

↑

The Plan

Luke, Late 1998

I remember vividly the night that Jean-Philippe told us about his plans to paddle from Mexico to Panama. It was late in the summer of 1997 and we were enjoying our lifestyles as settled expatriates in Sapporo, Japan. We'd both been there a couple of years and had easy jobs, spoke the language and hung out with a wonderfully diverse international community. Jean-Philippe chose the weekly Friday-night dinner party in my apartment as the moment to share his proposed adventure. About twenty people were chatting away in different directions when he started. All eventually stopped and turned to listen as snippets of his plan filtered through their own conversations. A few in the group, who thought many of his other tales to be outlandish and apocryphal, assumed he was bluffing. Someone asked if he'd ever been in a kayak. He hadn't. Someone asked if he spoke Spanish. He didn't. I asked him if I could come along and he flat out said no. "It's a solo expedition," he replied. "I've never met anyone who can handle the way I travel and go to the places I go." I was stunned. We were very close friends. We trained together. We raced together in ski marathons. He knew I was a hard-core endurance athlete yet he didn't think I could hack it?

His denial nagged at me and I resolved to change his mind, but I couldn't simply insist that I be allowed to join the expedition. I had to show him that his objectives required my input, or, better yet, come up with some of my own.

Over dinner another evening, I pried more details from him. His concept was to create a website with stunning photos and stories of extreme adventure and to add a cultural component by documenting native communities along the way. "I'm a writer," I suggested. "I can write," he replied. "But you're French," I argued. He frowned and answered curtly, "I was French! My current passport says different."

Needless to say, my first attempt ended poorly.

Over the next few months I was persistent. He listened patiently and I thought I could see his resolve begin to fade. I presented my own goals and reasons for wanting to go. I wanted to write a cookbook on Latin cuisine. I wanted to search for a few quirky stories that would make good magazine articles. I wanted to help him polish the content on the website into a professional product. He was concerned that I would never fully commit to the expedition, that he would do all the work and pull my weight, too. He was worried that I would start strong and then drop out at the first sign of hardship. He wanted assurances from me that I would invest myself both in the website and the mission to promote cultural preservation and that I could endure the physical demands of the trip day after day. So, as is his habit, he described in a hyperbolic fashion the endless hours on the water, camping in monsoons, malarial fevers and other horrors. I ignored his scare tactics and badgered him a couple of times a week, insisting that he needed a quality partner.

One day, after a completely draining cross-country ski training session, I told him point-blank, "I can't let you go alone on this expedition. It's the opportunity of a lifetime for me. I will never organize anything like this on my own and if I don't go now, I'll regret it for the rest of my life. I need to go with you."

He surprised me with his answer: "To be honest, I was already thinking about it. I wanted to test your commitment. Now that you're on board, we'll plan together. I'll come to your apartment next week and we'll work every night, really work! And when I work, I get things done!" I was very excited, but I had no idea what I was getting into: Jean-Philippe turned out to be a zealot.

That first night he showed up with a mountain of paperwork and a computer with a hard drive bursting with files and information. We immediately transformed my living room into an office. He had brochures and pamphlets on kayaks, camping gear, GPS navigational equipment, solar panels, dry bags, paddling shoes, clothing, everything you can imagine. He had done exhaustive research on each Latin American country that we planned to visit and wanted to meet and document every Indigenous community on the way. He spent eight months online joining mailing lists for survival skills, kayaking, Indigenous issues, asking questions of experienced members, establishing local contacts and creating a huge database of information to be used in constructing an itinerary. At 1:30 a.m., after four and a half hours of non-stop examination of his work, I was numb. Jean-Philippe looked at me and smiled smugly, "You look blown away."

I grinned weakly and said, "I'd like to dry up like a leaf and blow away, anything to avoid having to dive into that pile of stuff again."

"Welcome to my world," he replied.

And so it was. In October of 1997 we officially became a team. We planned to leave Japan by April 1998 at the latest and we had mountains to move before then.

One of our biggest dilemmas was training: how do two guys go from zero to expert in six months? Our plan was to leave Japan in April and launch the expedition at the end of September. Jean-Philippe had calculated all the wind and current patterns and we couldn't leave any later than that. It was already the end of November and we needed to have a destination, an instructor and a plan in place as soon as possible. So, naturally, Jean-Philippe thought of his fellow members of the sea kayaking mailing list, anticipating that they would embrace the idea of our expedition and offer support. He quickly learned, however, that novice paddlers must run the flaming gauntlet before being accepted into the community.

One debate in particular caused Jean-Philippe to reconsider using the list's public forum altogether. A young Canadian kid named Max was in the midst of an arduous paddle through massive surf from Canada to Mexico via the Pacific Coast. At one point he even shattered the bow of his Kevlar-reinforced kayak on a surf landing. His sponsor shipped him out a new one and he continued on undeterred. In his accounts of the journey, he made the grave error of mentioning that he had taken a brief ride on a sailboat through a particularly rough stretch. It caused a shocking uproar on the list. Some said that he had irreparably compromised the validity of his expedition by boarding the boat, that there would forever be an asterisk on his claim to have paddled the Pacific border-to-border. Others defended his persistence and courage. Some called his trip a suicide mission and inferred that it was detrimental to the responsible promotion of the sport of kayaking. A few aggressively asserted Max had real "balls" for even setting out on the adventure in the first place and that all armchair-warrior naysayers should "put up or shut up." The arguments went back and forth. Jean-Philippe sifted through all of this and decided that rather than risk being snowed with "advice" from the entire community, he would approach a few elder statesmen from the list privately. He planned initially to keep CASKE2000 under wraps and unveil it with the launch of our website and with our presence at a promotional booth at the summer TAPS Show (Trade Association of Paddle Sports) just prior to launch. And then, "come what may," any commentary would fall on deaf ears as we paddled for two months through the empty expanses of Baja.

There was one ubiquitous presence on the list whose comments, emanating from a far-off corner of Southeast Asia, never failed to generate waves of controversy. John "Caveman" Gray is often described in the same breath as a "brilliant pioneer of ecotourism, environmental preservation and kayaking" and as a "caustic, enigmatic bully on a power-trip." Nevertheless, he impressed Jean-Philippe as someone who possessed both a penchant for brutal honesty and a wealth of indisputable knowledge. Perhaps more than anyone else on the list, his commentary demonstrated a profound understanding of the ocean (we would later learn that he was a former lifeguard and experienced seaman). His tour company, Sea Canoe, was also a highly touted model for responsible ecotourism. However, the true deciding factor was the company's location. We needed a place where the costs of food and lodging wouldn't drain our coffers prior to the expedition. Training in the States or Japan, we would burn through our money. The southern islands of Thailand are breathtakingly beautiful and extremely cost-effective. It sounded perfect, so Jean-Philippe contacted him out of the blue and proposed a training sponsorship.

We were taken aback by Caveman's response. He called our plan suicidal and foolish and was unwilling to endorse it by training us. In so many words, he told us that during his thirty years of experience in and around the ocean he had rescued more than his fair share of idiots and unprepared, gung-ho yahoos. It would be irresponsible for him to give two more the tacit approval to go get into trouble. Combining courage and skills is one thing. Going on courage alone is insane. And in his mind, setting off into the blustery, unpredictable waters of Baja after only six months of training was lunacy, not to mention the three-year itinerary all the way to Panama. Even with world-class skills, he doubted that we could handle everything that the ocean would throw at us over such a long period.

Jean-Philippe sent a very strong reply and insisted that Caveman take us seriously. I remember standing behind him as he typed theemail.

"We're going with or without your endorsement. We'd like to go with some of your knowledge. We're not just a couple of jokers with zero experience in the wilderness. We may not have any kayak experience but we are top-level athletes and we will learn."

And then he bluffed and told Caveman that we had lined up major media coverage for our "big-time sponsored expedition" and that we could give Sea Canoe excellent exposure on our website. At that point, the website had received a total of a couple of dozen hits from friends and family and our only sponsorship was a wholesale discount from Feathercraft. He then closed the mail with a little flattery, hoping that it would seal the deal. "You have years of experience on the water and you are an esteemed authority on ecotourism and sustainable development; our website will promote much of the same ideology throughout Central America and our kayaking expedition is the only way we can make that happen. We need to learn what we will be up against. Nobody can teach us better than you. We would hate to go without your knowledge."

Caveman didn't bite. He responded again with an ultimatum: "Go check out the book *We Survived Yesterday*. I don't want to receive any more emails from you until you've read it."

Minutes after reading Caveman's email, Jean-Philippe ordered the book online. Three days later he had it in his hands and, over a twenty-four-hour period, he read and dissected it. The story was about a group of experienced middle-aged paddlers who waged war against the elements in a month-long, record-setting dash down the wave-strewn Pacific Coast of the Baja peninsula. All had been star athletes and/or adventurers through their teens and twenties. One was a former Navy Seal. One was a body-builder who spent his days in the gym. All of them were tough guys in some capacity. They decided to challenge the record for paddling the Baja peninsula from California to Cabo San Lucas. The four of them stuffed basic gear into two double kayaks and set out. They put in marathon thirty-five-mile days, ate their meals while paddling and only took two break days during the entire 1,000-mile traverse. They nearly died in the waves on multiple occasions. In their book, they recounted in provocative detail their daily battles with the elements, questioned their own sanity and discussed their survival methods and the fine points of the most diffi-cult maneuvers in sea kayaking: launching and landing in huge surf.

Jean-Philippe prepared a book report for Caveman along with a num-bered list of reasons why we would succeed where they had nearly failed. The first reason, which he explained very clearly, was that the nature of our expedition was completely different. We weren't racing. Our purpose was not to set a record. On days with wild weather, we could choose to rest on the beach rather than risk our lives on the water. There was no pressure on us. The second reason was that we were not planning to paddle the Pacific Coast (at least not until Costa Rica and Panama, a year and a half into the itinerary). The interior shore of Baja is much calmer. The third reason was that we had prepared for any and all contingencies. Jean-Philippe had researched the weather patterns, gear requirements and navigational difficulties. We would have everything necessary to survive for weeks if we got stranded or injured. The guys from *We Survived Yesterday* ran into surprises almost every day, as if they had just decided to go and do it without any detailed planning.

Eventually Jean-Philippe filled up a couple of pages with points and counterpoints and sent them off with another brash statement, "Our plans won't change. We're still going with or without your help."

Caveman capitulated a little and agreed to train us on one condition. He expressed serious doubt that we would be able to bring our kayaking skills to a high enough level to handle all the rough conditions along the way. So, we should be prepared to swim out of anything. His challenge was simple: if we could pass the Hawaiian lifeguard open-water swim test, he would train us. On the day we arrived in Thailand, he would take us out to an unprotected beach and we would have to swim 1,000 meters in the open surf without breaking stroke, in less than fourteen minutes. He was sure that his ultimatum would cause us to give up.

I watched Jean-Philippe's jaw drop as he read the email from Caveman. "Shit, I can't even swim the front crawl! I don't know how to breathe." With only four months remaining before our planned arrival in Thailand, we had some serious work to do. It was the last week of November and an early snowfall had already blanketed Sapporo in a beautiful carpet of white. The ski conditions were nearly perfect. Sadly, we put our boots and skis in the closet and headed for daily sessions in the pool.

Jean-Philippe's first phone call was to our buddy Steve, a former competitive swimmer. I could hear Steve roaring over the phone as he listened to Jean-Phi's predicament. "But you're a bloody diver! A certified diving instructor, for fuck's sake! I've seen you hold your breath underwater for two minutes," I could hear him say in his clipped British accent. "I know, I know," Jean-Philippe replied sheepishly, "give me a pair of fins and a snorkel and I'll kick anybody's ass. I just don't know how to work the arms and the breathing together. You have to help me."

The evening after Jean-Philippe's first swimming lesson we all got together for dinner to hear how it went. The two of them could not stop laughing.

"I've never seen anything like it," Steve explained. "The man can swim fifty yards underwater and breaststroke like a frog but you send him off on a lap of freestyle and he's exhausted and floundering before reaching the far wall."

Apparently, Jean-Philippe could not grasp the concept of twisting his head and breathing under his arm in the middle of the stroke. He drank so much water and flailed so wildly that he exhausted himself by twenty-five meters. Steve was pessimistic about his chances. "Man, conditioning is one thing but proper technique is another. You should be happy to swim five hundred meters in fourteen minutes. Forget about a thousand."

If there is one thing that Jean-Philippe hates more than anything else it's pessimism in regard to his abilities. He gets no bigger thrill than accomplishing something someone else said was impossible and doing it in an incomprehensibly short period of time. He is proud to a fault. He may laugh along at comments like that, but inside it burns him up. And although Steve certainly had no ill intentions with his comment, as soon as he said it, I knew I'd be hearing about it from Jean-Philippe almost every day until he proved it wrong.

After three weeks and less than ten lessons with Steve, Jean-Philippe learned functional technique and he began to focus on conditioning. I joined him three days a week at a dingy pool in downtown Sapporo for lap sessions. Both of us had competed at the highest levels in other sports—I had even finished a few triathlons—and in our minds we were talented athletes. Our initial accomplishments in the water proved otherwise. Our first goal was to complete four laps of freestyle without stopping and without lapsing into breaststroke. Little swim team kids watched the two of us, the big, tall *gaijin*, stroll into the locker room and they cowered in the corners tittering amongst themselves: "Sugeei na, aitsu! Mechakucha tsuyoi daroo!" ("Wow, check those guys out! They must be strong!") And then as soon as we jumped in the water and started swimming, the aura of invulnerability washed quickly away as we flailed away for four laps and then sagged into a lazy breaststroke just to keep moving. Needless to say, the tone of our former admirers quickly became one of mockery.

After the first week I completed the 1,000 meters in twenty-one minutes while Jean-Philippe struggled his way to twenty-eight minutes. Within two weeks, the two of us were keeping up with the adolescent group of the swim team. We could do six to eight laps without stopping and we'd throw in a half-lap of breaststroke now and again just to catch a breather. We even started joking around with the kids. Initially they were gun-shy when they realized that the two of us spoke Japanese and had understood all of their disparaging remarks about the "white whales" splashing about in their pool, but soon they were firing away and taking part in a rousing game of verbal one-upmanship. We soon began to taunt the fifteen- and sixteen-year-olds, "We're right behind you guys; the white whales are gonna be kickin' your asses soon!" I suppose it could be said that it was neither fair nor right for us to be battling boys for supremacy of the pool, that we ought to have set our sights a bit higher. But we were both proud and shameless and after a month we became the alpha males of the pool.

↑

Jean-Philippe

Caveman, his lieutenant, Dave Williams, and Ed Gillet ended up training us, but nothing could have prepared us for the shark attacks, brushes with armed bandits and guerillas and the corrupt officials that lie ahead, not to mention the high drama provided by our opposing personalities. In the end, we also survived the constant heat and humidity, insect bites and storms at sea to accomplish more than we had thought possible. It turned out to be a once-in-a-lifetime experience that neither one of us have the desire or the courage to repeat! It all started with our first paddle strokes in Baja, Mexico.

CHAPTER 1
BAJA, MEXICO

San Felipe to La Paz,
8 October – 13 December 1998

Jean-Philippe, 4 October 1998

IN BAJA, IT's feast or famine, Garden of Eden or barren desert, and it all depends on your luck and timing.

↑

I SPEND THE entire evening packing and repacking all our dry bags for our dawn departure and finally go to bed around 1:00 a.m. I am anxious; my mind races and I lie awake all night, flipping from one side to the other every fifteen minutes. The endless preparation and planning over the past few months has exhausted me: I've averaged four hours of sleep a night the whole time. I am tired enough to fall into an endless sleep as soon as my head hits the pillow, yet even my bone-deep fatigue cannot overcome my worry and excitement about the first day of the expedition. For two years I have looked forward to tomorrow. In this, our first attempt at expedition kayaking, we will ultimately go nearly 800 miles from San Felipe to La Paz on the Sea of Cortez. In just a few hours, Luke and I will get up with the sunrise, load our kayaks and begin our odyssey. I know there is no turning back, no matter what, and

I accept the prospect of the many difficulties we will face. I'm not one to invest this much time and not follow through; quitting would waste time, money and energy but those are things that I can find more of. No, for me, the real concern is abandoning a dream so I comfort myself that insomnia is a small price to pay for a dream coming true.

We have pledged to each other that we won't let fear affect our plans: we won't be turned around by it yet I can feel my heart pounding. My head feels thick and heavy, and pulses with more thoughts and worries than I can handle: *Did we forget anything? Do we have all the equipment we need? Do we have enough food and drinking water? Do we have the right camping gear? Do we have the skills necessary to paddle the Sea of Cortez?*

↑

Luke, 4 October 1998

The two of us are in no condition to squeeze ourselves into the kayaks tomorrow and shove off for three years and 3,000 miles, yet here we are. San Felipe has already become the point of no return. Our ride back to California peeled out at dawn yesterday in a cloud of dust. Two days ago, Eddie, our patron saint from San Diego, and his crew of friends delivered us with our mountain of gear to San Felipe, Baja, our launch site. Then they decided that a beer blast in the town's cantinas was an appropriate send-off. Still hung over and out of shape, I am in deep denial. Jean-Philippe appears worse off than I am and he had nothing to drink. Dark bags hang beneath his eyes and his skin looks pale and blotchy in the late-morning sun.

I worry about Jean-Philippe's condition. The eve of our departure is his first chance for a full night of sleep in three months. I worry about the weather, but maybe the storm forming tonight is an omen, forcing us to rest. Still, I resent being this uncomfortable so early in the expedition. My vision for Baja was to nudge the bow of my boat up on a barren stretch of beach, spear some fish for dinner, grill them over an open fire, unfurl my bedroll in the open and wake up with the sunrise. After months of deprivation, sleeping on friends' sofas, scrimping on food to pay for equipment and spending every moment on the phone and in front of the computer screen, that scenario is what we deserve. It's the promise of just such a payoff that kept me going.

↑

Jean-Philippe, 5 October 1998

The weather is not cooperating with us tonight. Outside the room's brick wall I can hear the howling winds growing stronger with each passing hour. It rattles the windows and puts me even more on edge. At dawn, when I step outside to check the water conditions, a full gale, thick with sand, blasts my bare chest and fills my eyes with grit. I look out to the beach and see Luke leaning into the wind trying to stay on his feet. We aren't going anywhere today.

↑

Luke, 5 October 1998

The past year of planning was an exhausting journey in itself: it was more than a full-time job. Weeks became months and months became an eternity; going through the motions for such a long time numbed me and now it takes me a few moments to fully register the wind. The sand stings my exposed skin, airborne gravel clunks painfully against my ankles and slowly, irreversibly, I begin to tremble in fear and anticipation—I'm awakening to reality.

↑

Jean-Philippe, 5 October 1998

The *norte* windstorms of Baja are notorious. They howl out of the Sonoran Desert, across the Fango Mud Flats and then escalate as they funnel through the northern stretch of the 1,000-mile corridor of the Sea of Cortez. What makes them most dangerous at sea is the speed at which they form: the worst winds rise from dead calm to full force in fifteen minutes, transforming the glassy, aquamarine waters of the Sea of Cortez into furious waves. Although the swells never reach the immense size seen in a Pacific storm, they are treacherous due to their irregularity, speed and high frequency. In the desert, those winds can completely cover a large truck with sand in a couple of hours.

Dragging our empty kayaks to the shore to observe the waves, we try in vain to protect our eyes from the stinging sand whipped around by forty-knot gusts, pelting our faces like shrapnel. This kind of northerly wind would push us quickly southward, but it's insane to even think of launching our fully loaded kayaks into these seas. We're not even sure they would stay afloat; we've never tested them with this much weight. The waves seem no bigger than five feet, but their peaks are being blown off in bursts of foam. We decide to launch with empty kayaks to test the conditions. Stroking hard for twenty minutes into the wind and against the breaking swell only gains us a few hundred yards, so before reaching total exhaustion, we turn back and surf in toward the beach. The wind is so strong that we have a hard time keeping a grip on our paddles. As I prepare to land, I lift my paddle too high and the wind catches the blade, capsizing me instantly. In waist-deep water, I stand up and drag my swamped kayak back onto the beach.

The storm is a mixed blessing. I dearly need sleep and am happy for the opportunity to get it, but the forced delay gives me too much time to think. What if a storm like that catches us in our overloaded kayaks in the middle of a large crossing far from shore?

I find that this break heightens my apprehension about the Sea of Cortez. I had chosen to add the Sea of Cortez to our route because I was attracted by one of its nicknames, the "Vermillion Sea," not because I had any wish to challenge myself in stormy conditions. I had read that the colors of the sky and sea merge into broad bands of spectacular colors at every sunrise and sunset. I had heard that the marine life is some of the most incredible on the planet and the area is also renowned for world-class spearfishing. As a scuba-diving and freediving enthusiast, I was enthralled with the idea of putting dinner on the table with a harpoon and a one-breath dive. I had visions of pelicans, frigate birds and desert landscapes. I saw us communing with the desert and the sea down this sparsely inhabited coast, adapting as we moved along. I thought the Baja stage would serve as our paddling school, a nice warm-up for the expedition and an introduction to a bigger dream. Yet more and more, it looks like Baja will turn out to be our proving ground, instead. As I stand on the beach shielding my eyes and leaning into the gale, I think to myself, *If we survive storms like this on our way to La Paz, Baja, nothing can stop us from reaching Panama.*

↑

Luke, 8 October 1998

Mike and Linda Schork, friends of a friend, are graciously hosting us at their beach house south of San Felipe. They were not expecting this weather, either. They have shown award-winning patience with us, but I still worry that our mounds of gear and continued presence are inconveniences. They both assure us that they love having guests. Mike tells us that it's a nice distraction from the normal routine of lounging and beach combing. Linda notices that we are going stir-crazy and takes us on a foray to the local market. It proves to be an eye-opening experience. Shopping for groceries in San Felipe could be more accurately described as foraging.

The rotund mustachioed clerk sits at the register of his dilapidated market and toys with us rookies. "Don't you have any *mas rojo* tomatoes?" I asked. "No, the weather is not so good. Anywhere you go, same tomatoes… have avocados, have eggs, have cilantro. Today's the best, delivery truck come last night. Have melons, have cantaloupe…" Small brown spots of decay, like cancerous moles, cover the exteriors of much of the produce and about a third of it looks completely inedible. What we do buy looks like seconds from suppliers over in mainland Mexico, as if they assume (and rightly so) that the *campesinos* out in the Baja frontier are so desperate for vegetable matter that they'll eat anything. According to Linda, it's one of the biggest downsides to life in the desert. But she'll trade green tomatoes and cancerous melons for ripe sunrises and peace and quiet any day.

Weaning myself from the comforts of civilization takes mental adjustment. The Schorks' little hacienda is more than just a shelter from the storm; it's the last set of walls separating us from the wide-open expanses of a three-year commitment to movement, progress, exposure and danger. Before this expedition, my longest camping trip was a week.

On the morning of October 8th, we awaken to absolute calm and sit on the beach to watch dawn break. The solid black curtain of the sky begins to peel away from the east, revealing bands of brown in progressively lighter gradations: opaque mahogany brown, milk chocolate and light khaki. The browns then shift into deep vermilion, violet, crimson and light pink hues that continue to evolve for half an hour until the buttery sun nudges up over the horizon.

It takes us over an hour to stuff the kayaks and lash the dry bags on to the bow and stern. On the beach, our small entourage, the Schorks and their neighbors, hug us and wave us onward. Linda hovers like a mother hen. Before we drag the boats into the water, she tucks sandwiches and Snickers bars into our deck bags and then stands there, anxiously wringing her hands. The foldable boats are so overloaded that it takes all our strength to drag a single craft across the sand to knee-deep water. We launch into flat glassy water and hold our breaths, waiting to see if our boats will float. The water inches up toward our cockpit coamings and we quickly seal our spray skirts. Whatever doubts we have we smother with false bravado. It's important to make a show of confidence for our nervous hosts, so we stroke briskly, trying to lend an air of lightness and agility to our struggle to maneuver the sluggish boats. "CASKE2000 hits the water!" we yell as we churn away from shore.

After ten miles we pull up on the beach and start to set up camp. The utter silence and desolation of the desert envelops us, but only briefly. Just as we're laying out the tarp and unpacking the cooking bag, I hear the percussive blatting of an engine and a few minutes later Mike, Linda and their neighbors show up in their converted VW bug beach cruiser, with barbecue fixings, pasta salad and box wine, for one last proper meal. It's a touching gesture. They stay for a couple of hours and, as the fire burns down, our hosts, satisfied that we're the capable, adventurous types we claimed to be, drain their cups, throw the cooler in the back and climb back into the buggy. The popping of the engine soon fades into the sibilance of the waves, the nocturnal desert insects and the sighing coals from the fire. The weight of anticipation and worry floated away during the first day paddling and I sleep like a baby. It's great to finally be out.

↑

Jean-Philippe, 8 – 14 October 1998

Our first paddling week has been a combination of beauty and intense suffering. The sunrises and sunsets are spectacular and so is our pain. All of our Thailand conditioning disappeared during the months of inconsistent training before departure. Fortunately, for the first three days, we paddled on glassy water and encountered neither wind nor waves; although those conditions make the heat incredible, they are good things since our kayaks are so overloaded they barely clear the water. The water line on mine is two inches from the cockpit rim and from a distance, all you can see are the large blue, green and red dry bags lashed to the front and rear decks. We must look like two colorful, giant snails inching our way along—and we're not paddling much faster than that, either.

In training we found we could maintain a pace of four and a half knots in choppy conditions. Here, even on flat water with no wind, we struggle to paddle at less than three. Our soft, wet hands chafe against the paddle shafts, opening a mess of split and bloody blisters. The joints of my fingers feel arthritic: they're not used to hours of constant gripping pressure. We have started slowly, covering seventy-five miles in seven days, only paddling an average of four hours a day, but I am suffering incredible lower back pain. The stress of pulling so much weight with each paddle stroke exhausts our upper backs, shoulders and triceps. I know that it's only the first week, but I hope my body adjusts quickly. As it stands, I can't function without the five ibuprofen pills I take at each meal.

Every morning we start paddling slowly for thirty minutes to warm up our sore muscles. My back is so stiff when I wake up in the morning that I can barely move. When the pain becomes unbearable out on the water, I accelerate and focus my mind on something else. A faster and more powerful stroke takes more effort and as a result my body creates more endorphins, which help kill the pain. After an hour of sustained high-level paddling, I no longer feel anything and the pain only returns after I stop, so I don't take many breaks. I know from my exhaustive mountaineering training that the body shuts off past a certain level of pain and exhaustion, leaving the mind in full control. My deep-snow experience of walk or die is quite different from Luke's training as an elite cross-country skier, where one responds to body fatigue and plans rest days as part of the training schedule. Luke can't comprehend my tactic for pain management. It's counter-intuitive to him that, at the moment I start complaining, I paddle harder and leave him behind. On calm seas, with all our bags piled high on deck, we can see each other more than a mile away. I often wait for Luke and when I lose sight of him, I jump in the water to cool off and stretch my back.

Both of us were paranoid about getting stranded without supplies in the desert; we figured we had to be totally self-sufficient for up to three months. Like a couple of car-campers, we completely overpacked. The Sea of Cortez isn't as cold as we thought it would be so, on our very first day, we unloaded my thick wetsuit and sixteen pounds of lead weight from my diving belt on the Schorks. We now have a growing list of equipment we wish we didn't have. At the top of that list is a ridiculous wheeled cart that is lashed to the stern of my boat. We expected to use it to tow our boats up and down the shoreline but now that we are here, we realize that it is completely useless. In the shallow northern waters of Baja, the beaches are rocky and uneven and the huge tides control when you can launch and land. The only thing we can do is time our arrivals and departures with the tide's cycles.

On our second day, we learned a hard lesson about the speed of northern Baja's tides. We stopped for what should have been a short break and partly unloaded our kayaks. We left them on the large slippery rocks covering the beach with sterns still in the water. By the time we decided to resume paddling, the water had already begun to recede. We raced to finish loading, but it was too late: the knee-deep water just behind the sterns drained away at high speed. In less than five minutes, the beach dried up into a wide rock garden and we found ourselves hundreds of yards from the shoreline. Again, the cart was of no help. The only thing we could do was to wait for the high tide to return. Stranded out in the open, we quickly learned our second lesson: we need shade. In Baja the nights may be cold, but the days are deathly hot. We stuck our paddles into the sand and used them as poles to rig the tarp into a tent. It gave us protection from the sun, but not from the heat and we baked for six long hours while waiting for the rising tide.

I had anticipated that paddling long hours would drain us and that we owed ourselves some comforts but it has taken us only a few days to realize that most of those "luxury" items I brought are useless. We know that we can't leave them as garbage on the beach, so it might be a week or two before we can unload them. Christmas will be arriving early this year for the first people we encounter in the few isolated fishing camps and settlements along the northern coast. We will be in danger in the waves if we don't lighten our loads.

↑

Jean-Philippe, 16 October 1998

Paddling five hours a day for over a week on flat water has tested our patience; not even a puff of wind has ever wrinkled the surface. Distances seem longer and temperatures hotter. The entire Sea of Cortez is unnaturally quiet, as if it's conserving its energy for something. On our first long crossing, a twenty-mile paddle out to the island of Miramar, we encounter a raucous sea lion colony. Their bellowing cries create a deafening amount of noise, as if they are warning us of some imminent danger.

↑

Jean-Philippe, 17 October 1998

Since day three, the scenery and marine life have been excellent, but other factors have prevented us from truly enjoying our Baja experience. Our kayaks are still severely overloaded. Our bodies have not yet adjusted to paddling long hours each day. I haven't yet found the right position for my kayak seat and every night my lower back aches. Our skin has not adjusted well to the constant exposure to sun and seawater, and salt is embedded in our pores. Our kayaking skills are rudimentary, so we still find ourselves fighting the conditions rather than adapting to them. And what really hurts us every morning is that it takes us nearly two hours to eat, break camp and repack our kayaks. The true beauty of wilderness paddling comes at a high price, the rate we have been paying for ten days. I hope we develop the toughness and efficiency necessary to complete this expedition soon.

†

Luke, 17 – 19 October 1998

In a way, Baja is a kind of hell. It is spectacularly beautiful and enticing and equally rugged and unforgiving. The coast is alternately edged with steep cliffs and scalloped with deep bays, shallow coves and patches of beach that beckon to boaters and offer them shelter. Stretches of flat desert are punctuated with rolling, eroded formations of red-gold sandstone and multi-hued sedimentary rock. Sunrises wash over you in great expanses of color that fade into lighter gradations all the way to the horizon: mahogany, burgundy, vermilion, crimson, chartreuse and pale straw. And from dawn to dusk, rarely does a wisp of cloud mar the azure blue canopy of sky. However, the stifling heat of the day, the numbing chill of the nights and the deadly windstorms that arise suddenly out of absolute calm temper enjoyment. It's as if Satan, the aspiring archangel, landscaped this stark but elegant rock garden, and upon falling out with God, created a chaotic weather specter that roams the land.

I read that fall is the best and safest time to paddle Baja: the raging summer inferno in the desert begins to cool and the weather is more consistent. All the books and travelers rave about southern Baja and so I remained a bit skeptical about the empty northern half as it receives so little attention. Yet one look at the maps reduced my anxiety. The region is full of place names that impart a sense of security: Islas Encantadas (Enchanted Islands), Puerto Refugio, Bahia de Los Angeles. However, as we approached the straits of Isla Angel de la Guardia (Guardian Angel Island), it began to dawn on us that the original explorers had employed a keen sense of irony when choosing names for many locations in northern Baja. Our bright, cheery outlook began to dim. We are extremely vulnerable here. We can't take anything for granted. We get the sense that were we to let down our guard, it would just as soon rear up and smite us.

Before we left, we had already begun to realize from the reports of Baja aficionados and locals that northern Baja has a bipolar temperament.

They assured us that we would encounter awe-inspiring wildlife and majestic landscapes but at the same time suggested that this area, especially the 100-mile approach to Bahia de Los Angeles, might prove to be the trickiest stretch of paddling in the entire Sea of Cortez.

Sure enough, as soon as we entered that stretch, our perspective changed from unbridled awe to wariness and we began to look for red flags. First were the impressions of our surroundings. The mountains lining the coast suddenly seemed menacing. The serrated, tawny peaks, flayed by arroyos and streaked with mineral greens, became the bony carapace of a sleeping dragon. The marine life seemed to have two faces, as well. During the first few days, we had marveled at pelicans gliding elegantly only inches above the water; golden grouper weaving fluidly through aquatic rock gardens; sea lions languidly bobbing and sunbathing with their fins in the air and dolphins and whales breaching next to us, spewing champagne geysers into the air. Yet soon what we began to notice more were the chaotic realities of the food chain, the feeding frenzies and the death. Pelicans and booby birds dive-bombed schools of yellowtail, large predatory fish chased small fry out of the water, turning it to froth, and occasionally the decomposing hulk of a dolphin or sea lion lay on the shore.

Before approaching the straits of Isla Angel de la Guardia, we spent a day and a half in the emerald cove of Bahia Willard, twenty miles further north. It lulled us into a false sense of peace and security. It's a magical little spot where you can dig clams on the south side of the bay and one out of five casts with your rod will net you a triggerfish or cabrilla sea bass for the evening's ceviche. The cove is a natural theater, with a show every few minutes. The main attractions are the five-foot-long roosterfish: with a brace of long spines that project above the surface of the water when they attack, they chase schools of minnows up and out of the water, shattering the glassy calm.

It's also the home of the Fernández clan, who owns much of the northern half of the bay. They rent cheap land to gringos, operate a restaurant and make tortillas that have become local legend. Papá Fernández, *el patron* and real estate don, is loath to leave such a place; he has spent most of his 107 years there. It is that beautiful.

We should have followed Papá Fernández's example and just stayed put, for our misadventures began as soon as we left Bahia Willard. The channel between Isla Angel de la Guardia and the Baja coast is a treacherous zone where peak tide currents run five to six knots and the winds shift constantly with no discernable pattern. Sure enough, the weather became increasingly blustery as we paddled toward the channel. An undulating satin surface gave way to ripples, then to small swells and, by mid-afternoon, it churned with six-foot rollers with white caps blown off the tops by thirty-knot winds.

The sheer cliffs lining that section of the coast were daunting in their own right, but when viewed from the lurching cockpit of a kayak they were downright sinister. They forced us to keep moving: there was no place to hide from the waves at the base of those walls. Splattered bird guano mocked us as we crept along searching in vain for a sheltered cove. At one point while I was struggling through choppy waves off a rocky point, a large pilot whale sounded twenty feet to my left, blowing a fountain of spray twelve feet in the air. Startled, I nearly fell out of my boat. But it was merely a temporary distraction from my fatigue. We were only halfway to our destination, and the conditions were exhausting me. I began to scour the coast for a protected landing site.

We encountered the first sheltered bay, Campo Calamajue, after eighteen miles. I headed in against Jean-Philippe's wishes—he wanted to continue to a point eight miles further than we had plotted on the map. We approached the shore to scout the landing and were relieved to find it manageable. After hours of battling choppy open seas, we were in no mood to land our overloaded kayaks through big surf. The beach was in the lee of a point and the waves offshore were barely a foot high. People had told us that this beach was nothing special, but even forewarned, we were unprepared for what we saw. Campo Calamajue was little more than a ramshackle collection of huts and fishermen's tents. After long stretches of pristine coast, we had forgotten about the detritus of human inhabitation. The rusty remains of a large fishing boat lay rotting on the sand. A quarter-mile down the shore, clouds of birds swarmed over piles of nets, tackle and heaps of mackerel and squid entrails. Empty food wrappers drifted into our campsite. Clanking cans being blown down the rocky strip startled us as we unpacked.

We made camp, cooked dinner as quickly as possible and, to put ourselves more at ease, we erected our tent to escape the scene before us. Humans often combat fear and disgust in funny ways, constructing flimsy physical barriers just to feel psychologically protected. Though these create little more than psychosomatic safety, they can make all the difference in attitude. Within our walls of nylon, we slumbered.

Then the winds came. Initially, they sneaked into the bay in furtive gusts from all directions, as if testing the outer defenses, and then they escalated in intensity all night long. Gusts rocked our tent, cracked the domed fabric like a whip, sandblasted the sides and bent the poles. After getting up numerous times to tie down and check our gear, we slept a total of one hour. The winds softened with the sunrise, a Baja meteorological phenomenon that happens almost every morning. For us, it was a savior.

We prepared pancakes and coffee and were a bit surprised to receive a visitor. A friendly old man in a worn paisley button-down wandered over. He introduced himself with *hola* and a million-dollar smile. And for a guy with no molars, he made quick work of our offering of sandy pancakes.

We didn't need to use our broken Spanish to understand that it's a tough lonely life out there. After a protracted explanation aided by many gestures, we learned that his wife and five children lived six hours away in Ensenada, on the Pacific Coast. He was here in Campo Calamajue, the biggest scallop operation in Baja, working for pennies a day to support them. We learned that the profits from sales to L.A. and San Diego go mainly to *El Jefe*, the chief of the camp, and to the middlemen, with little remaining for the guys on the lines.

He said *adios* and *buena suerte*, hung around, half amused and half concerned, and gestured to others from the camp. A small entourage had gathered on shore to see us off as we awkwardly loaded our boats in chest-deep water. We were afraid to push off from the steep, rocky beach through the rough shore break in overloaded kayaks, so Jean-Philippe held the boats a few feet beyond the break and loaded the bags as I ferried them out.

We started south out of the bay into a steady headwind. With only eight miles to go to the next camp, we thought it would be an easy day. The wind kept changing directions, blowing out from east-facing canyons on shore, then from the rear, pushing us down into swells, and occasionally from head-on, stinging our faces with spray. The workout was intense and for the last two miles, we progressed very slowly.

Jean-Philippe was suffering. His time in the Elite Mountain Commando Unit of the French Army, carrying half-frozen climbers out of the Alps, had irreparably damaged his lower back. After nearly four hours of struggle, we could see the point before our campsite only a few hundred yards away. His back was cramping and spasming and he drifted dangerously close to rocks on the point. Grimacing with pain, he pulled his boat up onto the first available stretch of beach, flopped onto his back and lay there moaning. In this way our campsite was chosen.

We spent the rest of the afternoon digging in to the rocky shore. Fist-sized rocks and small boulders provided perfect materials for a windbreak so we piled our bags, shored them up with the stones and settled in to follow the storm's development.

Encountering nature in action, I am awed by the physical endowments of wild animals that allow them to cope with the most horrific conditions. My relative frailty as a human being always leaves me feeling slighted by evolution: we must use tools and technology to overcome adversity and can never travel light. So, whenever I see animals struggling against the elements in the environments where they normally thrive, I watch enthralled, and I must admit, a bit vindicated. In contrast, when I'm in mortal danger from waves and a sea lion goes lollygagging by, I feel only resentment.

With no small sense of satisfaction, then, tucked into our niche on the beach, we watched a dozen birds' ludicrous attempts to make their way into the wind. They flapped madly for a few seconds against the constant forty-knot gale and then tucked in their wings and plunged into the waves to float for a moment and rest. They repeated the process ceaselessly but it gained them less than 200 yards in five minutes. What compelled them northward? If the rest of the animal kingdom were either holed up or headed downwind, why were they so stubborn? Surely they knew that the winter winds always blow to the south?

That night was unforgettable. By dusk the wind was gusting to a magnitude neither of us had ever experienced. Its gusts and direction were totally inconsistent, making the simple act of standing impossible. We would lean into the gale and it would suddenly die, letting us sprawl on our faces in the rocks. We anchored the bags and boats with boulders, the diving weight belt and anything else heavy we could find and hoped they would still be there in the morning. Without even considering the tent, we dug a pit as deep into the rocky beach as possible behind our constructed windbreak, then laid out the plastic tarp and our self-enclosed bivouac sacs and zipped our sleeping bags and bodies inside to ride out the night.

Through the tiny hole in the top of my bivy sac, on the dark eve of the new moon, I looked at the stars glistening like diamonds on black velvet. There wasn't a cloud in the sky to obscure my view. Phantom winds buffeted me all night and I watched Orion move across my field of vision in a lazy arc.

We awoke to howling winds and resigned ourselves to staying put for the day. We made it a rest and maintenance day. We lubed spear guns, greased the joints and seals of waterproof Pelican cases with silicon, cleaned camera lenses, recharged camera and laptop batteries with solar panels and filtered fresh water with a reverse-osmosis desalination pump, a handy device that, with much labor added, converts sea water into drinking water. We also thought about friends who were home imagining us, lounging on the beach in paradise, and realized that they have no idea of how much work it takes to keep gear intact and keep on moving.

After a full morning of work, we sat down for the afternoon to read and study Spanish and suddenly the wind changed. It made an about-face and started blowing directly south. We had to take advantage of it, so we began packing in a frenzy. This time, I held the boats steady in the water beyond the shore break while Jean-Philippe carried out the gear. We were such a sight that a passing pod of dolphins altered course to come take a look.

We paddled through the angular light of the afternoon to the next promising spot on the map. I trolled aimlessly for fish, getting nothing from the choppy water. A whale sounded twice next to us and disappeared. Soon after, we paddled up to a group of young sea lions. Immune to jostling from the waves, they were enjoying the last rays of sun, belly up and fins in the air. They appeared dead, only to roll over and dart away upon noticing our presence. Before dusk, we bumbled our way onto yet another beach with crashing surf and slippery rocks. We finished the day by refueling on a carbohydrate-heavy meal of couscous and oatmeal and then sat around the bonfire, sipping herbal tea in silence and lost in pensive reflection.

It seems that the Guardian Angel from the island only watches until her view is obscured by darkness—and demons only come after dark. You can keep the evil at bay for a while with a moat of orange light from the fire, but it's just postponing the inevitable, and wickedness encroaches as the glow from the embers dies. We went to sleep with a handful of coals left in the fire pit and were jolted awake three times in the next eight hours. We awoke first to the unexpected sound of waves crashing close to our heads. We had not expected the tide to rise so high. We bolted upright and ran in a panic to pull our boats higher and then tried to go back to sleep. Two subsequent nightmares left me wide-eyed and sweating in my bag despite the chill. I spent a haunted night on that beach and the long-anticipated dawn was a welcome sight. The crimson glow in the sky and the warmth on my face soothed my nerves.

Day eleven of the trip started like any other placid Baja morning. We were a few miles south of Punta Bluff, with the northern tip of the Angel standing guard. The chill burned off quickly so we shed our long sleeves only a half-hour after sunrise. In a light breeze, I set up the camp chair as best I could among the head-sized rocks washing and rolling around in the shore break and sat down to pump water while Jean-Philippe stretched and tried to work the kinks out of his aching back. My pumping session ended prematurely: I spent thirty minutes administering a deep tissue massage with my elbows since his muscle spasms were not responding to ibuprofen and stretching. Every time I touched him, he winced in pain. Meanwhile the tide rose, the wave troughs deepened and, despite the massage and medicine, both of us tensed up. Even the rocks on the beach seemed to be bracing themselves for some sort of impact.

Our boats were set up at the edge of the boulder field just below the high tide line. In theory, the encroaching tide and rising swell would lift our teetering boats off the shore and out into the shore break. From there, we would paddle like mad to clear the surf zone and be on our way. Jean-Philippe packed up and was ready to go first. Leaning into a northerly wind that tried to shove him sideways, he held the bow of his boat straight out toward the surf zone and nosed it into the first waves. As soon as it was afloat with no friction holding it on the rocks, the wind swept the stern downwind and foaming surf hit it broadside, filling the cockpit and rolling it. He stood, helpless, as the surf tossed and thrashed his submerged kayak on the rocks, ripping gear from the deck and scattering bags, bottles and straps. Watching several thousand dollars' worth of precious equipment being destroyed in front of his eyes, he launched into flailing cursing conniptions.

Fortunately, the Feathercraft lived up to its claims for ruggedness. We were surprised to find no damage to either his boat or gear so we re-gathered ourselves to try again. I watched the wave patterns closely and came up with another approach: a team launch for one boat and a solo push launch for the other. I'd get behind his stern and shove him through the break and then swim out, pushing my boat, and make a wet-entry beyond the surf zone. Yet even as I packed him back into his boat and helped him fasten his spray skirt, Jean-Philippe was doubtful. For lack of any other plan we went ahead and tried it. With a big push he started paddling like a windmill. Somehow he made it out through a series of six-footers that curled over his bow and blasted him in the face. He spent the next few minutes fixing his spray skirt and pumping water out of his flooded cockpit while I stood on shore, studying the wave sets.

It was my turn. I tried for five minutes to drag my boat off the rocks and into the waves lapping at the bow. I couldn't move it an inch. Finally, a larger set washed up under the hull and floated it just enough for me to get it out. I pulled it hard from the bow, aligned it straight into the waves and got around behind to push it out through the surf zone. I swam past the last set of waves and screamed for help. The cockpit was flooded and the boat was yawing to the side—I had to get in soon and pump it out or it would sink. Jean-Philippe paddled up to the side, I held the boats steady and he pumped out half the water. I swung my hips up and in and got ready to paddle. Now we were facing the beach and had to paddle backwards into the coming swell. My boat was swamped and unstable but there was no time to pump any more. We had to move. We quickly adjusted my deck gear that had nearly been torn off by the waves and stroked out into the deeper water.

By the time we started paddling toward our destination, I was already exhausted. Fortunately, the northerly wind and swell and an ebb tide pushed us along at a good rate. We quickly covered the ten miles to our next camp, where the beach lay at the back of a wide bay in the lee of a point. Spying the sandy shore and manageable waves, we sighed in relief, thinking that our ordeal was over.

Jean-Philippe landed without incident. He rode the small swell in, timed his landing and paddled hard on the backside of a wave onto the beach. He jumped out of the kayak smoothly, grabbed the bow and pulled it out of the water just before the next wave arrived. Very professional.

I was still on the water, judging and timing the wave sets. I back-paddled to avoid getting caught in a large breaker and waited for the right moment. From the beach, Jean-Philippe could see that the approaching set was smaller. He signaled to go but I hesitated. The following set proved much bigger so, stuck in the middle of what would soon be a breaking zone, I had no choice. I heaved against the paddle and pointed my bow straight for shore. I timed it well and hit the beach with no problems but in my hurry to jump out and pull the boat up, I capsized right in the foaming shallows. It would have been funny had a wave not taken the overloaded boat sideways and dumped it on the beach. The heavy kayak then washed around in the shore break, smashing and pounding the gear lashed to the deck.

Both of us rushed to the boat to try to move it up the beach. The next wave slammed it against our legs and swept us down into the water, too. When we surfaced, we saw that my dry bags, water bottles, life jacket, paddle float, bilge pump and deck bag were floating around loose and the kayak was still being thrashed around on shore. We didn't know what to grab first. Frenzied, we ran and picked up as much gear as possible and threw it onto the beach. Then we grabbed the kayak and pointed it toward the beach, hoping the waves would push it partway onto shore. Finally, after a five-minute struggle, we were able to pull it halfway to the sand, pump out all the water and drag it up the bank.

Exhausted, I began to unload slowly; when I reached down to undo the front hatch, what met my eye made me scream in anger and frustration. I called Jean-Philippe over to look. The wave had ripped out one of the deck rigging straps sewn into the seam at the edge of the bow, leaving a three-inch hole between deck and hull.

After a few minutes the adrenaline rush passed, my anger faded and we looked around and noticed the beauty of the site. The points on either side of us that formed the bay were narrow lips protruding from the mouth of a small canyon. To the left, the shore rose gradually up into sandstone hills layered in different shades of color. Out to sea we saw the jagged peaks of Isla Angel de la Guardia (whose inside shore we had followed for the last forty-six miles) illuminated by the soft orange light of late afternoon. The beach was a flat sand carpet, a welcome change from our rocky campsites of the past week. Another rough day had left us broken and battered, but delivered us to the shore of an idyllic haven.

We looked at each other silently, smiled in relief and resignation, and got to work. In the dying wind and warm light of the sunset, I set up camp while Jean-Philippe fixed my boat. With pliers from his multi-tool, a curved needle and ten-pound-test fishing line, he stitched the seam back into a remarkably effective seal. To patch our bodies back together, I prepared a hearty meal. After stuffing ourselves, we lay back in the descending chill of dusk with large steaming cups of tea and talked.

↑

Jean-Philippe, 19 October 1998

Coyotes are cautious creatures: occasionally we spot them early in the morning or in the evening, but they are shy during the day. They are most active at night, prowling around and sneaking in to check out our gear. Yesterday while camping under the stars in our bivy bags, 120 miles south of San Felipe, Luke shook me awake in the middle of the night and began yelling frantically. I was still half asleep and asked what was happening.

"Didn't you see the coyotes?" he asked. "I was sleeping and one came and licked my forehead!"

I laughed, but Luke continued, "I'm serious. I've been screaming and throwing stones at them and you didn't even wake up." In the morning, I could see that Luke had mud and a few claw marks on his forehead; he had not been licked but rather pawed by a coyote.

Coyotes in Baja have the reputation of being the thieves of the desert. We know they visit us almost every night for, at sunrise, their paw prints surround our campsite. One morning I woke up groggily to the sounds of Luke boiling water for our tea. When the water was ready, he asked me to fetch my cup. Our large plastic tumblers with travel lids are our most prized possessions in the kitchen bag. I had set it next to my head before going to sleep the night before. His question annoyed me—why couldn't he just reach over and grab it? I sat up and looked around, but it was gone. It didn't take me long to spot coyote tracks and then I realized what had happened. Although we always take great care to hide our food from the coyotes, it never occurred to me that they would steal my empty mug, which must have had some residue from sweet tea on the lid. I climbed a hill and walked around the beach to look for it. After ten minutes, I found the lid with deep tooth marks gouged into the edge and, a short distance away, the unmarked cup. I washed it and had my morning tea.

🌴

Jean-Philippe, 20 October 1998

Little by little our bodies are metamorphosing. We are lean and sinewy, almost back to the condition we achieved during our training in Thailand and our daily muscle aches have nearly disappeared. We have consumed a quantity of our dried food and drinking water and we can now pack more efficiently and move much faster. We are also learning to use the waves to our advantage and, on days with a following swell, we exceed four knots. Another motivation is that each paddle stroke takes us south over deeper and clearer water; we have left behind the vast tidal fluctuations and silty shallows. We are relieved to not worry anymore about timing our launches and landings with the cycles of the tides or carrying our gear hundreds of yards across tidal flats. Clearer water also means we can finally start freediving and spearfishing for food. Each day our outlook grows brighter as the conditions more closely resemble the paradise we had originally imagined Baja to be.

When we set off into the Sea of Cortez, we planned to be self-sufficient for three months. Because the interior shore of Baja is sparsely populated, we expected to be alone most of the time. Only three towns, Santa Rosalia, Mulege and Loreto, and a few fishing villages and camps lie along 1,200 miles of barren coast. So we had to carry enough food and water for up to three weeks to safely cover the distances between settled areas. Although we have storage capacity for ten days' worth of water, we knew from the outset that it would not be sufficient so we would have to rely upon seawater and our desalinator. For food, we had packed mostly dried staples such as pasta, rice and beans. What we seriously lacked, but could not carry with us, was protein; we couldn't thrive solely on starch and carbohydrates while paddling long distances every day. Supplying ourselves with fish was as important as covering distance or pumping water and I longed for the clearer water that would allow me to put on my mask and test my untried ability with a harpoon. At first, we struggled with everything. It took us an hour of effort to produce a gallon of drinking water with the pump. Our diet of dried goods from the food bag bored us and insufficient protein left us feeling undernourished and lethargic. The only two times I entered the murky water with the spear gun, I came back with barely edible bottom feeders. I am fast becoming desperate to encounter the legendary grouper, sea bass and yellowtail for which these waters are famous but today, our thirteenth day out, looks promising. I hope to finally experience the bounty of Baja's legendary fisheries.

I open the zipper of my bivy bag and poke my head out of my cocoon. The morning sun paints the sky with pinks and oranges, and the view of Isla Smith, twelve miles away, seems like an invitation to paddle out to it, so we tentatively make that our plan for the day. I get up, grab my goggles and go for a morning swim in the calm and pristine water. When I am waist-deep, I put my head underwater and spy a good-sized ray lying down flat on the sandy bottom, so I yell to Luke to bring me a spear gun. Rays are easy prey and I spear it on my first shot, our first catch in three days. Luke sautés its wings with Italian seasoning, garlic and a touch of lemon, an excellent substitute for our normal breakfast of granola and peanut butter.

Wasting no more time, we launch for Isla Smith. We follow the western shore of the long island until it opens into a protected bay with a beautiful sugar-sand beach kissing the water's edge. Overhead, pelicans circle, in search of fat little fish to fill their gullets with. We watch in awe as they swoop down like bombers to scoop up their morning catch. That is a sure sign of excellent fishing and, for the first time in northern Baja, the water is crystal clear. We land and quickly start unloading our kayaks. Suddenly a strange sound on the north side of the lagoon distracts us. The water appears to be in a full boil. The large roosterfish we had seen chasing hundreds of small fry out of the water in the bay of Punta Willard was an impressive sight, but this is truly awe-inspiring. We know it can't be dozens of roosterfish hunting together or we would have seen their rows of dorsal spines above the surface. This is different. The water simmers for several minutes over a surface area of more than 100 yards. The gyrations of these thousands of fish attract not only our attention, but also that of the pelicans diving on the south end of the lagoon. They take off in formation, do a half-circle in the sky over the roiling water and all plummet in a freefall simultaneously. We have no idea what kind of fish could move that much water, but we don't want to miss the party.

I finish unloading my kayak as fast as I can, grab our only fishing pole and paddle toward the activity. I am barely halfway there when everything suddenly stops. The pelicans sit, calmly floating on the surface, some of them choking down whole fish. The feast is over and I have missed it. I cast a couple of times with a spoon lure, but nothing happens. Disappointed, I decide to paddle a little further and try one more time. I soon give up and just as I pack my rod, the water starts bubbling right behind me. I quickly turn my kayak and cast into the middle of it. When I reel it in, there is strong resistance on the line and novice fisherman that I am, I get excited about my prize before checking to see what it is. An experienced fisherman would have known better. The melee moves on to another part of the lagoon and the only struggle remaining is mine as I try to free my hook from the stone it snagged upon. It finally comes loose and I go back to shore, frustrated and empty-handed.

Meanwhile, Luke has disappeared with his freediving equipment. I am about to do the same when the fish decide to have their party right next to the beach. I run with the rod and cast the lure in that direction, but my terrible luck continues. The line breaks when spoon and leader are still in the air and all I have left to hope for is Luke's success. My mood plunges rapidly when I see him come out of the water holding only a bent spear shaft. He missed a stingray in shallow water and hit the rocky bottom.

Dusk is coming quickly, fish are jumping all around us and we still have nothing more than plain rice to put on our plates. I throw down the fishing pole and grab my diving equipment. By the time I am all set in my wetsuit with weight belt around my waist, fins in one hand and spear gun in the other, the sun has already disappeared behind the mountain ridge behind us. The water temperature is chilly and the air temperature is plunging: I need to work quickly. Upon submerging, all I can see are rays; there is little time remaining before total darkness and I decide that they would make a fine dinner. I shoot at a small one and hit it but it twists around and unscrews the tip of my spear from the shaft, then swims away with it still embedded in its back. I can't let an injured fish go and I can't lose a precious spear tip, so I dive after it and try to subdue it. Its tail snaps around back and forth so violently that I can't hold it. I have to return to the surface to take another deep breath. I pull out my knife and dive again. It takes me nearly a minute to get into a position to cut its tail. I swim to shore with the body, give it to Luke and return for more food.

The second time I spear a larger ray. To prevent it from spinning away with my spear tip, I quickly drag it onto the beach. As I remove the spear, it snaps its tail with incredible speed and the five-inch dart barely misses my wrist. I am horrified. I had no idea that I had been spearing stingrays. Suddenly, I remember stories I had read about the terrible pain, infections and occasional death inflicted by stingrays. I look more closely at my glove and notice that the first small ray has cut halfway through the neoprene. I am lucky; my ignorance could have cost me much pain and serious injury. I sever the wildly flapping tail and take it to Luke, too.

It is already dark and I am getting cold, but we don't have quite enough meat to feed two hungry paddlers. I return to the water for one last try. In the increasing darkness, I can no longer see anything, but on my second dive, I am suddenly surrounded by hundreds of large fish that swim around me with incredible speed. I don't recognize them immediately. Then, as their curiosity brings them closer, I realize that I am in the middle of a large school of yellowtail. I have only a few seconds of air left and can't waste any time so I spin myself around, focus on one, aim and pull the trigger. Without waiting to see if I have speared the fish, I dash for the surface to breathe. As soon as I am up, I feel a strong pull and look down to see it fighting at the end of my spear. I swim immediately to shore and march triumphantly up to Luke with my first real catch, a twenty-inch, eight-pound tuna.

As we gorge ourselves on the decadently rich fish, we can't help but think of days in Japan when we paid a premium price for yellowtail sashimi. It is one of the biggest prizes in the ocean for the Japanese and the flesh from that fish alone would have cost $200. So, to honor that great tradition, we slice a portion of it into strips and eat it raw with some wasabi and soya sauce that Luke has stashed in the food bag. We cook the rest of the fish over a driftwood fire on its spear shaft spit and when we finish eating it, we're so full and so sleepy that we collapse into bed, faces and hands still covered in juices from the feast.

↑

Luke, 23 – 25 October 1998

During the first two weeks in northern Baja we have encountered only two inhabited places. At one point, we didn't see a soul for an entire ten-day period, so after 140 miles, we look forward to our arrival in the town of Bahia de Los Angeles, the only real outpost of civilization for 300 miles along the northern third of the Sea of Cortez. It is also famous as a nursery for a pod of friendly whale sharks. The calm, plankton-rich waters provide the perfect environment for mothers and their newborn calves. As we stroke into the outer reaches of the bay, I'm trembling with excitement at the prospect of cracking an ice-cold beer, sending a few emails and taking a swim with one of the most magnificent marine animals on the planet.

I am denied two out of the three: reliable email is a thing of the distant future here (the only phone is a microwave transmission system, no hard line) and the whale sharks prove too elusive. Beer, however, is readily available. It's the one constant anywhere you go in civilized Mexico, often more plentiful than drinking water. The country could be left a burning pile of rubble by a war and the beer trucks would still roll through. The public utilities and the wildlife are infinitely less predictable. We spend two days waiting for the phone to go back online and the whale sharks to appear.

We think the whale story is a conspiracy. All the locals and gringo regulars are in on it. They tell all the new guys about the dozen or so that feed in the bay for four months a year and ask you every day if you've seen them yet. We hear stories about people swimming with them, taking rides on their dorsal fins, etc. We go all the way to the estuary at the back of the bay three separate times and see nothing but flat water. To add injury to insult, while taking a swim after a long, hot morning of wanna-be whale watching, my right foot finds a couple of baby stingrays that lacerate the sole and arch with their spikes. To drown our disappointment and ease my pain, we gorge on fresh clams on the half-shell that we dig out of the sandy estuary flats.

Our headquarters is Guillermo's, a great little cantina next to the boat ramps at the western edge of town. Our waiter, Rey (how great to go through life named "King"), and the rest of the staff are gracious to a fault. We take advantage of their hospitality by parking ourselves at a table all day long until closing. There we use our portable computer brought along on the trip to document the entire expedition and post regular online updates. Afterwards, we camp on the beach in front of the restaurant.

Jean-Philippe spends a couple of hours talking with Wade, a marine biologist studying sharks in Baja. Wade has just arrived on a Zodiac from the small fishing settlement of San Francisquito, which is on our itinerary. After ordering parts for his marine radio he motored back south, where we hope to meet him in a few days to observe some of the shark-fishing activity.

Bahia de Los Angeles is a rustic, low-key place where people are always generous and happy to help. At one point, the high tide pulls my boat into the water and swamps it. Before I can even think about looking for someone to help, a fisherman and a boy are there, helping me bail. The same day, while shopping at a local market for supplies, we casually mention that we are in need of a wire grill for barbecuing fish and the clerk is soon out front, hack-sawing a section off a wire shelf.

This small outpost is little more than a stopover spot for travelers driving to points further south and Guillermo's seems to be the hub of it all. In the afternoon of our second day, two juiced-up dune buggies come screaming into town and pull up next to the cantina. The pilots are members of a team who are out scouting the course for the Baja 1000 off-road rally race. It turns out that the buggy manufacturer who sponsored the team had provided similar vehicles (high-speed, armed-attack versions) for Desert Storm. Interestingly, our expedition kayaks and paddling gear are as much of a curiosity for them as their race vehicles are for us.

On our second night in Bahia de Los Angeles, somebody stole my blue dry bag with most of my clothing and $250 from the deck of my boat. It isn't a huge loss, but it gives credence to comments that Jean-Philippe has often made about my cavalier attitude with my equipment. A wardrobe now consisting of only two T-shirts and two pairs of shorts will have to last me two and a half months and 500 miles until we reach La Paz. Getting dressed each day will serve as a reminder.

↑

Luke, 27 October 1998

For the past two days, we have paddled with a couple of natural historians for company. Eric and Bob, recent grads from Prescott College in Arizona, are both environmental studies majors and survival junkies and they know Baja very well. Around the campfire, they give us lessons in local ecology and history. They travel lightly, leave no sign of their passing and exude a confidence that they could survive any possible scenario in this inhospitable landscape. We learn that many of their desert survival techniques were learned directly from the Seri Indians.

The Seri were the lone Indigenous tribe in this area and victims of ongoing episodes of Baja history. They used to live autonomously on Isla Tiburon, on the other side of the Sea of Cortez, eking out an existence from the sea. In the days before reverse-osmosis desalination plants, they managed to find enough fresh water to survive in the desert. The Mexican army tried many times to subdue the tribe and force them into a settlement. Apparently, the Seri would retreat to the hills of Tiburon and hide. They knew of a few hidden springs of water, trapped birds and rodents and ate cactus fruits. They stymied their pursuers every time; the army inevitably ran out of water and returned to the mainland empty-handed.

Sadly, the tribe was eventually settled and Tiburon was declared an off-limits sanctuary by the Mexican government. Today the Seri are a marginalized community who live in cement block hovels over on the mainland. A few men still possess a wealth of knowledge about local flora and fauna and make a few pesos guiding students out on desert survival excursions. Prescott College supports one of these programs and Eric and Bob were star students; the time they spent with the Seri guides marked them and they plan to return. They're planning a courageous thirty-mile traverse in their double kayak from our current location on the western shore out across the open sea to Tiburon and to the coastal Seri settlements of the mainland. It makes me nervous just hearing about it. For Jean-Philippe and me it is not even a consideration, something we dearly regret, as we would have loved to join them and meet the last Seri Indians.

↑

Luke, 29 October 1998

We're now three days out of Bahia de Los Angeles and we leave this morning to cross San Rafael Bay. Crossing this eighteen-mile bay seems to take forever. The distances here are so hard to judge—eight miles or fifteen, you can't tell the difference. The clarity of the lines between land and ocean is so sharp that anything off in the distance appears as an unquantifiable gap that only seems to actually get smaller once nearer than three miles. It's psychologically devastating.

After an hour, the interior shore of the bay is on our right and miles off. We still have fifteen miles to go to the point ahead of us and in my mind's eye it stays there, regardless of our effort and the passage of time. There are no passing landmarks to give us a sense of progress. The water is smooth as glass. There is not a breath of wind to cool us and rivulets of sweat flood my eyes and run down my torso. In order to avoid insanity, I have to put myself in a meditative state. I repeat the stroking sound, swish, swish, in my head like a mantra and I fade out.

After three and a half hours, I am in the zone, machine-like, each stroke an exact repetition of the one before. On flat water I can almost go into mental stasis during these stretches, functioning on only a fraction of normal brainwave activity. A sharp noise registers through my foggy senses and I look up to see a point finally looming larger in front of me. It is only then that I notice that something has shattered the tranquility around me. It takes me a full ten seconds to realize what is happening. I find myself paddling through a garden of dark protruding fins. Little spouts of water emanate from a mass of twittering dark bodies. It's a several-hundred- strong pod of gray dolphins stretching in a narrow band through the water for more than a mile. The river of dolphins flows from my kayak off toward the point. They seem to be feeding on a massive school of yellowtail in a tidal current that snakes around the point and out into the bay. The dolphins launch themselves out of the water, spouting and squawking. Oblivious to the world, I have wandered right into the middle of them: I could reach out and touch dozens of them! At one point, I turn toward Jean-Philippe to make a comment and at that very moment one dives over the bow of his kayak. Neither of us can speak. I am awestruck as I thread my way through their midst and out the other side and I don't notice what is happening in the water 300 yards further ahead. The dolphins are not alone. A pod of pilot whales has joined the fray! The marine kingdom is staging a grand review in front of our kayaks.

Usually displays of this sort in the wild are harbingers of something notable, like animal stampedes on the savannah before an encroaching wildfire. It's difficult, however, to think logically and be wary at a time like this, so I don't read the signs. As soon as the whales pass, a breeze begins to riffle the water in front of me. Within two minutes, I find myself being blasted by thirty-knot winds, one of the legendary east-blowing winds we had heard about. They rage out of the arroyos on the Baja peninsula and blow boats out into the middle of the Sea of Cortez. The point we're trying to reach lies less than a mile away to the south, directly into the wind. Jean-Philippe is already halfway there, but I'm not sure I can make it. The wind is hitting hard, smacking me on the cheek at a position of two o'clock off the starboard bow. And it's getting stronger.

I keep my upper body bent into the wind, lower my paddle angle and rotate my torso as much as possible to get the maximum power out of each stroke. I'm cursing, spitting and whipping myself with verbal abuse to spur myself on. I can usually paddle a mile in under fifteen minutes with moderate effort. After nearly forty minutes, I finally muscle my way onto the beach at the point. Jean-Philippe is lounging on the sand when I arrive, frothing at the mouth, with all of my back muscles engorged with blood and throbbing. "Glad to see you made it," he says, smiling, "was worried there for a second, thought I might have to send out a rescue boat." "Back off!" I bark. Apparently, I'm not too fatigued for defensive machismo.

After a fifteen-minute break, we reboard and make our way around the point to the adjoining bay of San Francisquito. On the map, it looks like a little tiny indentation, so we expect a ten-minute paddle. We round the corner to see a mile-and-a-half-long bay foaming with breakers peaking at three to four feet blown up by howling winds.

The human mind, and not the body it inhabits, is a wellspring of fortitude. It is not only capable of second winds, but also third and fourth, and even more when necessary. The difference between endurance champions and also-rans, between survivors and casualties, is the ability to tap into mental reserves again and again and force the body to listen. In official jargon, it is described as endorphin production overcoming muscle fatigue and low blood sugar, but it's really just the drill sergeant of the brain kicking your ass to get you where you have to be. You either listen or die.

The final thirty minutes to the cliff-sheltered lee side of the lagoon is a brutal test of my will. We pass by a trimaran sailboat that bounces and tugs at its anchor in the bay. We take turns drafting off each other. The windblown spray stings our faces. Sunglasses offer little protection to my eyes and they stream with salty tears that turn everything in front of me into a blurry haze. Jean-Philippe aims for what appears to be a lighthouse and unable to fight the wind anymore, I tuck in behind him, struggling to stay in his protective wake. And then suddenly, we find ourselves in the wind shade of the cliffs and all is eerily calm. We pull up on shore, smiling and sighing with relief, and celebrate our efforts by clapping each other on the backs while in a big bear hug. A few fishermen from San Diego have watched our struggle and they come down to pat us on the shoulders as we walk up the shore. Sailors swear by this San Francisquito cove, as it is the only place to hide for thirty miles when storms hit. Marine guidebooks neglect to mention how hard it is to get there if you're already caught in the middle of one.

We also have the good fortune to run into our new marine-biologist friend, Wade, whom we met a few days ago in Bahia de Los Angeles. He and his two partners, Erin and Joe from Monterrey, California, pack us into his truck and we head off to a cantina a mile down the road for a heavenly meal of fish tacos. If we manage to leave tomorrow and paddle twelve miles south to El Barril, we'll get to join Wade, Joe and Erin on a research mission there. It's a rare opportunity but we're too tired to get excited. Despite the blowing sand and winds that threaten to peel our sleeping bags from our bodies, we slumber like babies all through the night.

↑

Jean-Philippe, 31 October 1998

El Barril is one of the biggest shark-fishing camps in Baja. It lies between San Francisquito and Santa Rosalia, just north of the twenty-eighth parallel that forms the boundary between North and South Baja. From a distance, it doesn't look like much. As we approached yesterday from the water, all we could see were a few tin roofs, a mess of fishing nets and, perched on the cliff above a gravel boat ramp, the crumbling concrete shell of an abandoned, unfinished hotel. After hearing so much about it, we were unimpressed.

Shark fishermen are a tough bunch. Up to forty men inhabit the camp for several months at a time but very few live here permanently. Wives and children come occasionally for a visit but most leave their families at home. Not even *El Jefe*, the chief of the camp, lives there. He visits once or twice a month from the town of El Rosario, a few hours away. The fishermen come from towns all over Baja and from states as far away as Chiapas in southern Mexico. To them, kayakers are a novelty. They were very curious when we pulled up next to the *pangas* (fifteen- to twenty-foot fiberglass fishing boats equipped with seventy-five-horse-power motors). They couldn't believe the quantity of gear we pulled from the boats as they helped us carry everything up the ramp. Wade, Joe and Erin then enthusiastically took us around the camp for a tour of what they called "the best shark processing facility in northern Baja." After an evening learning about the shark-fishing industry and preparation techniques, I lie in bed, letting my imagination run wild in anticipation of what I was going to see in the morning.

The big sharks are prized for their meat. Fishermen separate them into two types, red and white. The red meat of the mako, thresher and great hammerhead sharks is the most expensive and is sold directly to American distributors who haul it up to southern California in refrigerated trucks. Many of the shark steaks we find in supermarkets are from Baja. Other species like smoothhounds, hammerheads, blacktips, hornsharks and rays are all prepared together. The white meat is salted and dried and shipped off to all regions of Mexico, to be enjoyed as *machaca* for tacos, etc.

After sunrise, we are disappointed to learn that it is the end of the season. Not only have we arrived on the last day the fishermen will go out but also the moon is full, the worst time to fish. None of the boats have put out nets for the big sharks. The drift nets are attached to floats on the surface and the fishermen believe that sharks can see them by the light of the full moon. So, early in the morning, *pangas* roar out of the camp to pull in the nets they have set for bottom feeders, the smaller sharks and rays, in thirty to eighty feet of water.

At 6:30 a.m., we are up and waiting for the first boat to come in. They have a disappointing catch of small manta rays. The second boat comes in shortly after with a much wider array of species. They unload their catch onto a long wood table, weigh them (their wages are based on whole weight) and then set to work cleaning them.

Our friends, the marine biologists, sort through them first, trying to disturb the men as little as possible. They measure and weigh all species, identify males and females and record their approximate ages. The most important statistic they try to ascertain is the maturity level of the catch. They know the size-to-age ratio for all the species and thus are able to determine which have reached the age of reproduction and which are juveniles. Their data will be compiled later with that of other groups working on the Sea of Cortez to give feedback on the shark population and help to prevent overfishing.

The cleaning process is a fascinating display of efficiency. Already the cleaners have started to slice off all the fins. They constantly re-sharpen their knives on a whetstone while they work to remove the heads and intestines. Within minutes, the entire catch is off to a different station, leaving only a pile of entrails for the birds and insects.

The fins generate the most money per pound. The fishermen salt them and dry them for three days on cactus wood racks and then ship them off to Asia. Chinese and Japanese buyers will pay premium price for the entire lot, no questions asked. In Japan, shark fin soup is an expensive delicacy. The Chinese use the fins to make medicinal and aphrodisiacal powders. To us, the shriveled wafers of cartilage just look revolting.

The red meat sharks are selected out and sold whole and the white fish sharks go to the processing shack. Workers peel the skin off (once dried it makes excellent sandpaper), cut the flesh into thin filets and pass them on to the salters. At their station, they rub the filets with great handfuls of marine salt from 100-pound bags set next to the tables. Then packers pile the well-coated filets in crosshatched, square stacks. There, they stay for a day in the shade of the open-walled shack and then the fishermen repeat the salting process one more time. After the second time they are left in stacks for eight days. When the stacks are fully cured, workers spread them out to dry for a few hours on the cactus racks in the sun. *El Jefe* then ships it all off to Ensenada or Mexico City.

The camp of El Barril is very well organized. It operates from April to November, with the busiest months coming during the brutal heat of the summer. *El Jefe* makes occasional visits to supervise the operation. He sits in a hammock drinking beer and watching a TV powered by a gas generator. He receives anywhere from thirteen and a half to fifteen pesos per kilo and pays all the bills for the food, gas, and repairs. The fishermen are next on the ladder. They make five and a half pesos per kilo of red meat and five pesos per kilo of white filets. Expert fileters get the next best wages and salters are paid the least. When the season is over, the people from Chiapas return home for the shark season there. Others return to their families elsewhere in Baja, and a few remain to make a little money catching yellowtail by trolling with long lines from their *pangas*. It is a tough life, but the Sea of Cortez still provides plenty in a desert land where farming is impossible. Fishing is the only means of survival for people living between the desert and the sea.

↑

Jean-Philippe, 13 November 1998

Our duo is about to become a quintet. Nearly a week ago, just as we left the village of Santa Rosalita seventy miles south of El Baril, James, a fellow expedition paddler on his way to La Paz, joined us for a few days. He is a skilled kayaker with a background in extreme whitewater paddling. His day job as the manager of a climbing gym keeps him in shape and with his bushy blond beard and powerful shoulders, he looks and strokes like a Viking. Our combined energy has picked up the pace remarkably over the past couple of days. Last night when we arrived in Punta Bufeo, a young Canadian kayaker and his fellow paddler who were camping on the other side of the sandy point came over to introduce themselves. They turned out to be the infamous Max and his father.

Max and I have been in email contact for over a year, ever since I voiced my support for him during a controversial period on the online paddling mailing list. He started his kayak expedition a year ago in Vancouver, Canada, and is on his way down to Nicaragua, where he plans to cross the isthmus and go back up to Canada on the Atlantic side. His dad, a newly retired high school teacher who had led river canoe tours in Canada for many years, is now here to participate in a stage of his son's grand adventure.

Not long after sunrise, Max walks to our camp and asks us if they can join us for the ten-mile crossing to the town of Mulege. We tell them that we will launch and paddle by their camp.

By 9:00 a.m. the wind has picked up and the swell is big, even in our protected cove. It has blown hard all night, pushing in clouds from the north and filling the open sea with whitecaps. We can see eight-footers breaking out on the far side of our sheltered bay. The launch out through the small surf looks easy, but proves deceptive. Waves break over my bow, splash me in the face and fill up my cockpit. We can't drag our heavily loaded kayaks on the sand, so we must pull them out into the shore break and start paddling. Once in, we stop to pump out the cockpit and seal it closed with our spray skirts. When we look up, we have already drifted half the distance to Max's campsite; they stand up to watch us. We paddle close to the narrow sandy point and nearly get caught in the breaking surf. One large swell pops James' boat up in the air like a cork. The next one curls over my bow and swamps me and I narrowly avoid capsizing.

From the beach, Max's dad doesn't miss a second of this. After seeing the waves toss us around, he tightens up noticeably and we can see the two of them discussing whether or not to abort. They walk out on the point to get a better sense of the open-water conditions; Dad is hesitant to join us. We clear the point and surf into the protected side. Max reassures his dad and convinces him to portage their boats and launch in the calmer water of the protected side. We start paddling slowly toward the open sea, thinking that they will catch up.

Five minutes later, we look back to see that they have not followed us, instead they are hugging the protected shoreline. Dad must be scared out of his mind. We wait for twenty minutes, but lose sight of them as the thirty-five-knot wind quickly pushes us south, away from the point. There is no way for us to fight the wind and return so we shrug and continue forward. A large swell lifts my kayak from the rear and plunges my bow underwater until I pick up speed and begin to surf. In the trough of the wave, I paddle hard to catch the next one and find myself exhilarated by the challenge of the open sea. Luke and I have improved tremendously in a little over a month and we are now much more confident. I begin to experiment and play games, letting James get a little bit out in front and then waiting for a big one. With a few hard strokes, I drop down into the eight-foot swell, pick up speed and gain fifteen yards on James in a couple of seconds. One more and I'm abreast of him. He soon picks up on my enthusiasm and we play cat and mouse, paddling aggressively into the biggest swells and squirting out in front. We're dancing with the ocean.

Sometimes, though, a bigger series comes through that reminds us that we are not the masters of the ocean. At one point, a large swell lifts me and at the same time opens up a big hole off my bow. My boat teeters over the edge and I plunge over the ten-foot drop completely out of control. By some miracle I don't capsize, but I'm left in a precarious broadside position: I have to straighten the boat out into the direction of the waves or I'm finished. I put all my energy into sweep strokes to redirect the kayak while still in the trough of a wave. The boat is sluggish and I must lean over and brace into two walls of whitewater before my boat turns. Those few minutes change my focus entirely and I began to think more about arriving safely than having fun. I check my partners' positions and we establish a routine whereby we check on each other every five or ten minutes to make sure everybody is still up in their boats.

After an hour and a half, the swell grows even larger. The conditions are no longer fun; they are frightening and fatigue makes the situation that much worse. I feel like I am bracing almost as much as I am paddling;

Luke and James look grim and uncomfortable. There is no way out of this—the closest shore is five miles away. Luke stops a couple of times to pump the water out of his kayak and yells over that he has nearly capsized numerous times. After a few minutes of anxiety, I regroup and begin to repeat to myself like a mantra that I am strong enough and skilled enough to handle these conditions. "Anticipate, react. Anticipate, react." Today's conditions are one of the reasons why we chose to paddle the Sea of Cortez. We need rough-water experience under our belts before paddling the Pacific of Costa Rica and Panama.

I resume paddling vigorously, chasing after James, and a rogue wave nearly wipes me out. The huge ten-footer rockets me upward. The wind catches the lip, disintegrates it into white water, the entire wave releases beneath me and I plunge down into it. I find myself in water up to my neck. My full boat is submerged. Even my shoulders seem paralyzed by the weight of the water. For a few agonizing seconds, I can't move my paddle to brace. Luckily, the kayak pops back up and into position to meet the next wave. I wonder, however, how many times my foldable kayak can handle such pressure before collapsing.

Every second or third wave curls over and breaks on top of me and I am submerged, my upper body paralyzed again beneath the water. It is a miracle that my boat pops back up each time without breaking. Normally, in open water you only see swell so when the swell starts to break, it's time to worry. The only thing we have going for us is the direction of the wind and waves that push us straight toward Mulege.

Water has seeped through my spray skirt and into the sea sock lining my cockpit. The sea sock, a body bag that prevents water from flooding the bow and stern in a bulkhead-less foldable kayak, is no longer watertight and the kayak slowly fills up. With each stroke, the boat feels heavier and more difficult to handle. I will be in real danger if this continues. I aim for the entrance of the small bay and think that I am home free but one final obstacle, a half-submerged reef, almost ruins the entire day. I have to jam on my rudder and strain against my paddle with a full sweep stroke at the last minute to avoid it. I surf my way around its jagged edge and turn into the flat water of the river mouth. Grateful and relieved, I collapse over my cockpit and wait for James and Luke.

It is only after they join me that I look upriver toward the town and wonder about the place where we have just arrived. After five weeks in the desert, we have reached an oasis! Snarls of mangrove trees and fan-like palms line the shores of the river, one of the few on the entire desert coast of Baja. Further up we encounter wildflowers, patches of green grass and fields of dates and bananas. Snow-white egrets splash out of the shallow margins into flight and orange butterflies with brown and crimson spots dance around my head as we paddle by. Am I dreaming? Have we somehow landed in the Caribbean?

Everything is pungent, earthy and very real. Our last launch spot ten miles and two and a half hours back seems like a different planet. The Baja desert is beautiful, but after 400 miles of it, there is nothing as uplifting as the sight of greenery. We paddle up the shallow river at a slow pace, enjoying every bit of vibrancy. We understand what nomadic desert people must feel when they reach an oasis after weeks on the back of a dusty camel. Looking at the entire area, I flash back to my time in Egypt: as in the Nile valley where the vegetation ends abruptly at the edge of irrigation lines, the far hills flanking the Mulege valley are barren but for cacti and thorny scrub.

We fantasize that we have discovered an untouched oasis, but it is short-lived. The further we paddle upriver, the more development we see. Dilapidated wood cabanas with jetties and *panga* boats dot much of the shore. Occasionally, the beautifully manicured grounds and grander estates of wealthy American expatriates interrupt the mess. Then we arrive at the Orchards, an RV park and campground, the kind of place I would normally avoid; in this instance it's surprisingly pleasant. The grounds are full of date palms, bananas and mango trees and for us it is paradise and, for two dollars per person, a bargain indeed.

We take our first fresh-water shower in a month, leave our gear under the protection of the armed security guard and head into town, in dire need of a proper meal. We stop for an appetizer at a renowned bakery run by an expat American and his young Mexican wife. It more than lives up to its fame, the *empanada de pollo* is incredible. The decadent, crunchy exterior encases tender, succulently spiced chicken, roasted to perfection. We continue walking around, sampling various Mexican specialties at stands and little restaurants and, after a couple hours of stuffing our bellies, we waddle back to camp, dizzy with too much food.

Back at the campsite, we are astonished to see Max's kayaks. We were sure they had aborted the crossing. Max appears shortly after and explains their ordeal: his dad capsized four times in the first few minutes and although they had wanted to return to the beach, the southerly wind forced them out into the open sea. To survive, they tied their kayaks together to make a stable raft and then drifted the entire crossing. The wind and the waves pushed them at a pace of nearly two knots and they arrived after five hours.

We sit around sharing stories for hours before somebody happens to glance at his watch and notice that the date is Friday the 13th.

Later, I lie in my sleeping bag thinking about the events of the day. I make a list of all the things we have done wrong and all the reasons why we are fortunate to have arrived safely at all. We are still loaded with far too much gear to be truly safe. I imagine what would have happened if we had capsized in those conditions. Our ridiculous deck loads could have caused us serious problems. I have one medium-sized dry bag, a deck bag with compass and map case, my spear gun and a spare paddle strapped to my bow deck. My stern deck is even worse. Standing high behind my back, I have a pyramid made of two large dry bags, a Pelican case (for my camera), our video camera in its waterproof housing and a wetsuit. My freediving fins are tied to the riggings just in front of the rudder. I cringe as I envision all this precious gear ripped loose and floating around in rough seas while I struggle, inverted, trying to roll my waterlogged kayak back upright.

Words from the gurus we consulted in the past six months of training echo in my head:

"Know the ocean. Read the signs. Be able to swim out of anything. Combine caution with courage."

—Caveman Gray, Sea Canoe Thailand

"Brace stroke to stay upright. Roll to survive when you don't."

—Dave Williams, Paddle Asia, Phuket, Thailand

"Never have any gear on deck. Everything gets packed inside."

—Ed Gillet, Southwest Kayaks, San Diego

One might wonder if we had learned anything at all from our months of training.

↑

Divine Intervention at the Dinner Table

Luke, 22 – 23 November 1998

The stretch of coast south of Mulege, from Pulpito to Loreto, is stunningly beautiful. And contrary to other areas of Baja plagued by overfishing, it abounds with treasures that can be plucked from its waters and served up on a plate.

After two days of rough stuff in the big surf with no time or inclination to fish or dive, it is great to arrive in Pulpito and see the reefs, submerged rock gardens teeming with life in placid water. The afternoon we arrive, we set out with our spear guns to put some protein on the table after three days of dried packaged food. Jean-Philippe is a skilled hunter. I, however, am a late bloomer with the mask, fins, and gun and must take the role of scavenger. I usually pluck the stationary sea urchins or shellfish from the bottom and/or just take my rightful place by the camp stove to prepare the "bacon" that he brings home.

However, this place will prove to be different. There's a reef out in the middle of the cove that rises up out of fifteen feet of water and hosts a myriad of creatures. It's hard to find at high tide, but when the tide ebbs, waves seem to suddenly stumble and break over it, making it an easy mark for divers.

After missing my first three shots, I abandon the idea of spearing anything and begin looking for the elusive shellfish that everyone talks about. Scallops in this bay? Nope. Clams? Nope. Oysters? Nope. But what has eighteen-inch antennae and drives your dinner bill up into the stratosphere? Sure enough, lobster—Pacific lobster to be exact. No claws on this variety, alas, but ooh la la the tails! Although not my forte, I dive down quietly into the crack in the rocks and reach in to grab him, but my hand grazes only the tips of his antennae. Poof! He disappears out his back door, gone without a trace. I circle around the back and find him in no-crustacean's land, scooting along the sandy bottom toward another rock cluster. Gotcha!

The pole spear serves us well that day. We boil crabs and the lobster tail in water spiced with chicken bouillon, minced garlic, oregano and sage. I pluck out the shellfish and then use the same brine to boil macaroni as filler. A kayak tour group sharing the beach with us (they have a support boat with coolers, etc.) supplies us with cold beer and we sit with our new friends, ripping shells apart and sucking out bits of succulent meat. We make a royal mess.

The next day we paddle across a wide bay and pull into San Juanico Cove. What a jewel! Golden beaches are tucked into gaps in the cliffs. Grottos and underwater caves lattice the walls. Spires of volcanic rock protrude from the middle of the cove and underwater rock gardens create mottled shadows in clear turquoise water. It is so beautiful that we can't fathom why it has remained unsullied and quiet. Where are the jet skis, the dive boats, the huge resort hotels carved into the cliffs? Fortunately, all in Cabo San Lucas. In San Juanico, there is little more than the odd sailboat and a couple of car-campers who have made the gnarly drive out from Highway 1 on the bumpy dirt road.

Arriving in the afternoon, we don't have much time to dive for anything for the table, but when we stop to say hello to a couple on a yacht, they bestow upon us several gallons of fresh water and a steak! We share the beach that night with four other kayakers: a lovely Canadian couple, Paul and Sara, who are car-camping and day-paddling their way down to La Paz; and Solo Max and his dad, whom we had met earlier. They turn green with envy when we fry up our steak with garlic and soy sauce as they spoon down plain rice. There's a limit to generosity, I guess. Out in the desert sharing a cup of sugar or dry goods is one thing, but a hunk of fresh beef?

The following day we hit the water early. Rumor has it that there are rock scallops out there and we are determined to find them. A large rock garden in ten to twelve feet of water lies only 200 yards offshore from the beach, so we go straight for it. These scallops look like round, barnacle-covered rocks that cling to large boulders or are mixed in with a bed of similar-sized rocks. For rookies like us, they are too well camouflaged.

We swim down into the garden and start tapping randomly, looking for movement. Scallops sit with their shells open just a crack to filter-feed from the water that moves by, but when disturbed, they shut very quickly. Rocks all around us shudder and close—they are everywhere! All the shells are six to eight inches wide and the insides are filled with a couple tablespoons of guts and only a small thimble-sized lump of white meat. No wonder we pay a fortune for the bigger ivory medallions of flesh. They must be rare indeed—or so we think.

Jean-Philippe can't be bothered with scallop hunting for such a measly result, so he sets off with his gun. I continue, undaunted. On occasion I have seen what appear to be larger circular rock formations with a speckled yellow and black ribbon of something tucked up inside a long fissure. I had assumed it was a sea snake or something else unsavory and had never bothered to look closely. Tired of gut-filled, piddling little scallops, I decide to take a chance. I swim up to one of those large round rocks, shove my dive knife in and retreat quickly. The rock seems to release a little and then…nothing. I go back to look. It is indeed a scallop. Massive! The shell is the size of my head, and after cutting out the guts, the medallion of meat it produces is three inches in diameter and over an inch thick.

I now know what to look for and how to harvest. I swim around enthralled, examining every rock cluster for the telltale band of yellow and black. With my dive knife and a little mesh drawstring bag, I collect two pounds of medallions in an hour. All along we'd been looking for the wrong size! I never again looked at any shell smaller than a dinner plate and the biggest one I spied was the size of a cymbal.

My popularity peaks in camp that night; I have enough to stuff us and to share with Paul and Sara (Max and his dad have already left). Pan-fried in oil with garlic and salt, their density and sweetness are incredible! They are so satisfying by themselves that we struggle to finish off the portions of rice we had prepared to accompany them.

The next night is Thanksgiving, and we have more of the same—only the location has changed. I gather scallops in the morning before our departure and put them in a Ziploc bag with salt water. I store them in my deck bag and sauté them on the next beach in a garlic white sauce made with powdered milk. Divine!

It is certainly a week to remember, like four days of Thanksgiving, really. There is no comparison to the feeling of full-belly satisfaction and the after-glow of a decadent meal that you have gathered and prepared yourself out in the middle of nowhere.

⸙

The Food Chain

Luke, 25 November 1998

The ebb tide opens up a small sand bar twenty yards out from the beach. I throw some fish bones in the shallows near shore and watch a turkey vulture scavenge for them. Less than a minute later, another vulture joins the first one and a seagull joins the fray, hoping to get a few scraps. Seagulls fight over everything. Whenever we clean a fish they lie in wait screaming for the guts. At the same time, twenty yards away, a few dozen pelicans dive-bomb a small patch of water. Leading with their beaks, they break the surface of the water at great speed, creating a sound like rocks being dumped into the water from a high cliff. Most come up with fish and with little pause, they tilt their heads back and swallow them whole. The mad rush continues and more pelicans arrive. Flocks of booby birds follow them. Frigate birds and seagulls fly around and harass the hunters. The thunder of splashing reverberates off the hills behind me. It's a kill zone. People say that nothing compares to watching predators operate on the plains of Africa. Baja is without question the marine equivalent. With very few exceptions, each animal hunts and is hunted. And when we as humans enter the arena, we take our chances as well.

↑

Bahia San Juanico:
When the Hunter Becomes the Hunted

Jean-Philippe, 25 November 1998

A day paddling south of the majestic bay of Punta Pulpito took us to the equally spectacular Bahia San Juanico. When I researched Baja years ago, I heard countless stories about the incredible marine life: whales, dolphins, sea lions, fish, birds. Now that I am here, it exceeds my expectations. Every day nature gives us a lesson in beauty and harmony, but also in the raw violence of life.

Large predatory fish eat small ones and in turn are fed on by sharks, sea lions and dolphins. We, too, try to feed on big fish. We rely on spearfishing to fill our bellies and so go out nearly every day. This involves us in the mortal struggles of the food chain. I'm usually the spearfisherman (Luke is more effective with the rod) and I know that if I am caught in the middle of a hunt, there may be dangerous consequences.

Today, I intend to bring back dinner for four, as we're sharing the beach with Paul and Sara. After fifteen minutes, I spear a wrasse. I put it on my rope stringer and drag it ten feet behind me while looking for more. I miss a grouper and some yellowtail and after an hour in the water, I start to think that I may have to reduce my standards, go for the slower, easier and, unfortunately, less tasty ones. Just then a school of large striped mullets swims by. I choose the largest one, take a big breath, and dive in on the fish. They scatter in all directions but I get a good shot at the one I was aiming for and I quickly swim over to subdue it. I add it to my rope stringer and head for shore. Suddenly a strong pull on the stringer takes me underwater. Scared and swallowing seawater, I look down and notice that my rope is being pulled into a hole in the rock wall. My wrasse is still tied to the line higher up, but the bottom two feet with the striped mullet has disappeared into the hole. I pull strongly to try to break free and regain the surface. I know that it is most likely a large moray eel. By pulling hard I hope to sever the rope, but on the first few yanks it doesn't work.

I am already out of breath and have swallowed too much seawater. Throat burning with brine, I'm frantic to reach the surface that lies only a foot above my head. Before I can break loose, another large moray eel swims right at me. Frightened, I jerk on the rope, break free and explode through the surface, coughing and hacking. Already the moray with its razor-sharp teeth is biting the tip of my fins. I fend it off with my spear, but it keeps coming back at me. I swim away on my back, trying to keep the eel in sight and at my feet rather than let it get close to any vulnerable part of my body.

My rope and the mullet are gone. The other eel has swallowed it and cut half of the length off the stringer. He's sitting in his cave well fed and satisfied. This other one is still mad. The jagged teeth continue to come toward me and I do my best to keep my aggressor at bay by jabbing at it with my spear. I always thought that moray eels were not aggressive, but this one follows me for nearly 100 yards as I swim on my back, inhaling water through my inverted snorkel. I am so distressed I even consider spearing it. It is six feet long and as thick as my leg so I give up on the idea, but I need to move faster. I rotate onto my stomach and swim away as fast as I can. After fifty more yards, I turn back and see that I have finally lost my harasser. Now I understand how pelicans and boobies feel when frigates harass them and steal their food. Morays are violent opportunists.

Once the adrenaline rush fades, I'm upset about having lost my fish, but with additional thought and reflection, I realize that I was lucky. I should be relieved to have escaped unscathed.

Today the morays taught me a lesson. When we get in the water to feed, we don't just disrupt the food chain; we can become part of it.

From San Juanico Bay, three more days and twenty-eight miles of paddling took us to the village of Loreto, where we spent a day resting and enjoying the decadent pleasure of a shower, and filled up on food and gossip before escaping back to quieter grounds.

↑

To La Paz:
Finishing the "Training" Course

Luke, 29 November 1998

As we leave Loreto, we plan to paddle to Honeymoon Cove, what on a calm day should have been seventeen miles of smooth water through the strait between the Baja mainland and the imposing Isla Carmen.

As it turns out, we don't leave Loreto in the best sea conditions. We're already on the water when residual winds from the huge storm that thrashed the west coast of the U.S. from Seattle to San Diego come to town: poor timing for our spray skirts to go on strike.

We picked the REI tropical-weight spray skirt thinking it would be a great, lightweight, breathable, waterproof alternative to hot neoprene. For the first month it was. It kept us mostly dry and we didn't overheat in the sweltering daytime temperatures. During the second month of use, we began to find our cockpits half full of water before the end of the day. Now, a couple of weeks later, the waterproofing is almost gone. We can't blame it on REI, who had generously provided us with nearly $4,000 of equipment, including some of the very best we've packed, but this spray skirt clearly wasn't made to last the duration of such a demanding expedition. Now, any wave that splashes over us pools in the folds of the skirt and drips through. The leaky skirts leave us splashing about hip-deep in water and our boats become much more difficult to handle.

Refracted, choppy and windblown waves are the worst. They slop over the side of our boats and soak through. It looks like we will face this kind of swell for the entire paddle today. Fortunately, during the first two hours we only have to pump out once.

The wind in Baja seems to sense when we have reached the home stretch of a long crossing. Cruel and vindictive, it always blows harder when we have the destination in sight. Just past the halfway point, the waves and wind step it up a level. Every few seconds, a breaker washes over our decks and there is an almost constant stream of water coming through the folds in our skirt fabric. After fifteen minutes, we're up to our hips in water. The full sea sock puts pressure on the rudder's foot pedals, effectively locking them in position so the rudder is useless. We can't steer; we're at the mercy of the waves. As each one passes beneath us we veer off to the side and no amount of sweep strokes can correct the direction of our sluggish, waterlogged boat. The only solution is to peel back a tiny corner of the skirt, insert the pump and go at it like mad before another swell swamps us and fills us up entirely.

We must repeat this pattern for an hour and half. My right shoulder develops a cramp from frantic pumping and we don't seem to be making any forward progress. Finally, with the island near, I decide to make a run for it and try to get into the cove without any more pumping. I pay dearly for this decision. I am already half full when a large set of waves washes over the deck four consecutive times, almost filling the cockpit completely. The boat is riding extremely low and no amount of paddling will move it.

I open the skirt a crack and slide the pump through like a straw, and begin heaving up and down on the handle; I only have a few inches of clearance between the edge of the cockpit and the water. Another set of waves crests the rim and fills me up entirely. Suddenly the kayak lurches, teeters and gets caught in a swell that pushes it on a path away from the island. I find myself broadside to the waves and headed away from my destination.

I am stressed, frustrated and I feel like I'm losing it, but I do the only thing possible: I pump furiously. It takes five minutes before I make any headway. By the time I get the boat riding high enough that I can maneuver, my right shoulder is so tired that I can barely paddle.

I have to pump five more times in the last mile before I can get around the point into the calm protected water and onto the beach. In spite of the warmth and tranquility of the cove, I'm shaking with cold and shock. It takes me two hours to recover.

I realize that I came within inches of losing my entire boat and all my gear today. I won't forget this lesson. Heat be damned, a neoprene skirt is our only solution when we head to the Caribbean, from which the few remaining Central American Indigenous people can be visited.

↑

Agua Verde

Jean-Philippe, 1 December 1998

Two days of paddling takes us from the pristine Honeymoon cove to the village of Agua Verde. On the second day, we wake up at 4:30 a.m. and have a quick breakfast before loading our kayaks. We are counting on a nearly full moon to light our way, but residual clouds from the storm that originated on the northern Pacific Coast obscure the sky. We're on the water an hour later in total darkness.

Each paddle stroke stirs up constellations of bioluminescence in the water. We pass by Isla Danzante and head toward a string of islets dangling off its southern tip. The overcast sky is a myriad of blues and hazy blushes, typical of the pre-sunrise glory in Baja. For a few minutes, we watch the sun slip higher over the horizon until it disappears in the layers of clouds. We have made an early departure to avoid the heat of the twenty-three miles separating us from Agua Verde. The craggy mountains punch into the sky, their silhouettes along the shoreline reminding me of the majestic peaks in the Grand Canyon area. I'm so awestruck by Mother Nature's brazen display of beauty that I nearly miss a grand sea show. On different occasions, a giant manta ray more than twenty feet wide and weighing about 2,000 pounds and a half-dozen large bat rays launch themselves in the air, flip in a slow arc and land flat on their stomachs with great splashes.

After an easy paddle, we enter the protected bay in the early afternoon. We land next to a few *panga* boats and inquire about a place to get a meal. While we unload and pull our kayaks up the beach, a curious bystander approaches. He turns out to be a generous local who, after a few minutes of talking, leads us to his sister's place for a meal. We cross the village and weave our way through goats, pigs and frolicking children. We notice that each house is equipped with a solar panel. Agua Verde is immaculate and its inhabitants are very friendly. We wonder why this village contrasts so strongly with the fishing camps we have seen in other areas. We later learn that the locals are actually an Indigenous group that has been assimilated into Mexican society. Non-profit organizations from the States and the Mexican government gave them some support to develop their schools and construct self-sufficient solar plants.

A young woman named Veronica receives us with a big smile. Warned we were coming by the children, she has already started to cook us some tasty tortillas that she fills with beans and white sea bass. Her husband grabs two limes from a tree and we squeeze them over the grilled fish. Our host sits next to us and asks us many questions about the "where from" and "where to" of our kayak trip. Their little boy runs back from the *tienda* with two cold sodas. Our hosts are so talkative and our Spanish is so limited that we have a hard time understanding every-thing. It is a clear message to us that we have neglected our studies for too long. After our meal, we paddle over to the adjoining beach to find some seclusion and settle in for the evening, and we pull out our Spanish books.

Our campsite is on a small isolated beach separated from the village by a rocky point. We share the poorly protected bay with a thirty-foot aluminum yacht that rocks in the swell. When the crew lands on the beach, we introduce ourselves and ask if they could provide us with a few gallons of fresh water. Yachts usually carry large tanks and have electric desalination pumps. We are running low and have no desire to spend the next couple of hours hand-pumping ours. They invite us aboard for dinner, but in the chill of the evening, Luke prefers the warmth of his sleeping bag and chooses not to go. I paddle alone to the yacht to meet Marco and his family—his eldest daughter, his wife, their two small children and their friend, Pablo.

Born in Canada, Marco has spent most of his life traveling. While making a movie in Fiji, he met his Indian wife. They got married and had two children. For a year and a half, they lived on their boat in Canada to prepare for this sailing trip. As night falls, the strong wind kicks up more swell that rocks the boat severely. Marco's wife and eldest daughter are seasick and can't eat. The rest of us dine on a huge lobster and exchange diving and traveling stories. The family is soon going to make their way back to Fiji, where they will live a more sedentary life. His little girl loves sailing, but his wife and little boy want a house with goats. So they decide they will have both, a house in Fiji for the mother and son to retreat to when they get sick of sailing and a boat to take tourists on excursions for a few weeks at a time on the isolated islands of the archipelago. After a fantastic evening, I paddle back to the beach in the darkness.

†

Night Diving with Fishermen

Jean-Philippe, 4 December 1998

The next fifteen miles took us to Punta Botella, where we met a group of retired men on a kayak trip waiting to be motored back to civilization. With coolers full of cold beers, and edible goodies, they camp in style. A day later, our new friends' motorboat roars away, leaving us with more provisions and a new fishing rod on loan. A few days ago, a large fish had ripped our rod from Luke's kayak as he was trolling. With more food, we decide to stay an extra day. The amphitheater of red sandstone is a perfect place to catch up on some reading and writing. In the late morning, three fishermen—Monico, David and Pedro—set up camp 100 yards from us on an adjacent beach. We put our new Spanish vocabulary to practice, introduce ourselves and ask them what they are fishing for. We learn that they are waiting for nightfall to dive with lights for sea cucumbers, lobsters and fish. When I explain that in two months we have only been able to catch one small lobster, they laugh and say nonchalantly that they could get twenty-five kilograms in one night. They invite us to come along; I'm excited, but fear that my equipment will not be sufficient. They have thick three-piece wetsuits and very powerful lights. I have only a two-millimeter suit and a shorty to wear on top, and my only light is a little Petzl waterproof headlamp. They assure me that I will be fine as long as I don't dive too long.

In the afternoon, Luke goes off with his kayak to try out the new fishing rod. Soon after he disappears around the point, a large, abrasive Mexican guy lands on our beach. He walks toward me like a bandit character from a movie, sticking his chest out and swaggering. In a very imposing fashion, he introduces himself as Manuel. I know instantly that he is the notorious thief we have been warned of recently by numerous sailors. The local fishermen also dislike him—they call him a "*loco cabron*," or crazy asshole. He asks many questions and looks longingly at all our gear. I give him little attention and fortunately he soon leaves. Our fisherman friends, seeing his boat leave the bay, take their valuable diving equipment out from their hiding places and continue preparing for the evening's dive. Manuel disappears around the point but I worry as he's heading in Luke's direction.

A couple of hours later, Luke shows up and tells me of his encounter with the bandito. While Luke was snorkeling and searching for shellfish, Manuel rifled through his kayak, took out a few dry bags and broke open a Pelican case containing our computer. Not knowing how to unfasten the latches, he broke the box at the joints. Apparently, he realized that is was not an item he could resell easily and left it.

We spend the afternoon trying to solve the problem of our leaky spray skirts. Nothing has worked so far. This time, we try coating the undersides of the skirts with a layer of silicon glue that we spread using a flat shell. We hope it will create an impenetrable seal and allow us to paddle safely through rough conditions to La Paz, where we will have to get new equipment.

At the end of the afternoon, the trio of fishermen comes to pick me up. I load all my freediving gear and a dry bag with a change of clothes into their boat while Luke stays at the camp to keep an eye on all our belongings—we know Manuel is still around. We motor in the *panga* for eighteen miles. From the water, the landscape is spectacular. The half-overcast sky provides a blazing, technicolor sunset and the backdrop of mountains eerily bathed in shadow set off the whole composition. It is almost too perfect to look natural. It could be a closing scene from a Hollywood movie.

David maxes out the seventy-five-horsepower engine and blasts the boat through light chop. The waves slam the *panga* hard enough that the hull seems on the verge of disintegration. It's too noisy to hold a conversation. When we arrive at the foot of a cliff, David kills the engine while Pedro and Monico put on their layered wetsuits. One of them hoists what seems to be a secondary motor. It's old and rusty and looks completely unreliable. I move in for a closer inspection and realize that it's a diving air compressor. It's a crude system. They fix two fifty-yard rubber hoses to the output valves and attach the other ends to a couple of scuba second-stage regulators. I would never trust this setup but for them it's all they've ever known. They throw all the hoses overboard and spend the next ten minutes undoing all the knots. When their breathing apparatus is finally ready, they don the rest of their gear. We will all dive solo while David stays in the boat to check on the compressor and prevent the floating hoses from tangling. It's a demanding job; he must constantly restart the boat engine to follow after the divers moving across the bottom.

Monico briefs me on their light signals: when we want to approach the boat, we surface and flash twice so David can position the boat and relieve us of our loads. David sees that I am ready to dive and he laughs at my small headlight. He hands me his big dive light, then gives me the signal to dive. I roll back in the water and start my freedive into complete darkness. Monico and Pedro both take their spear guns to shoot the occasional big fish, but they focus mainly on the large sea cucumbers resting on the bottom. They can sell these strange sea creatures for eight times more than any fish.

They drop down to sixty feet and start their collection. I freedive by them a few times but am unable to stay more than a few seconds. I soon swim to a shallower area where rocks cover the bottom fifteen feet below me. All I can see are small patches of terrain illuminated by the narrow beam of my light. I am looking exclusively for lobsters. I don't want to waste my time with fish. I have never dived for lobsters before, so Monico tells me to look for their glowing eyes and explains to me three techniques for catching them. One is to grab both antennae at the base—but if you miss the base, the antennae will break. The lobster will grow them back but your plate will be empty. An easier way is to spear them using only one power band, or to just stab them with the full gun used like a pole spear.

I am pleased to see my first one after fifteen minutes. I spear it and struggle to put it in my homemade goodie bag. The bug grips the mesh with all of its legs and I can't stuff him in. It snaps its tail and one of its spines pierces my glove and sinks into the flesh of my hand. I don't have enough hands to do this well. I'm gripping the light and my spear gun in one hand and need two more to hold the goodie bag open and shove the lobster in. I send a light signal to David and swim to the boat. He grabs my catch and I return to hunt for more. It's like a game, totally captivating.

In the beam of light the lobster's eyes flash like lemon citrine gemstones. At first, I only notice the ones with open eyes and extended antennae. But then I start to see them better and understand their favorite hiding spots. I stay in the water for nearly two hours and only stop when I'm nearly hypothermic. The thin wetsuit I am wearing is clearly insufficient for night dives at this time of the year. I return to the *panga* after catching eleven lobsters.

I change into dry clothes in the dark and then grab my flashlight to look at the divers' catch. One section of the boat is entirely full of sea cucumbers. There are about thirty kilos of slimy invertebrates in a big pile. In the front of the boat are fifteen large parrotfish, a couple of giant pargo, a few sea bass and various others. Monico and Pedro have not wasted their time underwater. They return ten minutes later with their last loads that also contain over a dozen lobsters. We head back to our beach, trying to protect ourselves from the cold wind as the *panga* motors under full power.

Luke is sleeping when we get there, but he wakes up for a midnight lobster feast. Our friends fry most of the lobsters. It is our first ever all-you-can-eat lobster buffet. Luke pulls out a bottle of tequila he has saved and squeezes a few limes to make a margarita. Our friends boil the sea cucumbers in huge cauldrons made from oil drums to prepare them to be sold. We finish the evening drinking and talking around the fire, occasionally stirring the vats with a stick of driftwood. The night dive is a success, the dinner is divine and the margaritas are deadly. I go to bed with the odor of wood smoke in my hair and the lingering flavors of lobster and tequila on my palate.

The next morning, I go with the fishermen to pull their nets out of the water. The placement has not been good and the only fish they catch is a poisonous stonefish. They release it carefully and we return to camp for a breakfast of the remaining lobsters.

I have learned a lot from our new friends. The techniques they taught me for spotting and catching the prize of the sea will aid me for the rest of my trip. I have also learned a more efficient technique for gutting large fish that will improve our yields. But, more importantly, I have come to a deeper understanding of the fishermen's strong reliance on the sea. They have no other way to make money. They dive, collect and sell and will continue to do so. The risks are great, the rewards are few and, if the resources run out, they will be left with nothing. For most in Baja, such is life.

⚓

Jean-Philippe, 8 December 1998

On our third day out from Punta Botella, we leave the coast and choose to reach La Paz following a path of islands. In the morning, the wind comes in gusts. The sea is white with breakers but it looks manageable. We have to ferry angle east in order to reach our destination. It looks like we will have to contend with waves hitting us broadside and from the rear the entire way. In the last few weeks, I have begun to look upon these conditions as a positive challenge. I try to use the waves to my advantage no matter which direction they are rolling from. I now understand how to surf the side swell in crosswinds. I've learned how to surf down the backside of oncoming swells when they don't break. And, more and more, I find that I prefer rough conditions to calm water. I am no longer apprehensive about capsizing, even with our overloaded kayak. The Sea of Cortez has served us well as a training ground and we feel we're ready to paddle the rougher Atlantic Coast of Honduras and Nicaragua.

We spot a couple of small islands and realize that one has a lighthouse and what appears to be a collection of houses. On the map it's called Isla Coyote and we're curious, so we paddle directly to it. The islet is no longer than 150 yards and no wider than 75. It is little more than a rocky hill that supports a dozen houses. We land and are greeted by fisherman Jose and his son Umberto. We share stories and they take us on a tour. Six families, a total of twenty-seven people, live here. The island is equipped with solar panels and a desalination plant. There is a small school painted with bright murals of orcas and whales. The community, whose responsibility is the maintenance of the lighthouse, is largely self-sufficient.

After talking with the islanders, I realize that we are on sacred ground. Jose tells us that he is a friend of Jacques Cousteau; before his death, the famous French marine scientist often visited Jose on Coyote when he was filming in the Sea of Cortez. Cousteau has been one of my greatest heroes since childhood. I saw his documentary on the Amazon when I was eleven or twelve and his voyages have inspired my life and expeditions. In some respects I can say that I am here, on this journey, because of Jacques Cousteau. Realizing we have a common bond, Jose and I immediately hit it off.

When we leave the island, Jose offers us some pargo filets and wishes us well. He understands our journey and why we are on it. He tells us that one of his sons, also inspired by Cousteau, has headed out into the wilds as a biologist and explorer. On days when big storms rattle the roof and coat the windows with spray, he worries about his son. At the beginning, he was angry and forbade his son to leave, but he has come to respect and admire his son's accomplishments. If he comes home once a year to visit and shares many stories with the family, then Jose is happy. Luke and I nod at each other as we board the kayaks and paddle out into the open sea. We know what he is talking about.

We paddled out to our next destination, the island of San Francisquito.

†

Jean-Philippe, 9 December 1998

The end of our Baja leg is near and we are taking a rest day on the island of San Francisquito. In the morning the wind dies. It is our first calm day since we left Loreto. We plan to have our kayaks ready by nightfall in order to get up very early the next morning for our longest open-water crossing in Baja. We can barely see the foggy outline of Isla Partida, twenty nautical miles away. It's one of the last islands before reaching the mainland of south Baja; just beyond it is Punta Tecolote, which guards the mouth of the huge bay that leads to La Paz.

I have mixed feelings about arriving in La Paz. The adventure isn't over; it's merely the end of the first leg. In fact, the adventure will soon surge to a higher level. The tropics will certainly be more challenging in every way. The seas will be bigger. Insects and tropical diseases will be a concern. And the human factor will be less predictable. But the real crux of what I'm feeling at the moment is the idea of being in a large city with traffic, noise and pollution. La Paz, with a population of 200,000, will be the first city we have encountered since we left San Diego over three months ago. The only things I look forward to are a hot shower, an ice cream and a comfy bed.

†

Jean-Philippe, 10 December 1998

The alarm rings at 2:45 a.m., but neither of us move. Two minutes later, it rings again and still we don't move. We can feel the cold and hear the wind howling and are afraid of what we'll see if we get up. After the third alarm bell, we reluctantly leave the warmth of our sleeping bags. It takes us an hour to eat some breakfast and finish loading our kayaks. By 4:00 a.m., we are on the water and ready to paddle out of the protected bay. We know a lighthouse marks the north end of Isla Partida twenty nautical miles away, but as a backup I have entered the coordinates in our GPS receiver. The mainland is even further away, thirty miles as the crow flies. From our current location, even during the light of day, neither point is visible with the naked eye.

We paddle along the western shore of Isla San Francisco in the dark. We are now a party of three. Paul, a kayaking guide and ski instructor who is doing a solo crossing of the Sea of Cortez, joins us. We met a few days ago, and he asked if he could join us for this crossing, as he didn't feel he could attempt it by himself. Without us, he'd be hugging the coast.

The swell is big. It's difficult to say exactly how big in the pitch-dark of morning, but we feel it thrusting us up and down like an elevator. It feels about a story high. When we reach the south end of our island, we can't see the lighthouse that is supposed to guide us to our destination; the sea is too rough and it obscures our view of the horizon. All we can see is the churning black ocean immediately in front of our kayaks that fades into the gloom.

I try to check my GPS, but the rechargeable batteries die. Luckily, I have another set at hand and, once reloaded, I take a compass bearing. We have to paddle to 126 degrees. With my headlamp on, I check the compass and aim at a cluster of stars in that direction. Fortunately, the wind and waves are at our back. We surf and make good time but Luke seems tentative in the darkness. His silence means that he is not happy. Paul seems to feel comfortable with the conditions and I am loving them. The motion of the waves in the dark awakens a new sense in me. I can feel; I don't need to see. I let the swell push me and I focus on the stars. Sometimes they disappear behind clouds. I check the compass often and readjust our course to compensate for the earth's rotation and the displacement of my reference stars.

After an hour, the wind worsens, the swell grows bigger and the sky ominously clouds over. The stars disappear long before daybreak, leaving me without any guidance. It is still too dark for me to be able to monitor a compass heading. Holding the flashlight while paddling is impossible and leaving it on my forehead is uncomfortable, so I try to keep my bearings as best I can using nothing more than my senses and the angle of the waves.

When the sun rises, there is no land in sight. No islands south, no islands north and no mainland to the west, just the three of us in our small kayaks in the middle of a roiling sea. I take another GPS reading and it tells me to follow a new bearing of 135 degrees. Either we have drifted or paddled off course, but considering the wind and swell conditions, I am relatively pleased with our position. The waves are now visible and we estimate them at a constant eight feet, punctuated by the occasional ten-foot rogue. We surf for a while and when I finally sight the island six miles away, I adjust our course again.

As I'm surfing down a nice curling wave, I hear Luke's yell: "Man overboard, man overboard!" I turn back and see Paul upside down. He tries to roll but is unsuccessful. He attempts twice more and then pulls the ripcord. By the time we reach him, he is flipping his kayak back up and trying to flop his upper body over his cockpit. In the heavy swell, he waits for me to steady his kayak and scrambles back in. He is visibly shaken. His cockpit is full of water and the kayak is extremely unstable. He will capsize again if we don't pump it out immediately. To make things worse, Paul's kayak is a narrow performance craft, built more for speed and efficiency than stability. After putting his spray skirt on, I insert the pump through a gap and flush the water out as quickly as possible. Now we are all soaked and cold, so we quickly resume paddling. Paul is rattled to the core and it's all he can do to put his blades in the water. Luke is white as a ghost from nausea since he has spent the past twenty minutes looking down helping me steady Paul's boat instead of looking up at the horizon to steady his equilibrium. The bouncing and heaving has taken its toll on him. I am the only one still enjoying the conditions. After an hour our collective situation improves slightly. Luke now has the island to fix on and color returns to his face. I know he is feeling better when he starts talking about food. Paul, however, is not doing well. He initially regained confidence after his capsize and we made good progress toward our destination. But now, with four miles to go, I hear again: "Man overboard, man overboard!" When I turn back

Paul is rolling back up. His instincts and skills are still intact, but he looks on the verge of a breakdown. He had not seen this capsize coming. He is shell-shocked and not responding well; he can hardly paddle. This is bad. It's impossible to tow someone in these waves. All we can do is offer him moral support. We need to keep him talking and pump him up with encouragement. We take nearly two hours to paddle the final four miles, keeping Paul between us the entire time. When we finally touch down on shore, Paul takes an hour to compose himself and with a few sparse words and great humility he thanks us. We don't make a big deal of it because we know it has injured his pride. The whole experience gives us pause; it's humbling for us, too. We leave him alone and I call to Luke, "We need to talk."

Luke senses my unhappiness. "What's up?" he replies nonchalantly. And then I explode.

"What the hell was that on the ocean today?" Obviously not understanding, Luke barks defensively, "What are you talking about?"

"Two times, Paul was right in front of you, while I was leading the way hundreds of feet ahead. You called in man overboard and didn't move when he capsized. Both times I turned around and was at his side helping him out before you even thought about moving. Are you out of your mind?"

"Well, I thought he was okay, he's a professional kayak guide," Luke says.

"What the hell is wrong with you, Luke? Next time if I'm drowning, you're just going to stand still and watch, assuming I'm okay because I'm a tough mother fucker?" I had contained my rage while on the sea about Luke's lack of reaction so as not to add more stress on Paul's mental state, but now I had to let it out. Luke first stays speechless, until he finally explodes, too.

"Well, fuck you with your bossy leadership. I'm sick and tired of you patronizing me all the time. I'm sick of you telling me what to do every day, so fuck yourself."

"Fine," I say, "we're through. We reach La Paz and we split. I continue this expedition on my own. You do what you want, but I prefer to paddle alone than with an irresponsible and immature spoiled little kid." Luke and I had often quarreled, so much so that many people said we sounded like a married couple. But today was our first real fight. I want him to be responsible, and learn from his mistakes, but Luke isn't ready for that. He just wants me off his back, so we spend the entire day scouting opposite parts of the island. In the evening, we don't talk much. Paul does his best to cheer up our camp with jokes and stories, but this incident is a sharp dent in what had been an almost perfect expedition paddling the entire Sea of Cortez.

↑

Jean-Philippe, 11 December 1998

The next morning as I am preparing my kayak for another crossing, Luke comes to apologize. "I'm sorry, brother. I was really exhausted yesterday and didn't realize Paul was really in trouble." He also acknowledges that he is often too laid-back but says that he deeply values our friendship and wants to continue south with me. I apologize for lashing out at him and, after a big bear hug, we paddle on to the famous and touristy Isla Esperitu, our last camp before La Paz.

↑

La Paz: Viva la Expedicion

Luke, 13 December 1998

Yesterday we touched down on Tecolote Point and today we paddle into La Paz, the way we started out in San Felipe: just the two of us. Paul, who plans to continue south to Los Cabos, wants to avoid the twenty-two-mile paddle in and out of the bay, so he leaves his boat here at our campsite on a secluded dune, just around the point from the popular

Tecolote beach. To hide it, he buries his entire boat in the sand and then sets off to hitchhike into La Paz.

The scenery during the final paddle into town denies the wild, remote idyll of the rest of Baja. Our ears are attuned to the sounds of wind, water and wildlife. We've become accustomed to vast expanses of desert devoid of any structure made by man and it's a jolt to see the industrial trappings of a big city. We pass by a complex that looks like a refinery. Gleaming white Pemex petroleum tanks, like giant ivory lozenges, sit out front. Tankers and barges lie at the dock, their diesel engines clunking idly, exhaling blue fog. As we close in on La Paz, a few multi-story buildings—the first ones we've seen in three months—rise from the shoreline. The far-off blatting of outboard engines and metallic clanking of machinery filters through the sound of the breeze and waves. Both of us react, visibly tightening up.

The city turns out to be a quirky mix of industrial blue-collar energy and touristy charm. Palm trees wave over the *malecón* boardwalk. We stroll by a string of restaurants and discos blaring American top-forty and Mexican pop. We stop at a street stall for fried oyster tacos piled with pickled chiles and sautéed onions and oozing with three different kinds of salsa. Offshore, a shrimp trawler, stuffed to the gunwales, makes its way to a processing plant/fish market on the other side of town. Out in the bay a cargo ship churns toward the open sea.

We draw a lot of attention dragging our sodden gear over to a cheap hotel. We take pride in our haggard appearance. We fit in with the weather-beaten fishermen and laborers. Neither of us has shaved in three months. The backs of our hands are burned. Our skin is a dusty, matte bronze. We haven't had a fresh-water shower in weeks. When we tell fellow guests at the hostel that we've just paddled 800 miles and that we're going for 2,200 more, they look at us and see that there is no question that we speak the truth.

An evening of drinking and conversation in the hostel proves to be an affirmation of all our goals for the first stage of CASKE2000. People are curious about our adventures and interested in the much broader mission of our expedition. We look weathered and experienced and they take us seriously and listen to what we have to say. It's the kind of response we had tried to generate prior to departure from sponsors and the media. As we found out, our enthusiasm and drive didn't compensate for our lack of experience and fame so most people in the industry had brushed us aside. If only they could see us now. We're in rock-hard shape, our skills are sharp and we're accomplishing everything we said we would. Better yet, thanks to our burgeoning website, we're starting to touch people.

CHAPTER 2
BELIZE

Introduction

Jean-Philippe, 4 March 1999

BAJA WAS A fascinating experience on its own: Luke and I had learned how to handle the rough seas as well as our conflicting personalities there. We knew that we had to survive both to make this expedition a success—and that we needed breaks from each other even more than our bodies needed rest. Luke and I split up in La Paz after storing all our gear in the basement of a local kayak tour operator. Luke returned to the U.S. to try to secure more sponsorship while I worked on our website from South America.

It is the end of February by the time we return to La Paz. Happy to meet again and looking forward to returning to some action, our joy quickly ends when we find out that rats have chewed holes through half of our dry bags. It may have been funny if the rats had not also eaten through the fabric hulls of our kayaks. We put all our gear onto a cargo boat to cross to the mainland and, after three days of transferring 1,000 pounds of kayak and gear from one means of transportation to another, our last bus drops us in the Yucatan Peninsula close to the Belize border on the Atlantic Coast.

The thick vegetation of the coastal forest contrasts greatly with Baja so we're looking forward to this new adventure. The first few days we spend in a campground in Corozal, the Belize border town, fixing holes in our hypalon hulls and using a spare sponsoon (a small stabilization float) to patch all our dry bags. They end up looking pretty funky—red, green or yellow with white latex circles of various sizes spread all over them. During this task the first locals to welcome us are the mosquitoes and notorious sandflies; we haven't even touched the water and already look like we suffer from chickenpox. There isn't much happening in Corozal, but luckily this little Creole town is also the home of Snakeman.

↑

Snakeman and the Medicine of the Ancient Maya

Jean-Philippe, 5 March 1999

Snakes typically evoke fear and revulsion in western cultures. How is it that the same creature that represents the devil in the Bible was the symbol of medicine in ancient Greece and is still found today on ambulances and pharmacies in many countries?

In Central America, the ancient Mayan people revered snakes. Rattlesnake representations and drawings have been found on countless pieces of pottery and murals. A snake is also the most prominent feature on the headdress of one of their most important deities, the goddess of the healing arts, Ix Chel. Like the Chinese, they believed in the medicinal properties of certain species of snakes. The enduring legacy of the ancient Maya is a supposed cure-all snake bone medicine called *cascabel* that is still used today by a few traditional healers.

In the last ten years, new controversy over this ancient medicine has been brewing in the backroom lab/clinic of a man known as Snakeman. Twenty years ago, Peter Singfield's fascination with medical science, traditional healing and Mayan culture led him to Belize and an incredible discovery. A few days with this local legend in Belize served as an introduction to the world of Mayan medicine and gave me a revealing perspective on the skepticism and politics of the western medical establishment. Forgotten by most who now place their faith in western pharmaceuticals, these traditional remedies have no chemical side effects and they reputedly boost the immune system to help the body fight illness naturally. In a world of mutating diseases and increasingly resistant strains, modern medicine is losing ground: epidemics we thought long gone are now reappearing. Perhaps the one cure for all of them lies in new variations of old secrets preserved by a few healers who keep the faith.

I first came in contact with Peter two years ago while preparing for CASKE2000. We were both members of various mailing lists on tropical health issues. Peter often engaged other medical professionals in long discussions about the philosophy and science behind western medicines. He frequently posed questions about their toxic side effects, questionable efficacy and future obsolescence and, in the process, raised a storm of controversy. I found many of his arguments viable and I chimed in as well. We stayed in contact until arriving on our expedition in northern Belize.

It didn't take us long to find Snakeman. In the sweltering, sleepy town of Corozal near the border of Mexico, everybody seems to know everybody. The single mention of his name always elicited an immediate response, some enthusiastic and some dismissive. His medicine, passion and longwinded stories have built his fame. People warned us about Peter's ability to speak without pausing to breathe; our first meeting with him confirmed it.

We made a quick phone call and, a few minutes later, an old Volkswagen Rabbit stopped in front of our bungalow. A large man with a ponytail half hidden under a baseball cap climbed out while his diminutive Mayan wife remained sitting in the car. He walked over to us with a great big smile and we sat talking for a couple of hours in front of our bungalow.

Twenty years ago, he left Canada where he worked as a mechanical and electrical engineer at the National Research Institute. His study of chemistry and medicine as hobbies led to a fascination with medicinal plants and natural healing. He traveled extensively in Central America to pursue this passion and eventually moved to Belize to devote himself full-time to natural medicine. In the course of his studies and investigations, he became friendly with the elderly Mopan Mayan healer Don Eligio Panti. Panti—who has gained posthumous fame (he died in 1996 at the age of 103) as the mentor of Dr. Rosita Arvigo, the author of *Sastun*—was the last known Mayan shaman with the title "Doctor-Priest." Like Arvigo, Snakeman credits Panti with being an inspiration for some of his studies. It was Panti, in part, who gave Snakeman encouragement to pursue his greatest discovery, one rooted deeply in ancient Mayan lore.

During Peter's research into natural healing, and Mayan culture, science and history, he met a healer from El Salvador who introduced him to *cascabel*. In Spanish, the word literally means rattlesnake and, according to legends, the snake is the source of one of the most potent medicines known to the ancient Maya. Today, shamans and healers in many areas of Central America and Mexico tout different varieties of *cascabel*. Snakeman investigated dozens of them, but few proved effective in healing major ailments and none of them stood up to his battery of tests. That is, until Peter stumbled onto a rare sub-species of the tropical rattlesnake called *tzabcan* (Yucatec Mayan for "rattlesnake") and used it to produce his own. That medicine proved to be much more potent.

Singfield explains that the few existing Mayan codices (texts) actually refer to *cascabel*. In his estimation, other shamans who claim to make the medicine have missed a crucial aspect of the traditional preparation: the texts say that no "agitated" rattlesnakes shall be used. It was believed that the anger in the snake caused changes in the make-up of the medicine (not difficult to imagine when you consider what happens in the human body when we get angry, i.e., the release of adrenaline, endorphins and other chemicals), thus only calm ones were acceptable. The problem is that rattlesnakes, particularly tropical species, are quick, lean vipers known for their aggressive behavior. But, for some reason, the *tzabcan* is an exception. Singfield theorizes that this docile and meaty species is the rediscovered snake of lore. He brought in Wolfgang Wooster, a Ph.D. in herpetology. After two months of field study to verify the snake, Wooster officially classified it as a new sub-species, native only to that region.

For two decades now Singfield has produced the traditional Mayan *cascabel* powder by skinning, drying, baking, grinding and sifting Tzabcan snakes. Villagers who had always killed and discarded the snakes out of fear now bring them to Peter. It is the locals who have appropriately dubbed him Snakeman.

According to Singfield, *cascabel* doesn't treat any specific disease directly; rather it acts as a strong immune-system enhancer, promoting rapid, natural healing for a wide variety of ailments. Snakeman claims to have successfully treated patients with AIDS, cancer, terminal diabetes, ulcers and severe burns, infections and gangrene. One spoonful taken daily also boosts the immune system against most ailments including malaria, dengue fever and others. People who have taken his treatments, locals and foreigners alike, remain strong adherents. Scientists and health officials avert their eyes from a practice of medicine that doesn't conform to the western model. Snakeman explains that western doctors and the FDA require the identification of a pure chemical substance.

"How can you isolate an active ingredient when you don't know what you are looking for because we have no concept of a medicine that enhances the immune system, nor what combination of compounds augmenting and reacting with each other causes it? After baking the snake dry at 320 degrees Fahrenheit, no organic components are left; it's gone through the transformation, it's dehydrated, only minerals are left. The stuff looks like cement: you could mix that with sand and build with it. And the question arises, 'Well, how can a mineral be a medicine?' Well, God knows. When we put it in analysis with pharmaceutical researchers down here in the late 1980s that's what they were doing, culture tests and everything. I told them from the beginning that those tests don't apply. You can put it in a culture with a lethal disease and it doesn't kill the disease, it only works with the immune system. Well, it took them two years to figure that out. They spent more than a half-million dollars researching in that direction before they agreed with me."

I ate a mouthful of it and couldn't discern much taste more than that of toasted fish bones.

What Singfield does know is that his particular *cascabel* works well, miraculously so in some cases, but it won't make him rich. For years he tried to document it and share his discoveries, but gave up after realizing that western societies weren't ready to "make the leap of faith" to medicines they couldn't isolate or produce synthetically. His euphoria over his discovery faded over the years; he tired of what he referred to as "banging his head against an insurmountable wall of skepticism." Slowly, million-dollar dreams were replaced by realistic altruism. Snake-man returned his focus to the local patients and his few dedicated patients abroad and continued his studies on the efficacy of *cascabel* on other diseases.

His website features pictures of the impressive work of his medicine. Particularly striking is a photo sequence of a severe burn victim. The patient, a drug addict, had tried for the third time to steal from dealers and they taught him a brutal lesson by holding his hand in the flames of a campfire for nearly a minute. Embarrassed and in severe pain, he avoided medical treatment for four days. By the time he arrived on Peter's doorstep, serious gangrene and infection had advanced all the way up to the shoulder. The western solution would have been immediate amputation to be followed by a course of powerful antibiotics for weeks. Peter treated him with high dosages of *cascabel* and, within days, the infection and gangrene began to recede. By the second week tissue had started to regenerate. The time-lapse photos show the recovery to the point where the man regained full usage of the arm.

According to Singfield, another distinguishing characteristic of *cascabel* is its lack of toxicity and how that affects the recovery of patients. The side effects and after-effects of chemical medicines used to combat serious diseases and infections are so severe that they often have to be treated as well. *Cascabel,* however, is a natural immune-system enhancer; there are no toxic side effects. With great fervor he explained that things like chemotherapy, malaria prophylactics and strong antibiotics all do their job of destroying the foreign agent causing the disease. Unfortunately, in the process they also adversely affect the immune system and white blood cell count, in addition to the many other toxic side effects. The only byproduct of *cascabel* is blood sedimentation. It's unavoidable, he says, that when new tissues generate, dead tissues are reabsorbed into the body and in strong cases can produce a significant amount of byproduct. The dead cells being absorbed into the blood stream cause the blood sedimentation count to go up forty to sixty times above normal and the kidneys produce very thick urine. To aid the kidneys in cleansing the blood, he prescribes the highly effective and simple Mayan remedy, an infusion of corn silk, drunk like tea. The body then just excretes the excess dead cells. The patient can literally flush his/her problems down the toilet.

Snakeman's struggles for recognition and legitimacy over the years have marked him: he has become extremely cynical about the current state of affairs in the health care system in industrialized countries. He will tell you that the most difficult and disheartening part of his natural medicine practice is the constant battle to silence and/or convince the doubters. He is appalled at the amount of propaganda people accept as truth. The toughest decision he has had to make was to abandon his pursuit of mainstream acceptance and his dream of taking a place among the pantheon of great medical explorers. "I'm no saint," he will tell you, and he emphasizes that his original intention was to make money. He was convinced he had discovered the Holy Grail of medicine and would be suitably rewarded. These days he rarely even bothers to add more testimonials to his website and he disdains patients whom he calls "moderns," people from first-world societies. It is too much hassle with not enough reward.

"How do you convince somebody like that who is dying from terminal stomach cancer, that everything he thinks he knows about his disease, medical treatment, health care, etc., is bullshit? He should place absolute trust in a medicine that comes from a snake that some guy has dug out of a jungle? Even if he has exhausted all his options for treatment within accepted medical science, he is so brainwashed by the media and the AMA that he tries to hedge his bets by pursuing another course of treatment while on mine. That renders the cascabel completely ineffective because the chemical medicines neutralize any progress made by his immune system."

Apparently as the *cascabel* works to augment the immune system, the chemotherapy and antibiotics attack the disease agent and in the process tear down the body's natural defenses as well.

"Screw it, you know. I don't need to deal with that. I keep one 'modern' cancer patient a year to pay the bills. The rest are local people. They listen to what I say and it works and they're extremely grateful. The ancient Mayans didn't have chemistry to tell them why their medicines worked. There were no such things as chemically pure isolates."

He continued to explain that most ancient Mayans self-medicated with a number of bush remedies and herbal medicines for everyday problems and went to see the shaman for anything serious. People believed in the medicine; it cured them although nobody knew down to the exact atom why. A healthy society of millions flourished in this area, while the squalor of the cities in "civilized" Europe bred plagues and disease. They must have been doing something right.

Snakeman insists that medicine these days is all about marketing, propaganda, politics and money. He looks a little wistful about that last part, especially as he often barters with locals or sells them the medicine below production cost. He spends about thirty-five cents to produce a gram of cascabel. He sells it to local people, who mostly live subsistence lifestyles, for twenty-five cents; to friends and other Belizeans for fifty cents and to patients abroad for a dollar. As for his marketing and promotional budgets, they don't exist. The businessman in him dreams of multi-million-dollar investment capital to fund major case testing, push the medicine through FDA licensing procedures, start a promotional campaign and turn islands of mangrove into natural farms to breed and raise the snakes. "I could be fully operational within a year…," he says.

As we were talking, he walked around his overgrown garden picking bananas and cassava. His wife and her extended family milled around in the kitchen cooking. We visited his study/garage room and he tinkered with his dusty and finicky computer while we picked up various gadgets and bits of moldy electronics that he had constructed or salvaged. His hard drive crashed and his floppy drive malfunctioned as he tried to copy a file off a disk we'd given him. Unfazed, he opened a plastic bottle of home-brewed sugar cane wine, poured us some and proceeded to take the computer apart and fix it in front of our eyes. "That wine is a blood tonic. It'll make your head spin and it's good for you. Most of the snakes I get come from the cane fields. The workers bring them to me and I buy them and sometimes I get a little of this too."

With appropriate funding, he could have his name in lights, in print in medical journals or on the label of a bottle on the shelf of a chain store pharmacy. But he also might have to make himself more marketable. He'd have to tone down his notoriously provocative rhetoric and polish his ubiquitous and controversial presence on the Internet. With better facilities and equipment his life would be easier, more convenient and, dare we say it, more modern. But that's why he came to Belize, to get away from all that, to do what he wants and to be who he wants to be. Part of him revels in his role as the iconoclastic pundit of the medical world: after all, a snake in a farm isn't the same as a snake in the grass.

⸸

Luke, 10 March 1999

Belize is a funny place. You cross the border from Mexico into the first town, Corozal, and you see blacks, Chinese, Hispanics and whites all speaking at least two languages. One of them is usually Creole. I could pick up phrases and words here and there, but it is far enough from standard English to be an entirely distinct language. Verb conjugations are based on African grammar, everything is abbreviated and accented very heavily and idiom is the rule. They even use words that we would consider diminutive in everyday speech, like addressing each other as "boy." And when they're trying to be polite they call you "boss." "Baad" means good, and "haaht" means "hard." They abbreviate "and then I said…" to "an nen I seh…" It's fascinating, especially when someone, such as a clerk in a store, speaks to you in lilting but perfect English and then turns to a friend and fires off something in Creole. And when black people start speaking Spanish with their Caribbean swing, look out, because that is the true suave Latin sound. "Sabes, hombre? Yaaah, mahn."

When we were setting up and packing our kayaks on the water-taxi dock in Belize City, an old man sidled up and asked, "Wheh y' gwinta, baiy?" I had to ask him to repeat it three times. I still didn't get it and we had to talk in Spanish. After he left, a few minutes later it dawned on me that he'd said, "Where you going to, boy?"

Everyone in Belize has a ready smile and a cheery word to offer. This is especially true of the guys working the street, washing cars, doing errands, anything to make a buck. It's a combination of hustler's shtick and genuine friendliness and it's a perfect opportunity to train your ears to pick up the accent. Even when the inevitable moment comes—after they've introduced themselves and chatted gregariously for a few minutes—when they ask you for money, "Cahn I geht a dallah, boss?," it's hard not to empty your pockets into their outstretched hands. "Yah know whehn ya geev, ya geht, eet cum back in many way t'ya," they'll say. In response, I've learned to smile and say, "I jus' down yea travlin', mahn. Don' got many dallah. I gwin t'da islands," and then I shake their hand and say, "Nice t'meecha, boss."

†

Luke, 11 March 1999

In light of our mission and its goals, the etymology of the name "Belize" is appropriately symbolic. There are two theories on its origin. Some say that it was derived from a Hispanicized pronunciation of "Wallace," the surname of a prominent British settler. In the mid-1600s, he and his fellow pioneers carved one of the first permanent settlements on the mainland out of the swampy lowland forests. Their efforts inspired others to follow. The second, and more probable, theory is that the name comes from the Mayan word *Belikin*, meaning "road to the sea." And for us, the wide swath of calm shallows inside the 180-mile-long barrier reef will be like a gentle highway out to the open Caribbean further south.

Culturally and historically Belize offers much more than Baja. Although finding even electricity and phone, much less a line with reasonable transmission speed, is as challenging as the paddling at times, we're anxious to begin filling the website with all this new cultural content. The fertile jungle of this region was the petri dish for Mayan civilization. All the great cities of the High Classic Period in Mayan history were clustered throughout this area. Just over Belize's northern border in the Yucatan of Mexico lie the ruins of Chichen Itza, Tulum and Uxmal. On the western border is perhaps the greatest metropolis of the Mayan civilization, Tikal. And within the boundaries of Belize itself are the important sites of Lamanai and Xunantunich. Archaeologists estimate that even though the Mayan empire was well into decline when the first conquistadors arrived, over 400,000 people may have inhabited the area. The population today, although growing steadily again, is only 250,000.

Many different arrivals and political agendas have shaped Belize into one of the most ethnically diverse countries in Latin America. The first explorers, the Spanish, largely ignored the area. With their gaze already fixed on the gold in Mexico and Peru, Belize offered few obvious material resources. Later, British and Dutch pirates used the reef to play hide and seek with the Spanish Armada and the Cay islands as outposts for raids on the gold fleet throughout the Caribbean. As the flow of precious metals heading for Europe slowed to a trickle in the 1700s, many former buccaneers settled on the mainland. Logging of mahogany and logwood (used as a textile dye) replaced piracy as the foundation for the local economy. While the European settlements grew and thrived, the Mayan population was decimated by a host of foreign diseases imported by their new neighbors. Most of the rest immigrated to the highlands of Guatemala to the west.

At about the same time, Afro-Caribbeans began to arrive in Belize. Garifuna groups (mixed Afro-Indians) migrated up the southern coastline from Honduras, and slaves from Jamaica were brought in to work on sugar cane, banana and logging plantations.

More recently, Belizean independence has led to a shift in the ethnic make-up of the country. In the 1970s, with the logging industry in its death throes, the British government realized that they had tapped all the resources of "British Honduras." So, in 1981 they granted Belize full independence. Since then, many Asian and Middle Eastern immigrants, Mennonites from the States and a host of American and European expatriates have taken advantage of relaxed naturalization laws.

With little industry other than agriculture, the country remains remote and rural. The pace of life ambles along at the speed of its economic growth, half a step faster than neutral. Many communities still live pastoral, subsistence lifestyles, especially in the south, where Garifuna and Mayan villages preserve their heritage and traditions. But the odor of change, like the acrid sweetness of charred vegetation from slash-and-burn farms, is in the air.

We will spend two months here hopping from island to island. The climate and landscape are total departures from Baja: islands here yield a bounty of coconuts and seafood and it is no chore to be a castaway on a deserted isle.

†

Luke, 18 March 1999

Two weeks after entering Belize, our kayaks and the rest of our gear are fixed: with our papers in order and our website updated, our first day on the water has finally come. It has been three months since we last paddled.

Traveling and packing. Packing and traveling. It seems like we've done little else during the past three weeks as we've moved overland from Baja to Belize. Day one of the second stage of our expedition is supposed to be a change of scenery. I want to feel the motion of waves and taste their fresh brine; I'm ready for a little wind and spray in my face. No more shimmering waves of heat off the asphalt. No more dusty blasts from passing trucks. No more rust-colored droplets of sweat that stain our collars. Alas, this morning looks to be more of the same.

We leave our bungalow in Corozal to catch a 4:50 a.m. "express" bus to Belize City. We had already decided against paddling out of the murky bay of Corozal where the brackish water is shallow and full of half-submerged obstacles: wrecked boats, logs, dead coral and rocks. All visible land appears to be mangrove swamp, and we have just done more than our share of kayak hole patching so we decide to launch from the docks in the capital city instead.

"Downtown" Corozal is the first stop and we are two among six on the old converted school bus. We breathe a sigh of relief because we have all our gear, boats included, and the last thing we want to deal with now is a crowd. Unfortunately, our relief is short-lived. This bus turns out to be the commuter ride for all the day laborers in northern Belize. By 5:30 a.m., it is packed with people and bags from floor to ceiling. Contrary to its name there is nothing EXPRESS about this bus. We stop for every guy standing on the side of the road the whole way.

The driver and the money collector are very helpful. Looking at our ridiculous quantity of baggage, they gather that we are not standard "backpackers." So, they drop everyone off and then go out of their way to get us to the water-taxi dock at the mouth of the Belize River. We unload everything on the dock and start to set up the boats as the city awakens.

By 9:00 a.m., there is a large group standing around waiting for the boat out to Ambergris Cay. Everyone is very curious why we prefer to paddle out to the islands on our own power when there is a perfectly good motor launch to ride in. Ironically, the boat is late because of a mechanical problem, which gives all the passengers ample time to stare and ask many questions. One lady is so inspired by our journey that she runs out and buys us johnny cakes (an unleavened biscuit with ham and cheese) and presents us with hand-painted gourd cups which she inscribes with a message: "CASKE2000 Good Luck. Use only in an emergency." A guy catches her wink and informs us that a bottle of rum is appropriate for any such emergency. Another man even goes so far as to bring Jean-Philippe down to Belize Channel 5 for an interview. And, just before noon, a film crew shows up to film us packing on the docks.

It takes us an entire day of constant motion to get ready. Finding drinking water is our first challenge. I have to walk six blocks with two heavy, five-gallon containers of purified water to fill our water bags. Less than an hour later, I go to return the empty jugs and collect my deposit but the store that sold them to me won't take them back so I'm already frustrated when I go shopping for food. When I walk into the store, my mood deteriorates further. The so-called supermarket has less than half the food items I am looking for. I have to walk around in the brutal midday sun for two hours visiting various smaller markets to procure what we need. Our planned 2:00 p.m. departure comes and goes.

By the afternoon, we have an entourage of street kids gathered on the docks. They are very curious and helpful but all are jockeying for tips. No assistance or errand is free. As we finally push off from the dock at dusk, I begin a chorus of Bob Marley's "Exodus" and they finish it. We stroke out of the mouth of the river with no particular destination in mind; it is far too late in the day to make it to the point we plotted on the map. When we see a clump of islands less than five miles out, we head straight for them.

This is where the poor planning hurts us. When people tell you that Belize is a kayaker's paradise, they don't tell you that a large percentage of the islands are inhospitable mangrove swamps. Just after sunset we arrive to find a nightmare come true: there is no place to stop and we have no place to go back to in Belize City. Our only option is to grab the map, pick an island at random and continue out into the darkness.

The next closest group of islands is another four miles off. They are our only options so we go for it. Halfway across we become increasingly doubtful as it begins to thunder and then pour. Our only asset at this point is a large ship a mile offshore, where we hope to stop and ask for help and directions. It turns out to be a sugar freighter filling up its hold from two barges tethered to its hull. When we pull up to the side, four men approach. They are shocked to see us out at night in the stormy conditions and they help us aboard the barge.

Everything is coated in half-dissolved raw sugar. While Jean-Philippe asks their suggestions for an island to camp on, I stand shivering, wet and increasingly sticky in the wind. Clouds of sugar drift away from the large scoop moving between the barges and the hold of the mother ship. Nobody seems concerned that the downpour may turn the entire load into molasses and they work slowly and methodically. My skin is quickly developing a candy shell.

The men confer for a few minutes and direct us toward a small glow in the distance a few miles off. It's an island with a lodge and is a nice place to camp, they say. We are freezing and anxious to arrive so we hop in quickly and paddle off. But after an hour the light doesn't seem to get any closer. Jean-Philippe believes that it must be from a boat that is sailing away from us, not from an island.

He reassesses and decides to veer left toward islands that our map and GPS say are close. After a second hour, we arrive at another musty-smelling mangrove island. According to the map, a whole string of islands lies to the south but we are totally disheartened and we steel ourselves for the very real possibility that we may spend a wet, windy and cold night on the water.

At the southern tip of the mangrove island, we spy a few twinkling lights emanating from a dark mass a couple miles away. Boats? A lodge? It doesn't matter. We head straight for it. Ten minutes later all the lights wink out and we have no bearing. We get out the headlamps to check the compass. Neither of us, however, had the presence of mind to put in new batteries before setting out. We disposed of the dead ones back in La Paz when we finished Baja.

I try to scavenge batteries from the radio but find only the rechargeable pack inside. We need to keep batteries in the GPS, so the only option is the digital camera. In jostling waves, I try to keep the camera dry and the headlamp battery case from falling in the water. I manage to get two batteries transferred and everything sealed and repacked in waterproof cases.

We continue on the same heading for nearly an hour. By this point we've been out for over four and a half hours and we're wet, worried, frustrated and exhausted. Upon reaching the island we move slowly along the shore, scanning the twisted mangrove for openings. I spy something solid and gray in a gap in the vegetation. A small beach? No, a stone wall. We go in and find that it's a seawall protecting filled land: above it is a grassy clearing. We sigh in relief. We won't spend the night in the boats after all. Upon exiting the boats a bobbing flashlight comes toward us from the other side of the island. Someone, perhaps a security guard, has heard us. It could be a private island or even a small resort.

I preempt the guard and call out in a friendly voice, asking where it is that we have landed. It turns out to be not a guard but a trio of teenagers, members of a Presbyterian church group from Texas. They started a parish in a small community on the mainland and built a church. And to celebrate its completion, they are out on Spanish Cay for their last night before heading home. According to them, this cay is the only non-mangrove island in the area.

"What in God's name are you two fellas doin' out here?" they ask, as they shake our hands and help us with our gear. I don't have an appropriate answer for them. It's as if we've forgotten everything we'd learned in Baja. During our break in the expedition, all our ingrained habits and mental checklists have disintegrated. By the time we arrived in La Paz, we were two perfectly calibrated cogs in a machine, each with our own routine. We were quick, efficient and we overlooked nothing. Today, we needed the entire day to get ready—something that should have taken us a few hours—and then we forgot to double-check all our safety equipment and our route.

"Making lots of stupid mistakes apparently," I answer.

I take a bag of cookies from our food sack, lay out my bedroll on the floor of the lodge and collapse in exhaustion. One of the adult chaperones asks, "What lies in store for you boys after this?" By the tone of his voice, I sense he's of the opinion that something other than pure chance was at work out there this evening.

"Well, luck does favor the best prepared," I say. "Guess we'll do a little bit more about that as we head south." Everyone laughs as they settle in to sleep.

↑

To those who suffer, paradise awaits

Luke, 19 March 1999

It's no coincidence that the notion of reward for hardships is a tenet of most major religions. For most people, with the exception of the few cursed martyrs in the world, it is a truth. There is karmic balance in the world. If you have endured hardship, you are due something positive.

Today, on my birthday, we wake up feeling very sore. Over a leisurely breakfast, we look at the map and plot a relaxing seven-mile day. Our church-group hosts reluctantly pack up for their return to Texas. We can sense the envy from many of the younger members as we shove off for destinations further out into the cays.

An hour into the paddle we stumble upon a fantasy come true, a tiny little spit of sand less than 100 feet across with a half-dozen coconut palms. Our shoulders are sore so we decide to call it a day.

It is one of those islands that you see in cartoons, an idealized caricature: a hump of sand, four palm trees and two shipwrecked castaways in ragged clothes pondering their fate. The only difference is a small cruise ship parked off shore. Little do we know that our island is the passengers' destination for the day. Within an hour, the place is crawling with pale, fleshy retired couples and tourists, splashing about the reef in snorkeling gear and lying on the beach, basting themselves with sunscreen before cooking in the sun.

By 5:00 p.m. everyone has returned to the mother ship and the place is empty. Jean-Philippe spears a couple of fish and brings in a true prize for my birthday, a large crab. I climb one of the low-hanging palms to get fresh coconuts and we feast on coconut-chile rice, fish tacos and boiled crab. We now have total peace and quiet on our own deserted island. This is the Caribbean of my dreams.

↑

Jean-Philippe, 21 March 1999

Landing on Rendezvous Cay today, we meet only a dozen pelicans and a flock of little sanderlings. Our private island is a narrow, 200-yard-long oval of sand surrounded by coral reef and emerald water. On the island are a dozen coconut palms, two mangrove trees and a clump of beach grape trees that offer us shade; except for a soft, cool wind, nothing disturbs the peace. My only concerns are hunting for food and getting some coconuts—we're running a little low on water and we will need a few green coconuts from high up in the palms. During our training in Thailand we began to learn how to climb coconut trees but we never made it to the top. Here coconut juice is vital to our survival, so we have no choice but to succeed.

I send Luke off to make the first attempt. There is much potential for comedy so I pull out the video camera. He starts out strong, gets halfway up and loses his momentum. To save himself from a fall, he hugs the tree and rests in a modified frog-leg position with his knees out, feet tucked below his butt and soles pressed flat against the trunk. It takes him a couple of minutes to scale the remaining twelve feet to the canopy. He holds on tight and twists off three big coconuts but then his arm and leg muscles begin to twitch with exhaustion. The locals can scale a twenty-five-footer in less than thirty seconds—then they climb through the canopy, stand on top and knock off the coconuts with their heels. We're not nearly that skilled but we are improving and we're surviving. Our technique might not be pretty but it's effective.

After drinking coconut juice and taking a nap under the palms, Luke comes out of the water after his morning swim and tells me about his first encounter with a six-foot shark. He was too scared to look closely and identify it but I'm curious so I head off to take a look. In the process I intend to spear something to eat. Unfortunately, there is no sign of the magnificent marine creature Luke had run into, but I do manage to take down a meaty Nassau grouper.

I bring back my catch and we barbecue it on a fire of coconut palm fronds, using two spear shafts as a grill. Luke demonstrates his culinary expertise by preparing a unique sauce in which he sautés diced flesh of young coconuts with some fresh garlic and minced ginger, lime zest, chile paste and a bit of chicken bouillon. He then spoons the caramelized sauce over the fish and we have a king's meal in our private paradise.

In the afternoon, I return to the water to look for dinner. As I glide silently underwater, I sight three majestic spotted eagle rays and then find myself face to face with a barracuda nearly as long as I am tall. Razor-sharp teeth, similar to those of an alligator and long enough to take a chunk out of me, stick out of their half-open jaws; barracudas are as mean as they look. This one circles me a few times and I slowly retreat toward shallower water. It is then that I turn the tables and begin to stalk it. I was thinking about dinner, but I didn't want to risk shooting it in deep water. If I only injured the animal, it would give me a serious fight, and I'd like to be able to drag it to shore quickly. Unfortunately, it doesn't follow me all the way into the shallows. It returns toward deeper water, trolling slowly for prey. After following it for a minute, I give up and turn back. Just then, for no apparent reason, it comes right back at me—I'm dealing with a very smart fish and a potentially dangerous predator. Other fishermen have always told me to never spear a barracuda unless I'm sure I can kill it instantly. When I'm so close I am sure I can spear it in the head, I fire my gun and hit it right in the cheek, but the spear bounces off without even drawing blood.

It occurs to me that I might have been at the limit of the range for my gun's spear leash and that the spear had merely been yanked back but that can't be right. I saw it hit. The unfortunate truth is that we have chosen our spear guns poorly. They simply lack the power to bring home such fish. The barracuda flees unscathed and I come out of the water empty-handed.

↑

Jean-Philippe, 23 March 1999

Two days and a world away from Rendezvous Cay, we wake up to the sound of lapping water and muffled thuds: our boats are bumping against the posts of the dock beneath us. We had to sleep on these uneven wooden slats out over the water last night because it was the only dry place we found on this mangrove-covered island.

The breeze changes direction and it looks like we will have to paddle against a headwind today. When kayaking, there is nothing worse than a strong headwind. Its only saving grace is the relief it provides from insects. We are coming to understand what locals have told us about sandflies here. They inhabit most of the cays in Belize and, on the days without wind, they are a menace. They are almost invisible but their painful bites leave bloody marks that swell up and leave people looking like victims of chickenpox. The flies usually hover in a zone that extends only a few feet above ground. When attacked, locals stop their work and seek refuge in their shacks raised up on stilts. But we have to sit, cook, sleep and do everything on the ground. We pray for a breeze whenever we're on land and hope it translates into a tailwind when we paddle; we're not always that lucky.

We leave Colson Cay by 9:15 a.m. and paddle the first nine miles against the wind. Luckily, the waves that hit us on the front port side are small. We are still within the protective shield of Belize's famous barrier reef where the water conditions remain manageable even on the windiest of days.

In two hours, we cover less than a third of the planned distance. Our back and shoulder muscles are already sore. Down here, our visibility doesn't extend as far as it did in Baja. There, most of the islands were mountainous and we could see them from over ten miles away. In Belize, all the islands are tiny patches of white sand with no topography other than coconut trees or mangroves. They don't appear until the last minute, forcing us to monitor our GPS heading closely on the compass. When we start paddling, we rarely see the next island we're going to. We take a heading and then paddle out into what seems to be a yawning stretch of nothing but blue ocean. When we arrive at a point about four nautical miles off the island, a small blemish of shadow appears on the horizon. At first glance, it is impossible to discern whether it's inhospitable mangroves or beautiful sand and coconut palms. As we paddle closer, dense vegetation indicates more mangroves.

After nine miles and three and a half hours, we land on the first island. With the exception of a small clearing and a trio of coconut palms, it is pure mangroves. The place is an abandoned fish camp and we are surprised to find that the fishermen were sporting fellows with a sense of humor. There in the middle of nowhere, they constructed a basketball hoop made of woven reeds and plywood. Luke jokes around and does his best approximation of an NBA highlight reel, dunking a coconut repeatedly through the eight-foot hoop. After a short snack of coconut juice, we quickly resume paddling, chased away by insatiable mosquitoes.

We aim for another island we can't see, Tobacco Cay, six miles away. When the shape of the island appears, I see what seems to be dense vegetation. It's amazing what our minds do to us when we're dehydrated. As I stare at our destination, at first I think I can see coconut trees, then they seem to dissolve into a gnarled mass of green mangroves. That's the last thing we want: to arrive, exhausted, on an island where we can't camp. We keep forcing the paddles through the water. The wind has died, which means faster paddling but also much more heat to cope with. I stop every ten minutes to splash myself. My muscles protest and I feel like I am hallucinating. Finally Tobacco Cay is close enough that I think I can see a small strip of white sand.

We struggle for the last half-hour, but to our great relief we land on a perfect island. Alas, we aren't the first people to discover it. The land is divided into fifteen lots with expensive-looking bungalows on each. We aren't even planning to pitch a tent but people want to charge us ten dollars merely to sleep out in the open next to our kayaks. Tired and frustrated, we paddle instead out to a pile of dead coral that has been erected as a reef to protect the island. We set up camp separated by a fifty-yard stretch of water from the expensive resorts, within view of tourists cracking open cold beers on their chaise lounges on the sundeck. We unroll our plastic tarp onto the bed of sharp coral and look with envy upon the beach where we are unwelcome. This island fails to be the paradise we had read about in the guidebooks; we hope that some spectacular snorkeling will make up for it.

Our respective roles on the expedition have been established and are based on skills and interests. While we both scavenge and forage, I am the hunter and Luke is the chef. Since Baja, my underwater hunting skills have improved significantly and I enjoy spending two or three hours freediving every day. Luke has become a master at creating fine cuisine with spare ingredients and rudimentary camp cookery. We are comfortable in our roles and they are now habitual. As usual, Luke seems relaxed and cheerful as he sets up the camp kitchen. I slip in to my diving booties, grab my spear and fins and head for the water. In an hour or so we should be eating well once again.

†

Jean-Philippe, 23 March 1999

In the wake of the movie *The Big Blue*, the sports of freediving and spearfishing received international recognition and are now surging in popularity. For us, spearfishing began as recreation—a natural extension of diving—but it has become a means of survival: it is our only way to obtain protein during our expedition. While diving, I often encounter sharks, mainly non-aggressive species such as blacktip reef sharks, nurse sharks and hammerheads. When I see them, I know that the hunting must be good. To be safe, however, I wait for them to move on before I start spearing fish. People have often asked me, "Aren't you afraid to freedive with sharks?" I have always told them, "No," that they don't usually threaten humans. As a sensible and observant diver, I have been able to swim with and safely observe them for many years. As I would learn, however, a spear gun radically alters the equation; when divers become hunters by spilling blood, things change.

We have arrived at our camping spot late today. I don't get into the water with my spear gun until 5:00 p.m., less than an hour before sunset. The coral is unspectacular, but I continue swimming through a channel in the reef. I know that marine life congregates in channels where the currents run and that dusk is feeding time. I sense that I may see some sharks. Generally, they fascinate me. Their shapes and the way they move underwater are magnificent. Here in the Caribbean, I see them daily; it is usually something I look forward to.

After a few minutes I see my first prey, a ten-inch, plump blue parrotfish fifteen feet below me. I dive straight down and move in from behind so it can't see me. My first shot is on the mark. I hit it next to the head and it bleeds profusely, leaving a thick trail of green (blood appears green underwater). I quickly pull my stringer from my right bootie, run it through the gills and then let it drag on the rope ten feet behind me. It makes me nervous to be towing along a fresh kill in shark territory. I want to get out of the water and give the bloody fish to Luke before resuming my hunting.

On my way back to shore, a huge spotted eagle ray glides gracefully by me, less than five feet away. Its wingspan is wider than my arm span and its tail must be ten feet long. Next I see a small squid and I shoot it without hesitation, narrowly avoiding the black cloud of ink as it bursts underwater. On shore I call to Luke and hand him my catch and return to the water. We don't have quite enough to feed two hungry kayakers.

It is now after dusk and the visibility is less than fifteen feet. Back in the channel, I spot my third prey, another blue parrot. I dive and take a shot, but the fish sees me and surges at the last moment. My spear grazes it, leaving a gash in its flank. The injured fish spins and thrashes around, spreading blood everywhere. Back on the surface to breathe, I quickly reset my spear and line, restretch the two power bands and dive after the injured fish. I hit it squarely with my second shot. As I head back to the surface, large gray masses move in around me with lightning speed and I fear they are sharks but, when I break the surface, they come in closer and I realize that it is merely a school of twenty to thirty tarpons. A few come within four feet of me. Had my spear been free from the parrot-fish and my gun armed, I could have hit one easily.

By the time I get the second parrotfish on the stringer, the sky is nearly dark and the water visibility is down to ten feet. The tarpons disappear. My fish has now been streaming blood for a couple of minutes. I am in twelve-foot deep water but I can't see the bottom anymore. I re-arm my spear gun, just in case, and before I can swim one more stroke, I glimpse a gray torpedo coming right at me. I aim my gun, thinking it might be a large tarpon. Then I choke on my snorkel, swallowing water and kicking madly in reverse as a huge ten-foot bull shark stops just six feet from me. The predator is almost as long as my kayak, and much wider than I am. I am hoping that the two bursts from my fins have startled him as much as he startled me, but before I can make any more progress, the shark comes right back at me, shaking its head from side to side. I can see that it is much larger than I am. It veers off at the last second and disappears into the rapidly darkening water, but in a few seconds it is back again and I am frozen, unable to swim. I know that it is after my injured fish, not me, but the blood in the water is driving it crazy. I can't take my eyes off it to look down to my hip to unclip the stringer. All I can do is grip my spear gun tightly and try to fend it off.

Each time I lose sight of it, I spin quickly, rotate my head and try to predict the direction from which it will attack next. I try to stay composed and continue swimming slowly toward shallow water. I must swim on my back; I need to be able to see in all directions. When I look down to my feet I realize that my stringer is entangled in my knife just next to my ankle. I can't stop moving, let down my guard and reach down to release it. So, the dead fish bouncing around by my feet spreads clouds of blood in the water. To the shark I must appear to be the bleeding prey; it wants to get at my legs. The shark charges a few more times. With each charge I try to stab its nose, but it stays just beyond the tip of my spear—a weapon that now feels like nothing more than a toy in my hand. I know that the shallow coral reef must be very close, but I can't risk turning on my stomach.

Although less than two minutes have passed since the first encounter, I am now completely out of breath. Both my calves are cramping from the exertion of kicking my long, stiff, freediving fins, but when I get near the edge of the reef flanking the channel and into shallower water, an adrenaline rush drowns the pain and exhaustion. I'm almost to safety. I dash for the shore still swimming on my back and aiming the spear gun toward deeper water. When I reach water less than waist-deep, I let loose all the panic that I had contained in the water, tearing my fins off and running to shore, shredding my neoprene booties on the dead coral. I stand ten feet from the water's edge, staring at the dark blankness of the channel. The shark is gone; the surface is placid, rippling only slightly in the wind. My heart is pounding, my stomach clenches and I want to vomit.

I head down the coral strip toward camp, in shock and still trembling from the adrenaline. I walk laps to discharge all my emotions before sitting down to skin the squid and clean the fish but I still can't find the words to tell Luke what has happened to me. He calmly cuts the squid into sashimi and whips up a sauce of ginger and soya. The ginger settles my stomach and I start my tale. I watch his eyebrows rise and his jaw drop. He doesn't know what to say so he silently opens up the food bag and takes out a small flask of rum and makes a long pour into one of the painted "good-luck/emergency" gourds given to us by the lady on the docks in Belize City. "I was saving this for a special occasion," he says.

For years I've been trying to dispel the myth of *Jaws*, for few other marine creatures captivate me in the way that sharks do. Before this encounter, I have never felt threatened in any way by them. When I think about what happened, all I can say is that I made several serious mistakes. I went spearfishing at dusk, which is feeding time for marine predators. I was freediving without a partner. I also knew that channels were favorite hunting areas for sharks and rays; sighting the eagle ray should have reinforced this. Then, I let my first fish bleed for a long time before I came out of the water to give it to Luke. Sharks have an incredible sense of smell and there is no doubt that my first kill lured him in.

Still, I think the shark was probably more interested in the fish than me. I know that almost all shark attacks worldwide are accidents. Even bull sharks, which are one of the most aggressive species, usually do not go after humans; they mistakenly identify them as prey only on occasion.

As I sit by the camp stove eating, I wonder if I will ever be able to get back in the water again. But then I recall some advice a fisherman gave me recently about sharks: the best defense is offense. He said I should unscrew the tip of the spear and shoot the shark with the blunt spear. Apparently, they don't like challenging hunting, and will abandon the chase if it's too much work to subdue their prey. I vow to remember that a smart, sensible, observant diver is a safe diver.

†

Jean-Philippe, 5 April 1999

Days go by, and we cover very little distance. It isn't due to inclement weather, but rather to the fact that every five to eight miles we find a new deserted island, each more beautiful than the previous. The crystal-clear water abounds with fish and, in spite of my previous shark experience, I spend more time in the water than paddling. I admit that for a couple of days I was haunted by thoughts of bullsharks; I imagined them sneaking up from behind, and I was constantly turning around to check but found nothing except the clear water and dozens of thousands of multicolored fish. Magenta creole wrasse, glasseye snapper painted in pastel pink, zebra-striped highhats, and Spanish hogfish, burnt orange transitioning to a blazing yellow like the sunrise. It's a feast for the eyes. Beauty appreciation quickly replaced fear and, once again, I had a hard time leaving the water. Our lunch break often ended up being our campsite but we finally returned to coastal paddling to meet locals.

After visiting Hopkins, a friendly Garifuna community, we reach Placencia, a low-key tourist destination where we meet Debb, an American woman, married to Dave, a Creole guide who also works on the Board of Tourism for the Belize government. They take us under their wing, offering us good discounts in their guesthouses, free meals and, more importantly, great information about Belize's hidden secrets. Dave recommends that we leave our gear at his place and go visit Blue Creek, an inland Mayan community. He assures us that there we won't find the artificial tourist setting we just experienced a few days ago at the Mayan Center.

↑

Luke, 6 April 1999

There are times when we arrive in a place, look around and just know that we are meant to be there, that something profound and formative awaits us. We've been waiting for that kind of revelation since the beginning of the expedition. All through Baja and northern Belize there were plenty of beautiful landscapes and interesting communities, but nothing that compelled us to pull out the cameras and impulsively decide to stay for a week. Until today.

Blue Creek is a gem. It's a poor village of Mayan farmers (inland west of Punta Gorda in southern Belize) who have returned to the land of their ancestors. Most of the Mayans fled the plagues and violence of the early colonial period in the 1600s and settled in the highlands of Guatemala. It is only within the last century that some groups have begun to return. Most of the early returnees settled in the northwest, carving out *milpas*, or small farms, from flat, featureless expanses of secondary forest and brush, the stubble left over after the deforestation of the high-canopy jungle that once covered the land. During the rainy season, that land becomes a bog, and during the dry season, it's a dust bowl with little shade. When the first Mayan homesteaders arrived 100 years ago, the only assets of that area, as far as I can tell, were availability and affordability. The group that founded Blue Creek is made up of more recent arrivals. There was little land available in the northwest, so they kept on moving. Fortune smiled on them and led them to an unoccupied idyll.

The river, Blue Creek, is the most prominent feature of the land. At the head of a narrow valley, jade waters flow out of a cave system through a rare tract of primary rainforest. Just below the caves, the river forms a wide, deep, slow-moving pool. One-hundred-foot canopy shades the pool and provides habitat for birds, monkeys, iguana, butterflies, snakes, peccary and a stunning array of other wildlife. On the banks of the river is a small lodge, managed by one of the village's prominent sons, Ignacio Coc, and his family.

When we hopped out of the back of a communal pickup truck this morning and looked around, we knew at that very moment that we would be spending some time here. There was a palpable sense of identity and a unifying similarity in the movements of the people, as if they were following daily rituals dating back hundreds of years. A group of women, all in loose dresses, sat on blankets flanking a trail leading up toward the head of the valley. They hoped to sell woven baskets and crafts to the few visitors staying at the lodge. An elderly matron patted out balls of *masa* into tortillas and grilled them on a clay *comal*. A young girl toasted cacao beans and ground them with a pestle in a stone mortar. Men with hoes and machetes tended rows of corn and beans on slash-and-burn plots. We could see the inertia of history and tradition in the village.

Jean-Philippe felt it first. Before we even started up the path, upriver into the forest, he knew unequivocally: "This is it. This is our first big project. There's a lot to see and learn here."

↑

Luke, 7 April 1999

Jean-Philippe has hit it off well with Ignacio and Maura, an American naturalist volunteering at the lodge. We have a week of activities and documentary projects lined up for us, starting with some adventure and ecology and then delving into the culture.

After breakfast, Maura shows up carrying a headlamp and wearing a swimsuit and water moccasins. "Get your gear on. We're doing the caves." Ten minutes later, we arrive at the gaping maw of a huge cave system at the head of the river valley. Jungle vines and vegetation dangle from the cliffs above down into the seventy-five-foot-high cave mouth. "We'll be swimming and scrambling, so make sure your batteries are good and take care with your hands and feet." And with that, we slip into a deep pool and breaststroke into the dark grotto. Over the gurgling of the river we can hear the twittering of bats, and in the water schools of tiny fish nibble at our legs. We swim, occasionally clambering over rocks and small cascades and, twenty minutes later, we emerge into a wide chamber. Twenty feet up on the wall, a waterfall gushes from a narrow split in the rocks. We can go no further.

On our way out, Maura explains that Belize is full of caves. The Blue Creek network may contain more than twenty miles of underground passages, and although many of them are only now being rediscovered and explored, the caves have a long history with the native Mayans. Shaman/priests used many of the caves for religious rituals and human sacrifice. Archaeologists are finding bones, bits of pottery and other artifacts in grottos all over the country.

In the afternoon we head out with Pepe, a guide, on the other marquee tour in Blue Creek, the iguana hunt. It's ecotourism here, so we're not hunting to kill; it's a catch-and-release tour. We follow the river down out of the high-canopy forest into the secondary growth, past many of the houses in the village. Pepe's son and their three dogs push through the brushy margins of the river and disappear. We hear much rustling and then nothing. A minute later we hear rustling again but it's much higher up. Pepe's son is now fifty feet up in a tree shaking the branches. Iguanas nap in the sun on the high boughs of trees. Two large ones tumble through the leaves and thump into the underbrush—apparently there is little risk of injury as they can withstand falls of more than 100 feet by filling up their soft ribcages with air to absorb the shock. The dogs lie in wait behind the tree and chase them toward the river. Pepe is there, waiting with his diving mask, and as soon as they splash into the river, he plunges in after them. After a minute, he comes up with a six-foot-long Godzilla-like creature. The face is nearly identical to that of the monster that destroyed Tokyo in the movies. Fortunately, once caught, iguanas are docile. Even though they have three-inch razor-sharp claws, we can hold them in our hands without risk. Jean-Philippe's film is whirring as I hold the reptile and mug for the camera.

Today's tours are perfect examples of locally controlled ecotourism and Ignacio and Maura want to train more guides and promote the village and the lodge. Blue Creek survives primarily on agriculture, a rough subsistence living: a little more tourism would measurably increase the quality of life. Activities like these reinforce the importance and long-term viability of running educational and ecological tours in the rainforest instead of exploiting it. The community would be able to preserve its culture, which is the first thing to disappear in other villages as more and more young people leave to work on plantations or move to larger towns to take menial, low-paying jobs.

All of this is affecting Jean-Philippe deeply. I can see him brainstorming and reviewing his extensive travels and interactions with native communities in other countries. In his mind, there is more that can be done here. There is a treasure, a sustainable resource that is not being harnessed. "Cultural tourism," he explains to Maura and Ignacio at the dinner table, "has a lot of potential." They agree.

✦

Jean-Philippe, 10 April 1999

Our first three days in Blue Creek are filled with educational experiences. We learn about local harvest, and slowly sink into the community's daily activities. Today, Pepe invites us to his farm to sip a local specialty.

There is a delicious incentive to visit Mayan villages in Belize: chocolate. *Cacao*, as the plant is known, may be the most enduring and pervasive contribution Mayan culture has made to the world. But what you recognize as chocolate when you unwrap your Swiss confections or stir up a glass of chocolate milk is far from the original.

In ancient Mayan society a warm beverage made from *cacao* was revered as the "Drink of the Gods." The beans themselves were used as currency, thus only the elite of Mayan society could afford to drink it. Colonists discovered *cacao* and brought it back to Europe, where it became a fashionable drink in high society. The drink has evolved into a variety of chocolate products that incorporate many extra ingredients but to find it in its pure form, to get the original recipe, you have to go back to the heartland. The Mayan communities still prepare it and drink it the way their ancestors did.

Cocoa comes from the seeds (beans) of a fruit pod, the same shape and half the size of an American football. The green pods sprout directly from the trunk and main branches of the low-hanging *cacao* trees. They turn yellow or red as they ripen. Inside the pods, the seeds are embedded in a white fleshy pulp that is fragrant, sweet and tart. The local kids suck on the flesh-covered beans like sourball candies.

After the beans are washed off in the river, they are set out to dry on sheets of corrugated tin or wood planks set in the sun. Over a period of approximately a week, they will darken into a deep brown color. Once dried, they are roasted on a *comal*, a clay disk set over a fire made in a clay hearth. At this stage the beans are very strong and bitter, similar in my mind to the taste of coffee beans. The cooled beans are ground by hand using a stone mortar and pestle. The raw cocoa is either preserved as powder or mixed with a dash of water to form a solid block of paste.

It's a lengthy process to reach the final "drink" stage but it is worth the wait. We watch as Pepe's wife puts a few spoonfuls of powder into a *calabasa* or gourd bowl and adds a few grains of black pepper for extra kick. With a dash of hot water she mixes it into a paste. From here, as the consumers, we have options: cold or hot water, sweetened or unsweetened. Without question, we choose hot water and homemade cane syrup. The mealy texture is pleasant and it has just the right balance of bitterness, sweetness and deep, toasty cocoa flavors that warm us to our very bones. It is like no other chocolate we have ever tasted. We feel like gods drinking it.

†

Luke, 21 April 1999

The past two weeks have been a stroll back in time; Jean-Philippe and I are documenting many aspects of the traditional lifestyle of Blue Creek, from agriculture and jungle survival to art and oral history. As I sit in the darkening lodge in a post-meal stupor, I wonder, *What can we possibly do with all this material?*

An exhausting system of agriculture is the foundation for everything here. They grow corn, yucca (cassava), beans, cocoa, coffee and sugar cane as their staples. The whole process is done by hand. The villagers tried to form a cooperative and buy a used tractor but they couldn't afford the payments and it got repossessed. They clear land, plant and harvest by hand. They mill corn, press sugar cane, grind coffee and cocoa by hand. It's a stunning amount of work.

The culmination of our agricultural immersion was a meal with Ignacio's family. His mother, Valentina, rounded up a rooster from the yard, butchered, cleaned and chopped it up and put it in the soup pot. She added corn kernels, onions, garlic, chiles, achiote and dried herbs. Meanwhile Ignacio's daughters made hot chocolate from freshly ground cocoa powder, raw cane juice and hot water. While the *caldo kash* (chicken soup) was cooking, Valentina grilled corn tortillas on the *comal*. Survival skills have to be relearned depending on the flora and fauna of the local environment, and Ignacio and his friends are undeniably sage survivalists in this corner of the woods. Over two days we learn about water vines, edible *cohune*, *jippi jappa* and *waree* palm hearts, wild *pokonoboy* and hog plum fruits, emergency shelter building, trapping birds, moles and ground rodents and other survival techniques. Jean-Philippe is completely engrossed in the minutiae of every explanation. I, on the other hand, at the end of both days, am glad that we have a lodge and a meal to go back to. I hope we never get lost. Another day, we spend time with a group of women and discover their special creative talents. They use the *jippi jappa* palm for an entirely different purpose. The inedible parts of the palm, the fronds, are used as fibers for basket weaving. The fronds are separated into long, narrow strands that are boiled and dried in the sun, then twisted into lengths of twine and woven into tight, intricate coil baskets using a needle and single fibers as thread. The result is a light-jade colored basket that is so well made it can hold water.

Like a scientist, Jean-Philippe is meticulous and driven to perfection as he collects all this material on film and in his journal. He sits down each night after dinner and spends a few hours recording notes on little scraps of paper to insert in each canister of film. He records the events of the day in a notebook, and asks Ignacio or one of the guides to clarify a detail or provide a more specific explanation when he has questions. And then, he opens the computer. The generator stays on until 8:00 p.m. and he works with electricity until then, charging the computer in the process. At that point I go to bed while he puts in two more hours of work until the computer's battery runs out. Every night for the past week has been the same.

I know when Jean-Philippe, unsatisfied with something, has a big idea brewing. There's a glint in his eye, a hint of urgency in his step and an agenda to his questions, as if he's had an epiphany about a way in which he can do more, be proactive, step up and leave his mark. He tells me only that he's working on the website a little. I know better. I sense that he is plotting, projecting and imagining how he will completely transform it. The few dozen pages we have online encapsulate all the planning for the expedition and the four months of adventuring through Baja and northern Belize up to this point. However, the current format will not accommodate all the material we have collected this week. We've enjoyed a privileged perspective on the culture, traditions and history of Blue Creek, and in order to do it justice when we present it online, Jean-Philippe wants to make sense of it all first.

At this point, we are a team of two, with one tiny palmtop computer packed with software, connecting to the Internet when we can, trying to produce an ambitious website from our remote location. Something will have to change but I'm hesitant to contemplate too deeply how. It's one of those moments when I see Jean-Philippe embody the motto of our expedition: "Paddling into the past with an eye on the future." Part of me is inspired, but part of me wonders more and more what I've gotten myself into.

↑

Jean-Philippe, 22 April 1999

The electricity has gone off and I am left alone, typing on the tiny keyboard of our palmtop with a headlight, around which a whining cloud of bugs swirls, driving me insane. It is our last night in the Mayan village and I reflect on our experience and what makes this such a magical place.

Blue Creek wouldn't be the same without its children. If you arrive during a school break, the children will be the first ones to welcome you with smiles and energetic greetings. You will see them bathing in the river, and a few riding old bicycles three times too big for them. Older girls help their mothers washing the laundry next to toddlers sitting naked in the water. The kids quickly adopted us and some even joined us in jungle walks. Others proudly showed us some of their latest animal or map drawings. We visited their school and attended their classes for a morning.

The ninety-five students are divided in three classrooms. The three Garifuna teachers from Punta Gorda are kept busy. The first class is divided into two rows, one facing each direction with a blackboard on each side. The teacher teaches grade one while the grade two is drawing, then the teacher changes sides and teaches the other half. The two other classes contain U.S. grades three to eight with each instructor teaching three grades in the same class.

During recess the boys like to play soccer and the girls softball. The problem is that this equipment doesn't last forever. I went looking for some but even in the town of Punta Gorda (capital of the Toledo district), I couldn't find any. Even if available, families in Blue Creek live from their own farming and usually don't have the financial means to purchase sports equipment. The government operates the school, but small villages aren't a priority. Some students aspire to go to high school but, unlike elementary and junior high, high school costs $400 per term, a fee most families can't afford.

Out of all the teenagers in Blue Creek, only three families send one of their children to high school in Punta Gorda. The students first have to ride their old bikes for twelve miles on a dirt road to the paved main road where they catch the bus to the big town. No child from Blue Creek has yet entered a university. Ignacio hopes it will change. He explained that the village needs more educated people and he wishes those people to be natives from the village. He hopes to attract educational bodies or NGOs to help them provide some scholarships.

The future of Blue Creek is still uncertain. Blue Creek is a small town that has kept much of its culture and many traditions because farmers are still able to provide for their kids. But, with electricity coming to the village, many things may change. Blue Creek will either become an eco-tourism success or, as in so many villages, the children may be forced to leave to look for low-paying jobs in factories or on plantations. In the worst case, some will end up in the streets of Belize City: this is what Ignacio would like to prevent. He understands the potential of Blue Creek's natural beauty and cultural heritage and also knows the importance of modern education in a modernizing world. The children of Blue Creek are its future and they should be given a chance so Ignacio is working on various projects for the town: library, scholarship programs and limited tourism development, as well as lobbying for governmental or NGO support to obtain more services for the village.

I wonder how CASKE2000 can help. We will certainly mention Blue Creek on our site and promote it as a not-to-be-missed destination, but can't we do more? Without funds or resources, we are limited in the scope of assistance we can bring—but, if our expedition attracts the media, maybe we can do more. Perhaps we can become a real voice for

Blue Creek's struggle for education, cultural preservation and self-managed ecotourism. As the computer battery dies, I go to bed with a vision of what CASKE2000 could become beyond kayaking—I have no doubt that CASKE2000 can make people aware of these many needs, but can we touch their hearts enough to get them involved?

↑

Jean-Philippe, 15 May 1999

We spend three weeks in and around Placencia. I spend the time mostly behind the computer compiling the information we gathered in Blue Creek, taking breaks to talk with our hosts, Deb and Dave, about the history, ecology and future of Belize and eating the sweet, succulent mangos that cover the ground in the village. My father also comes to visit for a week, and I take him to Blue Creek for three days. But we've been off the water for over a month, and I worry that the next few paddling days will be painful reminders.

↑

Luke, 16 May 1999

My entire head is throbbing: I've never had an ear/sinus infection this bad. I can barely chew and sleep is impossible. Tomorrow we plan to re-board the kayaks and paddle south toward Punta Gorda and the Guatemalan border, but I'm not sure I'm capable.

The Creole village of Placencia has been our base of operations in southern Belize. It's a beautiful spot right on the water, rare for the coast of the mainland that is normally covered in mangroves. If we were still in Blue Creek, I'd be in trouble. There are no medical facilities anywhere close to that village. Placencia is more prominently placed on the tourist routes, thus the stores here are better stocked. At the little market down the street, I buy tetracycline, a powerful antibiotic, over the counter.

At this point, I'll need a few days before it has any effect on my infection. I pray for calm winds and small waves. My equilibrium is off and I don't feel well enough to paddle hard. The exertion makes the blood pump faster and the pain becomes unbearable.

Jean-Philippe is not much better off. His father came for a brief visit a week ago and stepped on Jean-Philippe's foot, fracturing his little toe while walking down the boardwalk along the beach here in Placencia. To stabilize the bone, he has taped the three smallest toes together, but he can barely walk. Together, the two of us are going through ibuprofen like candy, four each at every meal. Tomorrow will be an ordeal.

↑

Luke, 20 May 1999

The karmic scales of justice must stay balanced. We've had so many positive experiences over the past month that it stands to reason that calamities and discomfort now erupt with greater frequency.

We are now one day's paddle south of Placencia in the aptly named village Monkey River. Howler monkeys and birds in the trees wake us at dawn. We are on the water at 6:30 a.m. According to our map we have a relatively easy day, twelve or fifteen miles, half the distance to Punta Gorda. Initially, ideal morning temperatures, a light breeze and low angular light make for beautiful paddling. We make it eight miles to Punta Negra, our first checkpoint and rest stop, before most people in the world eat breakfast. Our planned stopping point is four miles off so we're in a great position to arrive early, find a shady spot and rest for the day.

We pass the next point and enter another shallow bay and begin to scour the coast for a campable beach. From the water, as far as the eye can see, the shore is lush green and full of life. We don't have to set foot on shore to know that up close, it will prove to be dank, insect-infested and utterly uninhabitable. We have to keep moving.

At the seventeen-mile point, we spy another group of islands. We get our hopes up for nothing. They too turn out to be covered in mangroves.

We have eaten our only snack food and there is no place to stop and cook. It becomes a mind game to fend off total fatigue and keep plunging the paddles into the water to make progress. I note and register points off in the distance as references only, not places to stop. I know that it's just more mangroves.

After hours of sustained exertion, muscles no longer protest and my body passes through the exhaustion stage into semi-conscious automation. I use regularly spaced landmarks as reminders to pause for a drink of water. My body forgets that there is any reality other than paddling and any speed other than very slow. Fortunately, we have a slight tail wind and following seas that allow us to make forward progress. We arrive in Punta Gorda at 3:00 p.m. after twenty-eight nautical miles and nearly nine hours on the water. We stop immediately at a waterfront restaurant for food. Never again in my life will I find comparable joy in a bland meal of rice, beans and stewed chicken!

Our plan is to spend as little time here as possible. There is nothing redeeming about Punta Gorda. The only reason we are here is to check out of the country and make a long eighteen-mile night crossing (to avoid pirates and the heat of the day) over to Livingston, Guatemala, on the opposite side of the bay.

Stamping out at immigration and customs in a port town in the Caribbean is supposed to be a simple matter and to give you a pleasant sense of closure. After they ink your passport, you have twenty-four hours to be out of the country. Simple. A friendly exchange with the officers is what you expect and immigration proves to be exactly that way. The tall, striking, black Garifuna woman whom we had met a few weeks before when renewing our visas gives us a friendly hello and wishes us good luck as we paddle on. Her counterpart over in customs is her opposite in every way.

He's a short Latino man who must feel emasculated by our friend in immigration. He witnessed our exchange and immediately gives us a hassle. He starts grilling us about our intentions to leave in the middle of the night. Showing false concern for our safety, he tells us apocryphal stories of other sailors who have come to unfortunate ends in this area. He talks in circles and parries every logical point we make with ridiculous and impertinent counterpoints. He invents new regulations on the spot just to stymie us. He asks me to put myself in his position. He says something about a "two-sided coin" and that it would be very "difficult" to stamp out our kayaks and let us leave in the middle of the night, at which point he pulls out a coin, looks me in the eyes and places it deliberately on the table. I've never seen a customs officer work so hard for bribe money.

Refusing to stamp us out on the spot, he reluctantly agrees to meet us at the police station at 3:00 a.m. before our night crossing. I can see in his eyes that he doesn't think we're serious.

↑

Luke, 21 May 1999

It's seventeen miles across the Bay of Honduras to Livingston, Guatemala. I am manifestly morose at the prospect of spending six hours in a kayak to cross it tonight. Thunderstorms are roiling on the horizon, and negative thoughts are roiling in my mind.

We spend the evening in a restaurant sharing stories with the owner, a Canadian expat with a flair for the dramatic. He tells about three Swedes who came through just after the hurricane last year. They purchased a sailboat, hoping to sail off south through Honduras and the Caribbean. When they stopped in at his restaurant the night before their departure, he warned them that going into Honduras in the aftermath of Hurricane Mitch with a nice boat full of fresh water and supplies would make them a prime target for dispossessed and desperate storm survivors. They were very confident and dismissed his concerns.

The Swedish embassy knocked on his door a few weeks later, following a paper trail the trio had left. The last place they had been seen was his restaurant (credit card receipt). Apparently the boat had been found adrift off the coast of Honduras, minus passports, visas, money, supplies and bodies. Nothing has been seen of them since. It is not the kind of story we need before heading off on a similar course.

Just as John and his Belizean wife close down the restaurant at 11:00 p.m., a squall pounds down, making us more ill at ease. We try to sleep for a few hours on the cement patio of the restaurant. Jean-Philippe awakens numerous times to check on the kayaks and deal with a sudden onset of diarrhea.

We arrive at the police station at 3:00 a.m. (the hour of our planned departure) and the customs official is not there. The officers are sympathetic to our cause and it gives us great satisfaction when they dispatch an officer to roust the guy from his house. Angry and groggy, he grudgingly stamps us out, knowing that he will get neither bribe money nor a full night's sleep. He glares at us and sends us off with pleasantries dripping with sarcasm: "Thank you for visiting Belize and travel safely. This country needs more travelers like you who follow the rules and regulations. We hope no harm comes to you on your way out." It's an obvious reference to the missing Swedes.

We don't get on the water until 4:00 a.m.—under stormy skies it is so dark I can't see Jean-Philippe's kayak twenty feet in front of me. There are no stars and no visible bearings, so for an hour, until the sky begins to lighten, Jean-Philippe navigates according to GPS and compass heading, and we listen for each other's paddle strokes to stay close.

By daylight we realize that we have covered less than eight miles in nearly three hours; the current is working against us. Jean-Philippe's rumbling guts have also forced him to jump over the side of his boat and relieve himself twice. Just before dawn the storm that has been mocking us from afar slides in over our heads. Thick sheets of rain pound the ripples in the water flat. It immediately obscures our view of land and all colors disappear in a surreal wash of gray.

The storm passes quickly and the Guatemalan shoreline materializes out in front of us. Although separated by less than twenty miles, the topography looks completely different from that of Belize. It's psychologically uplifting to see a spur of low mountains and deep green foliage appear out of the fog. We begin to paddle more energetically.

By 8:00 a.m. the sun is already hot. The shore seems to hover out there the same distance away, no matter how much we paddle; for an hour we have no sense that we are progressing. My blood sugar is low, energy levels are sagging and my back muscles are on the verge of shutdown. Jean-Philippe can barely rotate his torso because of the stomach cramps from diarrhea.

We pull up on shore by the wide mouth of the Rio Dulce just before 10:00 a.m. After a five-minute break, we paddle around the first bend to the main docks of Livingston to check in at immigration. A mixed crowd of Garifuna and Latinos stand on the edge and marvel at our boats laden with gear. They pepper us with questions in Spanish. My Spanish has improved over the past six months, but it's far from fluent and at the moment I'm too tired to make an effort. I just pretend that I don't understand.

Everything is so much more vibrant here than in Punta Gorda. People volunteer information and give us directions without asking for money. It feels good to be in a new country.

↑

Jean-Philippe, 21 May 1999

Getting sick while traveling is never fun, but getting sick in the middle of an expedition is atrocious. Dysentery is probably the most frequent ailment we will have to deal with, and as I kept having to jump in the water to relieve myself, I couldn't help but think about all the occasions on which I got sick in foreign countries. All those uncomfortable, or sometimes shameful, moments when cultural differences seem to accentuate the ailments, and then I think that in spite of afflicting a large number of people, when nature calls in foreign lands, it remains a taboo subject that I'm about to break. I decided to spend my first day in Guatemala coating my stomach with plain rice and bananas, and just write on the subject.

↑

When Nature Calls in Foreign Lands

Jean-Philippe, 22 May 1999

Thailand is famous for its white sand beaches, plunging cliffs of limestone surrounded by lush rainforests and warm turquoise water. The bay of Phang Nga has quickly become a kayaker's paradise. Your best friends invite you to join them on their paddling trip around the bay. You're now paddling the longest stretch from the resort of Krabi to the famous island of Koh Phi Phi. The day breaks with the sun reflecting its orange beams of light in the water. The only ripples are the ones from your paddle strokes. You think you're in paradise when you start feeling strange movements in your bowels. You shut your mind to it but soon stomach cramps alter your paddling. You remember the delicious spicy food of the previous night and have no choice but to jump in the water...

It isn't difficult to imagine this scenario. Most travelers and adventurers have had experiences similar to this. People often ask me, "What do you do when you need to go to the bathroom?" or, "How do you keep your toilet paper dry in your kayak?" even, "How much paper do you pack for a month in the wilderness?" I wonder if the people who are curious enough to ask are ready to accept the answers?

During one of my first travels I met a young British couple in Thailand. They had spent a year touring India and recounted to me fantastic tales. Somehow our discussion moved toward the subject of daily necessities. Shocked and horrified, I listened to this charming woman saying, "Now I'm so used to using my left hand that I don't want to use toilet paper anymore. You feel so much cleaner with water." Even though more than half of the world population has never used any toilet paper, my upbringing and ingrained squeamishness kept me from accepting that she could be right.

My subsequent travels have taken me around the world and I have come to wonder which is more absurd: the hang-ups that we have developed or others' habits that offend us. I have learned that a taboo in one culture is a norm in another, just as a culinary delicacy in one country is considered inedible somewhere else. While it is natural that we all think differently, we usually are strongly influenced by the education we receive and the social habits we are taught. This early bias makes it hard, if not impossible, to judge the good from the bad, for it is just a matter of customs.

Education starts at an early age. In Nepal, the Sherpa children are dressed in pants with the crotch seam left un-sewn. When kids stand up, the pants are naturally closed. When they squat down, they automatically split open and the youngsters don't need any help to relieve themselves. Of course, Sherpa children spend most of their time outside and house floors are made of packed earth that are easier to clean than a Persian carpet. In "modern" countries, toddlers "benefit" from the latest thing in diapers that ensure a good hermetic seal that lets the toddler stew in its own excretions for hours. *Which is cleaner?* I wonder.

Westerners have gone a long way to hide these small natural disasters for as long as possible. Perhaps we develop a phobia of feces as a reaction to the experiences we undergo at an early age. We see our parents' expression of disgust at a particularly messy diaper. We hear others react to the stench. It's understandable that after sitting in one's own waste and enduring disparaging remarks every day for a few years that, as adults, we develop a hypersensitivity to the matter.

As little puppies grow up, they are trained to be clean; people too are trained to "hold it" until they reach a special place. For some people it is a hygienic bathroom with a toilet, for others it may be a place that does not always appear clean to the eyes of outsiders. In small Indonesian fishing villages, a narrow dock over the sea takes you to a small space surrounded by boards. When you look down, crabs and fish are all waiting to be fed. On the side, you notice some old coconut shells. Although I have never tried the coconut shells, I can imagine that it would be similar to using sandpaper. In China you squat down in a communal room over a tube from which a strange snorting sound comes out. A closer examination reveals the moving snout of a pig impatiently waiting at the other end. In African villages, vultures pick the streets clean. The precocious birds can sometimes come too close to your hind flesh before you have even finished with your business. If you take a taxi through the poorest part of Kathmandu, the capital of Nepal, you will be blessed with the sight of dozens of butts squatting over the ditch by the road.

In other places people use stones, sometimes leaves from various plants, but most people still use water. Toilet paper, commonly referred to as TP, is a modern invention that is always evolving. You can choose from single, double, or triple ply with a full array of colors, patterns, and softness. I'm not sure what particular purpose the large selection of scents serves, but they definitely would benefit from such aromatic variety in Latin America. There, TP is commonly used, but the plumbing can't handle the paper, so you are provided with a small plastic garbage container in which you dump the used paper for the visual and olfactory pleasure of your successor. Of course, TP also needs to be disposed of, and you may find that you need to remind your hotel host a few times. All of this makes me think that, after all, perhaps the British lady wasn't entirely wrong.

Sometimes a person's dedication to the use of toilet paper can be taken to extremes. The most absurd thing I've seen on the subject took place years ago in San Francisco. I was jogging early on a winter morning when I saw an old lady walking her little poodle that was dressed in a hand-woven wool jacket. After the dog defecated on the sidewalk the lady picked her dog up under one arm and opened her handbag. I expected her, like all good urban Americans, to pull out a Ziploc bag and clean up. Instead she pulled out some tissue, lifted the tail and very thoroughly wiped her dog. She repeated the operation two more times, put the dog back on its feet and nonchalantly threw the used tissues on the street before resuming her morning walk.

Modern toilets, most notably public ones, are built to complex specifications. In the U.S., thin disposable paper seat covers are being replaced by rotating plastic wrapping operated by an electrical motor and a conveniently positioned button. That way, people don't have to touch anything that has been touched by another human being. In France, public pay-toilets are self-cleaning, not only the bowl but the full cabin is washed with pressure jets. When you close the door after use, make sure you get out quickly or you might be disinfected and cleaned up yourself! If you happen upon the strong smell of urine in a Paris subway don't worry, it isn't a leak from the modern toilets. The homeless simply can't afford to pay the fees.

Japanese public toilets show technology at its best and their use is free. The seats are heated in cold areas. Toilets come with a full console. You have to read Japanese to make sense of all the possibilities or you could have fun experimenting a little on your own. One of the most utilized features is the sound track. At the push of a button, a flushing sound conveniently covers the sound of your excretions. This feature is important for without it, people might know what you are doing.

It seems like the more modern the country, the more self-conscious its people are about the most natural of things.

This hypersensitivity, which comes from rigid perceptions of hygiene, isn't easy to set aside. When you travel, sometimes things happen that will shake the most unflappable person. On a solo trek into the wilderness of Irian Jaya, I was more of a novelty to the small Papuans than they were to me. Dani and Yali people believe that a man with a long beard is a great spirit as very few of them are able to grow long facial hair. Adorned with boar tusks through their noses and dressed in nothing but their penis gourds and grass skirts, they followed every move I made. I ate and went to sleep under the gaze of hundreds of eyes. After a couple of weeks I got used to it, but once I was in a village where nobody spoke a word of Indonesian. Half of the village was following me so closely that I had begun to feel claustrophobic. When nature called, I tried to communicate my desire to be left alone but nothing worked. After trying to escape for an hour, I resigned myself to squatting behind a small bush with all the people surrounding me to see if excrement from the white giant were similar to theirs. I remember feeling humiliated, but at least I wasn't sick. That might have destroyed their image of a strong bearded spirit.

Being sick is another issue most travelers worry about, and for good reason, as most of us get sick eventually. It varies from a little diarrhea to bloody or watery dysentery. In Kathmandu, I lost twenty pounds in two weeks. Another time in Indonesia, my self-consciousness was pushed beyond its limit. I was on a local bus crossing the long island of Flores driving through terrible roads. The bus was hours late. I was sitting in the last row, holding my stomach as best as I could. Cramps became unbearable and when I felt like I couldn't hold any longer, I discretely told my neighbor to immediately stop the bus. His response wasn't the one I was hoping for. From the rear he screamed loudly to the driver, "Hey, the tourist is sick, stop the bus." Before the driver could even touch the brake, the fifty heads were turned back and staring at me. The bus stopped, the rear door opened, and I wasn't able to go farther than two steps before abandoning all decorum and going right on the road. All the people came out of the bus to urinate, forming a half-circle all around me as I was relieving myself. To me it was another shameful experience, but to them it didn't seem to be anything out of the ordinary. I was learning to fight my hang-ups the hard way.

These experiences don't always happen in front of perfect strangers. Yesterday, when Luke and I were paddling from the border of Belize to Guatemala, I had to hastily throw myself into the water three different times. Because we were paddling through a storm on rough seas, I needed Luke's help to stabilize my kayak while I was holding on to it with one hand from the water. Do you think I asked him for some toilet paper?

To better understand the sanitary conditions of a long expedition, one needs to have a better understanding of multicultural differences. What you need to pack depends on your needs and ability to adapt. You might want to trade some TP for insect repellent. Sometimes when nature calls, you have to expose some flesh to painful bites.

One day you might run out of paper or your TP might be wet. You might be forced into trying something you would have never considered otherwise. You may even come to the conclusion that the British lady was right. **WATER IS JUST MUCH CLEANER.**

CHAPTER 3
GUATEMALA

Introduction

Jean-Philippe 25 May 1999

Livingston, the only Guatemalan town on the Atlantic Coast, is a remote port accessible from the capital only by plane or a long trip on buses and boats. For us, it was only a brief stop before we began paddling down the peninsula that would take us to northern Honduras, where we planned to take our first break. The most diverse and best-preserved Mayan culture is found on the Guatemalan *altiplano*, so I intend to travel overland there from Honduras. On the evening of May 25th, after three rest days and a few more computer entries, we pack our gear, planning an early start paddling for Honduras. It is essential that we leave no later than 5:00 a.m. to avoid the early afternoon heat and headwinds.

This evening, we suddenly realize that we forgot to get our passports stamped. Although it is 7:30 p.m., we immediately run to the immigration office and knock on the door. It is closed but the generous officer agrees to wait for us in the street for half an hour until we can get our customs clearance. We run to Customs only to find it closed too, and then we learn that we also need a clearance from the Port Captain because we're leaving by sea. Resigned to delaying our departure another day, we return to our guesthouse. From there, a Swiss expat takes us to the immigration officer's house and explains for us that our expedition is humanitarian, thus our kayaks and equipment have nothing to do with customs.

This leads to an interesting conversation:

"Okay, let's see if we can do it. Please give me the registration papers for your kayaks," the officer says.

"We don't have any," I reply.

"Well, what flags do you fly?"

"We don't fly any flags, we just paddle kayaks."

"Well, you can't navigate and cross borders with unregistered boats and no flags. Where did you buy them? Do you have ownership records or receipts?"

I couldn't tell him we bought our kayaks for $4,500 apiece—no one should ever know that we are traveling with $40,000 worth of equipment—so I stretch the truth: "We don't have any receipts, we're a fully sponsored expedition. We're famous, we have a big website to promote tourism in your country."

He shakes his head, stamps our passport and wishes us good luck, saying, "Beware of bandits. Honduras is very poor, especially after Hurricane Mitch. You could be mugged on the beach or at sea."

We thank our new Swiss friend by inviting him for a drink and afterwards enjoy the comfort of a real bed for the last night.

↑

My Fear of Crocodiles

Jean-Philippe, 26 May 1999

My original plan was to paddle around the large peninsula separating Livingston from Omoa, the first northern port in Honduras. It would have taken six or seven days and we knew we would be fighting strong currents, swell and winds on the other side of the point. Potentially, we might also create problems with Honduran immigration by checking in more than a week after the date of our Guatemala exit stamp. When locals told us about a canal, unmarked on any maps, that cuts across the entire peninsula, we instantly opted for it. In addition to shortening the distance and protecting us from wind and waves, our paddling through rainforests would be a welcome change.

At 5:00 a.m., as we're about to launch, a former Guatemalan navy man warns us to be careful of the large aggressive crocodiles in the canal that have been known to attack canoes. We start paddling across the Rio Dulce, a dark threatening sky moving just above us, and I feel anxious; the words "beware of the crocodiles" resonate in my head. Between that warning and knowing that normally only motorized wooden canoes go through the canal, I start doubting the wisdom of my plan. Maybe we should just go around the point? Finally, I decide that I will have to face my fear of crocodiles sooner or later anyway, so we choose the canal. After paddling for only four hours, the storm has passed over us without incident and we have covered the full fourteen miles across the bay to the small settlement of Graciosa. The current, which gave us such a hard time when we paddled from Belize, made this day very easy.

In Graciosa, we find several thatch houses with graceful covered decks on stilts over the water. We prepare our mosquito nets for the night and spend the rest of the day resting in the shade. Friendly people bring us mangos. I climb a coconut tree and get delicious green coconuts. As we buy tortillas, we ask the locals for directions to the canal and its notorious crocodiles. They confirm what we were told earlier: large crocodiles live in the canal, especially at its mouth, but they tell us that the crocs aren't usually aggressive. And I think, *Sure, not aggressive if you're in a wooden boat traveling full speed with an engine. But we're in narrow unstable fabric kayaks, barely above the waterline, and there is no way we can outpaddle a hungry crocodile.* I fall asleep tormented by visions of crocodiles.

Crocodiles frighten me more than any other animal. I freedive with sharks, fondle tarantulas, catch snakes, play with scorpions and would love to pet lions or tigers, but I've always been deeply afraid of crocodiles. Tonight, for the first time, I remember that when I was a child, the only nightmares that awakened me were those where a giant crocodile was eating me. Today I don't believe that nightmares materialize, but even the thought of facing a crocodile in the water remains something with which I have a hard time. I just can't imagine how one could fend off those charging beasts. Crocodiles seem to be sublimely efficient killing machines: they can run faster than a 100-meter Olympic champion, swim far more quickly than we can paddle and jump much higher into a tree than we could climb in a few seconds. Documentaries I saw where large crocodiles would leap out of the water and quickly kill powerful African buffalo forever secured their nightmare status with me.

↑

Jean-Philippe, 27 May 1999

People told us it would take less than an hour and a half to paddle to the canal and then the rest would be in the shade. Knowing that crocs feed primarily from dusk to dawn, we decided that, despite the heat, we would start late.

Luke and I go over our strategies for fending off aggressive crocodiles and helping each other in the event of an attack. Although the crocodiles were no danger to us as long as they were sleeping on shore, if they entered the water we would immediately join one another as fast as possible so that we could face them together. First we would try a flare, a tactic of decidedly questionable value, as our flares had gotten damp several times in the past year. The next step would be to attempt to push them off with our paddles, then would come the spears from our guns, tips unscrewed and relocated close at hand on the deck. Those blunt-ended shafts might discourage an aggressor and, if we were really attacked, would come in handy to poke at their eyes. We also moved machetes and dive knives nearby as a last line of defense; we planned to defend our lives ferociously.

When we leave at 7:30 a.m., the sun is already as high as the temperature. After a hot hour and a half of paddling across a small bay into a smaller lagoon, we find the canal entrance. It is a little stream blocked by trunks that force us to duck; many of the fallen trees over it have been cut with a chainsaw. Sinuous as a snake, it grows narrower and narrower with each paddle stroke. We arm our flare gun and spearguns and I lead the way, trying to watch everywhere at once in anticipation of an attack. Luke follows so close behind me that he rams into me every time I stop paddling. As I face my phobia, I think it has spread; Luke seems as terrified as I am.

As the river narrows, a flurry of sudden surface splashing just in front of me spooks us. All we saw was the wildly agitated water and then everything returned to a silence that feels almost too heavy. We're afraid that maybe it is small crocs feeding on fish. We quickly paddle through the murky water, turbulent only moments before, without spying the cause. A minute later, it happens again right behind Luke, then in front of me, then on all sides. We look everywhere but see nothing—then dig our paddles into the water as hard and fast as we can. Later, we can clearly see schools of fish fighting for food; reassured, we slow our pace and, at least for the time being, feel a little safer.

Minutes later, we squeeze through channels in floating carpets of thick grass and roots so narrow that we can't even get our paddles into the water. Instead, we have to push on the grass that slowly sinks under the pressure of our paddles. The river keeps snaking its way through the swamp, sometimes opening to a few feet wide, sometimes narrowing to leave only a few inches of clearance for the kayaks. Unidentified fruit trees heavy with large brown pods hang over the water, yellow, white, and blood-red wild orchids grow on the riverbanks and snowy white egrets poised on spindly, black legs are easily approached in our silent kayaks. This river is magnificent!

We are lost in nature, away from all civilization, until we hear an outboard motor roaring. As we pull over to the side just before one of those narrow channels through the floating grass, the motor canoe cuts through. The grass spreads a little to let the canoe through, and then eases back over the water. We see three canoes during our crossing; without daily traffic keeping these channels clear, we probably wouldn't be able to paddle through this dense floating vegetation. The presence of the motorboats reassures us because we know that, at least for a few minutes after their passage, there is no risk of seeing any crocs in the water.

On rare solid ground, we stand to stretch our legs and are instantly attacked by an army of mosquitoes. As we prepare to re-enter our kayaks, another canoe comes by and the astonished passengers check us out. When we inquire how much longer it will take us to reach the ocean, the boatman gives us directions and reassures us that we are almost there.

As soon as we start hearing the waves, I put the flare gun back into its dry box and secure the speargun on deck once again. The boatman described the waves as very large at the river mouth, where we remember that most of the large crocodiles live. Anxious not to capsize in the middle of crocodile-infested water, we put on our spray skirts.

The ocean soon appears in front of us although we are protected by a sandy spit; we decide to stop on it to check out the waves. As we paddle closer to the spit, we see the few thatch houses of the settlement of San Francisco. After five hours of paddling in the heat with no breeze, nerves on edge, we have made it all the way through the English Canal without ever seeing a croc. Curious children swim across the river mouth to meet us and we gape at them and ask, "Aren't you afraid to swim here with all the crocodiles?" They laugh and tell us, "Crocodiles only come here at night; there's too much motorboat traffic during the day." Their parents tell us later that the largest and most dangerous crocodiles are found at the Honduran border on the Montagua River and that we will need to be careful there.

Happy to be back at the ocean, we go bodysurfing and then set up camp under the scrutiny of all the villagers. I contemplate my phobia and in hindsight find it comical that I was so terrified that I even sucked Luke into it. We looked so foolish with our flares, spearguns, machetes and diving knives at hand on deck that I decide to use part of our next expedition break to learn more about crocodiles. I will fly to the Brazilian Pantanal to seek firsthand experience.

↑

Jean-Philippe, 28 May 1999

We awaken before dawn hearing waves breaking on the beach but the moon has disappeared and we can't see much. The sandflies are terrible and attack any exposed flesh to feast upon; the 100% DEET "jungle juice" helps but isn't enough to protect us from the voracious insects. How can people stand to live here? As the sky starts to lighten at 5:00 a.m., we leave through waves significantly bigger than the previous evening, but apparently still manageable. Although strong winds prevail from mid-morning until evening, the swell is largest in the morning when there is no wind. Unable to paddle against such strong gusts and needing to avoid the exhausting heat, we have no alternative but to launch through the large surf of early mornings.

After a breakfast of leftover rice, we push our kayaks into the river's mouth and start paddling through into the ocean. The first breaking surf isn't big and only splashes enough to wake us up, but the more break zones we cross, the bigger the waves become. We soon find ourselves in the biggest breaking surf we have ever experienced. I miss my timing, nearly do a rear endo (kayak backflip) on an eight-foot curling wall and take a vigorous spanking on the chest while paddling hard to punch through the last set. We have barely begun the day and I am already tired. Past all the breakers, the swell here isn't nearly as big as that we had experienced in Baja, but there we often found small protected bays where we could launch and land without encountering the largest surf. This experience is a rude awakening and not-too-subtle reminder of the power of the ocean, where man is small and of little significance. As we paddle against the current, enervated, dehydrated and feeling as if we're making no progress, we worry about our landing: strong trashing surf could destroy our loaded kayaks. Fortunately, most of the coast appears to be made up of sandy beaches.

When I stop for a water break, and turn to Luke to tell him my energy is already gone, he looks like a ghost. It is clear that he, too, has suffered on this brief paddle. As we get closer to the Honduran border, my mind starts playing tricks on me and the words of the immigration officer resonate in my head. I can almost hear him warning us about Honduras, where people are attacked with guns or machete and you can't even camp on the beach. After only two hours of this tough paddling, I am already demoralized.

The combination of physical exhaustion, anxiety and fear in the last couple of days is taking its toll: for the first time since we left San Felipe last October, I have doubts about this expedition. Although my goals remain strong ones, today I wonder if we really are ready for all the challenges still awaiting us. Suddenly I desperately need a break, some time to regroup and reevaluate the next leg of our expedition. I don't want Luke to lose his mind just because I am losing mine. We decide that Luke will go to the Bay Islands and learn to scuba dive, while I go to Guatemala, study Spanish, visit the *altiplano*, and then fly on to Brazil.

This evening, a strong breeze keeps the insects at bay, so we decide to sleep in our bivy bags rather than pitching the tent. I wake up in the middle of the night, in pain from hundreds of sandfly bites only to see Luke, deeply and comfortably asleep after awakening and closing the mosquito net to protect his face. I can't believe that, concerned only with his own welfare, he didn't wake me up when the wind died. I am furious as I wonder what kind of a "friend" would do a thing like that.

🌴

Jean-Philippe, 29 May 1999

We wake up and pack our gear in the dark, the sandflies worse than ever. Luke, speaking as if his face is paralyzed, tells me that he slept with his mouth next to the mosquito net, and his lips are swollen after being bitten through it. With absolutely no sympathy, I reply, "Ironic, hey? Maybe that'll teach you to wake me up when the bugs start attacking."

In total darkness, I am first to launch through heavy waves and then I wait for Luke outside the surf zone. We had agreed to wait for each other for five minutes and, if we didn't meet on the water, to return to shore to regroup, but the waves are huge and it was too much work to get out here. After five minutes, I pull out my flashing emergency beacon waiting a little longer, until I hear, "Where are you?" I yell back, "Over here. See my light?" and we begin stroking toward the bay of Honduras.

When day breaks, Luke calls me and says, "Look at my lips." I burst out laughing and immediately feel bad about it because Luke's lips are so swollen that he looks like a comic character. By 7:00 a.m., we reach the calm bay of Omoa, the first port of Honduras.

We check all our gear in a friendly German-owned guesthouse, then clear immigration and the port captain's office with no problems. I make a phone call to Richard, an American who had made his home in Honduras for the last thirty years. He lives in Puerto Cortes, the next port as well as the largest one in Honduras, and has agreed to help us during our stay here. After enjoying his hospitality and before starting the next stage of CASKE2000, we split off for a few months of well-deserved break.

My "vacation" is well spent. Guatemala turns out to be so captivating that I decide I must return on future breaks and the Brazilian Pantanal delivers what I need most, a remedy for my croc phobia.

†

Dispelling the Crocodile Myth

Jean-Philippe, 25 July 1999

Imagine that you are trekking through a tropical jungle. Heat and humidity produce drops of salty sweat that sting your eyes while mosquitoes are biting every inch of exposed flesh that you thought you had protected. This is the lush green hell described by so many explorers but you've made it this far into the wilderness and you're determined that nothing will make you turn back. That is, until you reach a river too wide to throw a tree over and you have no choice but to wade across it. Your backpack over your head, you start walking and, when you are chest-deep, large splashes behind you attract your attention. As you turn and look back, you see nothing but agitated murky water and you fear for your life, knowing that it is most likely a crocodile. If you're not scared, you certainly have more nerve than I do!

During our exploration of the Central American rainforests, we have had to paddle and camp in places inhabited by crocodiles and alligators. Warnings from locals were commonplace and frequently my fear adversely affected my mental state. The next stages through the jungles of La Moskitia in Honduras, Nicaragua and Costa Rica would expose us to even more of these saurians. To overcome my fear of crocodiles once and for all, I flew to the Brazilian Pantanal, where there are so many alligators that one can never swim without meeting them. I learned how the local people live with these creatures and my guide, Paulo, taught me how to catch them. That experience added to my knowledge and, more importantly, bolstered my confidence.

Driving 120 miles through the world's largest wetland, we observed much wildlife as we crossed the large cattle ranches. The nature reserve there is most famous for its variety of birds, and the first day was enough to understand why. Over the course of just a few hours, I saw large, white jabiru storks, crimson throats on full display, toucans with their almost cartoonishly vibrant beaks, and gloriously plumed macaws. We came across parakeets, egrets and even rheas, a cousin of the ostrich, which fled alongside fleet-footed deer as the car approached. Howler monkeys hung in trees and raccoon-like coatimundis, armadillos, foxes, wild pigs and capybaras (pig-sized rodents) crossed the road in front of us. I felt as if I were on an African safari, the only difference being the vast herds of cattle and hundreds of horses grazing everywhere.

The atmosphere reminded me of an old Wild West movie. My guide explained that although the Pantanal is a nature reserve, all of it is used for cattle ranching. I was surprised to see a six-year-old boy astride a horse fully loaded with lassos and bags, accompanying two cowboys. My guide pointed his finger and said, "That was me as a kid." Paulo's father was a Duruvao Indian from Hauta Foresta, a region of the Amazon, and his mother was from Corumba, the main town on the border of the Pantanal. He grew up as a cowboy, the wild reaches of the Pantanal his school.

Paulo explained that people here know nature intimately and can catch most animals with only their bare hands. The elders come from a generation that hunted alligators, armadillos, deer and wild pigs for their meat. Alligators also proved valuable for their leather. Today, the only animals hunted are the wild boars that destroy agriculture. Sons of accomplished hunters have become the ecotour guides of the reserve. They capture the most unique animals for the photographic pleasure of tourists and then release them, unharmed, back into the wilderness.

During my travels with Paulo, I saw hundreds of alligators. They seem to live in every small pool of water, in every ditch, swamp and river. As the Pantanal is composed entirely of this kind of landscape, they are everywhere. My guide assured me that it was safe to swim in the rivers; all the locals do it, despite the fact that all rivers host alligators. I learned later that *jacare*, the Pantanal alligators, mainly feed on piranhas, a fact that did not help reassure me about swimming.

Paulo took me for morning and evening walks to observe the wildlife. I was fascinated by these large reptiles, seemingly sound asleep on the banks of the rivers, but was never able to get close enough for the photos I wanted to take. Each time they saw me coming they were back in the water with a large splash and quickly disappeared. Paulo informed me that their amazing vision is the only highly developed sense they can use on land and they are extremely conscious of movement. When I wondered aloud how we could ever come close enough to catch one, Paulo looked at me and said confidently, "Don't worry, we are going to catch alligators."

One day, on our way to a new camp, we stopped our truck in front of a large pool of water. Before attempting to cross it, Paulo went to check its depth and bottom consistency. He walked barefoot into a knee-deep mixture of floating vegetation and murky water; a big splash caught my attention and Paulo immediately started searching for the already-hidden alligator. Seeing it beneath the vegetation in a few inches of water, he moved toward it like a cat, slowly placing one foot on each side of the animal. Suddenly, he leaped forward, plunging his hands in and dragging out a five-foot-long alligator by its neck.

He walked toward me with a smile and asked, "Do you want to hold it?"

"Yes," I answered. "But wait a minute. I've run out of film, and if I don't load a new roll and immortalize this, nobody will ever believe me." The alligator's powerful jaw was armed with razor-sharp teeth; I wrapped my hands around its neck and held it up with pride and more than a little anxiety.

"As long as you keep strong pressure on the neck, the alligator can't open its mouth," Paulo assured me. "Because you hold it in front of you in the air, it can't whip you with its tail. There's no problem. As long as you hold it with both hands very close to its skull, it's harmless."

In spite of my guide's faith, I still worried that the alligator would jerk around and, if my grip relaxed even slightly, my arm might be its next meal. However, since the purpose was to control my fear, I continued to hold it. After a few seconds, it looked so harmless I began to feel ashamed of my exaggerated fear. When we released it close to the water, the alligator stayed still for several seconds and I managed to take a couple of photos. As I was taking a close up shot of its head, it ran a few steps toward me and I jumped back, surprised. It changed direction quickly and disappeared into the water.

Paulo described his catching technique: "Don't go to the side of the crocodile. If you do, you'll get bitten. Walk slowly from behind, put one leg on each side of its body and grab its neck with your hands. Make sure you keep a good grip just behind its head where the skin is the softest and then press the crocodile against the bottom to immobilize it. As you do, make sure your legs are spread apart and in a position well in front of its posterior legs to avoid the sharp and powerful tail as it whips. Once immobilized, if it's small enough, you quickly lift it up in front of you."

I was impressed by Paulo, who walked barefoot through the floating vegetation in the murky water full of alligators and piranhas. It was natural for him, but I didn't immediately forget my prejudices; it would take several more encounters for me to lose my fear.

The technique for catching larger alligators is different. They have so much power it isn't possible to immobilize them against the ground or the bottom of the swamp. They can also lash you with their tails and escape from your grip so it would be dangerous to even try to catch them by hand. Paulo showed me how to use a noose tied to a stick.

Paulo always walks barefoot in the middle of swamps, so I asked him if he'd ever had a problem with alligators. He denied it, but a day later I noticed scars, clearly left by teeth, on his leg. When I questioned him about those scars, he responded, "Once, a large alligator caught my leg, but you see it didn't destroy it."

I asked, "What did you do?"

He answered, "Nothing."

"What do you mean nothing?" I said incredulously. "Can't you do anything if you're being bitten by an alligator?"

"The best thing to do is not move," he explained. "Alligators have no sense of taste and they will bite anything that moves in front of them, sometimes even branches. Nothing can make them open their jaws once they are closed; they will only release if they think they have mistakenly bitten something inedible. If you move your leg, the flesh will be shredded. If you try to wrestle the alligator, the same thing will happen. It is best to be still and suffer the pain until the alligator releases you."

This is what Paulo did; the scars on his leg are very clean and he suffered no complications from his injury. His explanation left me thoughtful. Not a Pantanal native, I might not possess the same level of pain tolerance as Paulo. If caught, would I be able to remain still until released? I can only hope this question will remain unanswered.

One morning, we sighted a large alligator on the bank of a small pool of water. As usual, it dove instantly at our approach, and disappeared into the depths of the muddy green pool.

Paulo said, "It's a big one, but we can catch it. Stay here, I'll go get a rope."

He came back with the rope and made a lasso. The alligator had stayed submerged, hidden in aquatic vegetation. With a long stick, Paulo poked around in the water, but the alligator seemed to have disappeared. Paulo stepped knee-deep into the pool, poking here and there with his stick, and suddenly a huge jaw broke the surface with a fast snapping movement and showing the tip of its nose. Paulo turned his lasso in the air and threw it; on the second try, the lasso made it over the alligator's head, but was not yet around it. With the long stick, he poked the alligator, which bit the open noose. Paulo pulled the noose tight, moved quickly toward the shore and said, "Take it, it's yours!"

"What?"

"Take it!"

I took the rope and started pulling, but as soon as the alligator's feet touched the bottom, it fought back with its tail and pulled.

"Pull it strongly but slowly," said Paulo.

I did and forced it up out of the water. Once on firm ground, alligators are much slower and more vulnerable, so while I held the rope tight, my guide went around and wrapped a double loop around the dangerous jaw. Then he grabbed its posterior leg, lifted the gator up and said, "It's a big male, about 220 pounds and eight and half feet long."

I proudly lifted it, well bound with rope, up into my arms. Noticing scars on its back, I asked Paulo, "Fight with another *jacare*?"

During the driest month, too many alligators share very small pools and often fight. I was also surprised to learn that humans are not their only predators. Paulo told me that jaguars sometimes attack juveniles or small adults, and large anacondas attack them, although they don't always win the fight.

My week in the Pantanal with Paulo was enlightening. I learned much about its wildlife in general and particularly about alligators. I realized that they fear humans much more than we fear them and, unlike their cousins in Australia and Africa, they don't prey on people. Mishaps are rare and usually involve a defensive reaction during a surprise encounter. The twenty-one-hour bus ride back to Sao Paulo was filled with memories of hundreds of alligators and thousands of tropical birds. The Pantanal did me good: I am now ready to paddle the jungle rivers of La Moskitia with much more confidence. Twelve months in the jungle with the Miskitos and Pech Indians in Honduras and Nicaragua await me and I'm looking forward to meeting Luke and getting back into my kayak.

CHAPTER 4
HONDURAS

The West Coast

Luke, 11 August 1999

IT HAS BEEN two months since we last paddled a kayak. We've used the time to document our expedition while I learned how to scuba dive in the Bay Islands and Jean-Philippe learned Spanish in Guatemala and to catch alligators in Brazil. Now we are hitting the water again for what we expect to be a ten-day, ninety-mile-long paddle to reach the town of La Ceiba and the Mosquito Coast. Today though, we only plan to paddle twelve miles before looking for a camping spot around Punta Ula.

There is no gentle way to reintroduce our bodies to distance paddling, so yesterday we were incredibly sore from our first long day but the elements showed us no sympathy. At 3:30 a.m. we awoke for an early departure, only to hear rumbling thunder and see the sky being torn apart by bolts of lightning. We should have paddled because we needed to make some progress but, without even getting out of bed to check the conditions, we decided to make it a rest day.

Fed and rested, we push off the next morning at 6 a.m. After a couple of hours, we are sore and sweltering but there is no shade to be found for thirteen miles along this barren strip of beach southeast of Puerto

Cortes. When we stop mid-morning, we erect a sunshade by stretching the plastic tarp between pieces of driftwood plunged into the sand. It is shady but certainly not cool. The morning breeze dies and the sun bakes the thin plastic, passing all of its heat to the stagnant air below it. We aren't getting sunburned but the shelter is convection-cooking us. The only time we move is to roll over and drink water. We go to sleep early and wake up late the next morning, missing our customary pre-dawn departure. We launch at 7:30 a.m., looking forward to an easy seven-mile leg to Laguna Diamante.

Just before 10:00 a.m., we pull into the lush and picturesque Laguna Diamante but soon realize that some gems are best appreciated from afar. All we want is a nice spot in the shade to nap and relax but, to our horror, we discover a ravenous insect empire that attacks us with abandon. On the windless beach, we rub 100% DEET into the sheen of our sweat-covered bodies and sit sweltering in the shade of a vine-draped tree. Hordes of whining tiger-striped mosquitoes, sandflies, yellow-winged doctor flies and wasps descend upon us. They sting us through the fabric of our long pants and through the mesh of our Bug Shirts. Meanwhile, howler monkeys in the tops of trees on the other side of the lagoon roar at us, as if to mock our pain.

The confines of our sandfly-proof mosquito net let us sleep, but our night is cramped and uncomfortable. We've rigged up a roof with the tarp and a rain fly but it offers scant protection from a midnight rain-squall. Stiff and damp, we arise at 3:00 a.m. to get an early start on a long day. Whirring with constant motion—slapping bugs, shoving equipment in bags, making breakfast, packing the boats—the process that usually takes us two hours is finished quickly and we launch by 4:30 a.m. Our consolation for a night of extreme discomfort is the view out on the horizon as a gorgeous sunrise turns the last wispy clouds of the retreating squall into cotton candy.

†

Jean-Philippe, 18 August 1999

On our second morning out from Tela, nine days into our paddle from Puerto Cortes to La Ceiba, the alarm rings at 4:00 a.m. but lightning flashes in the sky and thunder booms in our ears and we decide to stay put until dawn. We get up at 6:00 a.m. and see a low thick layer of black clouds. We can see fishermen hurrying back home against a strong headwind that has risen up from the north. We know that a big storm is coming and, though most seafarers find these conditions forbidding, for us it means a free ride south. We quickly eat some breakfast and pack and, as we finish loading our kayaks, the frequency of the lightning increases. The wind turns into a constant gale and it begins to rain thick drops of water that feel like small stones falling on my head.

The sea is rough but nothing we can't handle. We punch through the surf and start paddling but the wind abruptly changes direction. A strong easterly gale hits us from the side, creating large breaking swell. To avoid capsizing, we have to brace constantly into waves breaking over us broadside. With such powerful forces aligned against us, our kayaks are pushed off course. We expend a lot of energy to cover a short distance.

After an hour, the wind changes again, this time coming at us head-on. The large swell that had been washing over us broadside has disappeared into messy chop. Combined with the strong headwind, these water conditions hinder our progress even more. It is now pointless to be out here.

Although the conditions are exhausting, they don't scare me; Baja prepared us well. We've been on worse seas. What really intimidates me, though, is the frequency and intensity of the lightning. I think to myself that being struck by lightning is a shameful and inglorious way to die but I remember something a local told me: "When down in the troughs, the kayak is lower than the peaks of the waves. The risk of being struck by lightning is minimal." Those words are small comfort though; logic doesn't always calm the nerves.

Another hour passes, the storm subsides and, mercifully, the sky clears. Eventually, the swell decreases and the wind disappears all together. After four hours, we are drained, hot and dehydrated and our muscles are sore from the sustained effort. We need to get to shore for a break. We soon spy a beach with a thick margin of coconut trees lining the shore; it looks promising, so we land and quickly move on to other pressing concerns such as eating and sleeping. Almost immediately, two armed cowboys on horses hail us. One has a big knife strapped to his belt, a bandolier full of bullets across his chest and a shotgun in his hands. The other has a .45 automatic handgun and a long ammunition belt. I recall hearing that .45-caliber guns are illegal in Honduras, only the army is allowed to use them. These two, unshaven and wearing rags, certainly don't look like military men.

We get the feeling that we have stumbled onto a drug plantation and Luke innocently asks them if we have landed on a "farm." They reply brusquely that indeed we have and that we should leave as quickly as we appeared. We are exhausted and tell them we just want to rest and camp on the beach and ask where there might be a better spot. They make it clear that no such place exists close by. I can see one of them eyeing my hat and the other looking intently at our bags of gear. There is no need to push our luck here, so we turn to leave.

We have no choice but to ignore the protests of our muscles and keep paddling on in the heat. Finally, after more than twenty miles, we land, exhausted, on a deserted beach. We jump in the water to cool off and just float motionless for twenty minutes.

Amazingly, the beach turns out to be our best campsite in Honduras yet. In the evening we can see the lights of La Ceiba, another eighteen miles away. One more day and our ocean paddling will be over for the year; we'll stay off the open water during the rainy season from September through the end of March. Beyond La Ceiba, the jungle rivers, lagoons and remote communities of La Moskitia await us.

†

Luke, 3 September 1999

Since arriving in La Ceiba two weeks ago, we have busied ourselves with making preparations for our trip to the Rio Platano Biosphere and tomorrow we plan to depart by plane for Palacios. La Ceiba has always been a portal; its name comes from a legendary *ceiba* tree of such stature that colonists and local Indians used to gather beneath its broad canopy to trade. The diverse mix of people and peddlers and their wares still found there today reflects that history. The town is an ideal place to launch and land, fill up, rest, recuperate and exfoliate travel calluses. It's the gateway to the Bay Islands of Utila, Roatan and Guanaja, thirty-five miles off the coast, and also the launching pad for excursions into the wild outback towns of the south. For us, it will be a home base to return to once every four weeks for the next six to eight months of our exploration into the Mosquito Coast to renew our visas.

Today is a typical multinational one in La Ceiba. We wake up in an *hospedaje* run by a retired Dutch sailor, stop by a restaurant/inn run by a U.S.-educated Honduran, munch some bread made by his French expat baker, eat a lunch of falafel in Cafe Shalom, which is run by a former Israeli ship's cook, and spend the afternoon talking with a half-Miskito adventure-tour operator and his Garifuna guides.

†

Jean-Philippe, 3 September 1999

The Mosquito Coast gained some recognition from the novel of the same name by Paul Theroux and its movie adaptation starring Harrison Ford. Although the movie was actually filmed on the Sibun River in Belize, it gives viewers some appreciation for the conditions in Central America's jungles during the rainy season. The Mosquito Coast, La Moskitia in Spanish, is the largest and most unspoiled rainforest in

Central America. It covers the entire southeast part of Honduras (nearly a third of the country's landmass) and extends into the northern half of Nicaragua. The name, although appropriate for the many parts of the region that are infested with the notorious malaria-carrying insect, actually comes from its inhabitants, the Miskito Indians. Since the days of the first European explorers, the land of the Miskito has been known as the Mosquito Coast.

For us, La Moskitia is a major highlight of our trip. We hope to gather photos and stories for a powerful documentary about the Pech who, along with subsistence-farming Miskitos and a smaller Indigenous group called the Tahwaka, live along the many rivers of the interior. Along the coast, there are a few Garifuna villages scattered in the north and Miskito communities occupy the rest. Some of the largest villages have attracted a growing number of Latinos, tempted by the opportunities for commerce or by the potential for the exploitation of natural resources.

As I was preparing our itinerary for this area, I came across an excellent book by Derek Parent, a Canadian professor and cartographer who had fallen in love with the area. As an advocate and expert on La Moskitia, he became one of CASKE 2000's strongest supporters. It is from him that I first became aware of the history of this fascinating place and he has continued to provide us with a constant flow of information and contacts as we move along the coast and prepare to go deeper into the jungle.

It is believed that the Miskito and Pech people moved to La Moskitia from the Amazon and Orinoco regions of Ecuador and Venezuela from 750 to 1,000 years ago. During the colonial period, English and Dutch buccaneers used the region's extensive network of lagoons and estuaries as bases from which to stage raids on Spanish forts and the gold fleet because large warships couldn't enter the shallow lagoons to chase them down. The pirates, along with their Miskito allies, used their smaller boats and strategically placed batteries of cannons very effectively. The British were happy to let these privateers operate without regulation in the area as it effectively extended their influence throughout the region. The area where we are headed, near the mouth of the Rio Platano Biosphere, is full of names that date from that era: Laguna Ibans is named after an English pirate, Evans, and Brus Laguna is named after the notorious buccaneer, "Bloody" Brewer. Another pirate legacy left can be seen in the faces and occasional blue eyes and blond hair of the local people. The buccaneers commingled with local Miskito people; many of them are now of mixed heritage and a large percentage of them speak English, especially throughout the Nicaraguan portion of La Moskitia.

We're in the middle of hurricane season and we're being careful because the disastrous aftermath of Mitch still marks this land a year later. It has made us wary of continuing to paddle the coast at this time of year; instead, we have decided to fly into the interior and explore the rainforest, paddling through the canals and then upriver to the community of Las Marias. Later, when the weather stabilizes, we will resume our paddle down the coast from La Ceiba.

We work late into the night preparing our gear. With only four hours to go before the time set on our alarm, we are still struggling to compress the contents and close the zippers on our large duffel bags.

At 4:45 a.m., the second alarm forces me to raise my head. Luke tells me that the taxi driver has just knocked on the door. We had asked the hotel manager to reserve us a station wagon taxi with a roof rack. I go out to negotiate the price with the driver because I don't want him to see all our gear. If he knows what we have, he will ask for five times the normal fare. He agrees to a fair price and, as we unveil our cargo, I can hear him curse under his breath. We stuff the old car to the roof—and beyond. Its suspension is non-existent and the car bottoms out the entire way to the airport as we crawl along at a top speed of twenty-five miles an hour.

Getting the gear to the airport is not our only concern; we have to get it on the airplane too. Between the two of us we have over 300 pounds of baggage, unfortunately our combined allowance is only 100 pounds. To our relief, the scene at check-in is chaotic and when the desk clerk finally gets around to calculating our extra costs, the bags are already out the door and loaded. With a smile, I insist that there must have been a weighing error. There is no way now to double-check and we end up paying only a ten-dollar penalty.

The difficulties will start soon enough once we arrive. After paddling from Palacios to Barra Platano through lagoons and canals hand-cut through mangrove swamp, we will have to fight the current to go thirty-five miles further upriver to the settlement of Las Marias. In between, we will need to camp at least once in the wet, insect-infested jungle but I know the trip will be worth it. Las Marias is home to the last remaining Pech population in La Moskitia. The village should be the setting for a spectacular documentary; however, it makes me sore and itchy just thinking about the trip to get there.

⸸

Luke, 3 September 1999

The twin-engine plane descends low over a carpet of green savannah that opens abruptly on to the tea-colored expanse of a large lagoon. Almost skimming its surface, we approach the Palacios airstrip on the far side of the lagoon and touch down with a jolt. The pilot throws the plane into a full reverse throttle and the landing gear bounces rapidly as we slow to a stop on the bumpy grass and dirt runway. Out of the starboard porthole, I read a faded sign off to the side of the clearing: "Welcome to the Rio Platano Biosphere."

Ducking under the low arch of the door and stepping out of the plane, the second thing I notice is a soccer goal and a group of children. Apparently, the runway doubles as the town sports field. I look at my watch: it's only 7:30 a.m. The smiling rag-tag bunch of black Garifuna and dark Miskito kids, aged between six and ten, can't have come this early for a game. As soon as my feet touch the ground, I understand why they have congregated here. Six or seven of them immediately offer their services as porters. Most of them are barely waist-high. They are very eager and hopeful, that is, until the pilot's assistant pulls our gear from the hold of the plane. The two huge black bags containing our folded-up kayaks and a massive green duffel stuffed with most of the rest of the gear thump to the grass. Most of the kids smile sheepishly and move on to the only other gringos on the plane, a Dutch couple. It's the only flight of the day and their last chance for a tip. As we load up, two courageous boys, one Latino and one Garifuna, ask to be our porters. Fully aware of the size and mass of the bags, they still seem up for the challenge. How do you say no to the pleading eyes and toothy smiles of two ten-year-olds? Besides, we are curious to see if they will be able to lug the bags the 200 yards across the field to the boarding house.

Although fearful that their tips might need to be shared, they grudgingly recruit help from two young girls and, together, the four of them trundle the 100-pound bags over to the *hospedaje* and up the steps to our room. Sweat streams down their faces and into the corners of their smiles as they struggle. We are very impressed, so we hand them their hard-earned *lempiras* with pleasure, knowing that they will be buying staples such as sugar and flour for their households rather than candy.

Our preconceived notions of the Mosquito Coast turn out to be largely incorrect. We expected the weather and living conditions to be tougher, with more humidity and more insects. We were sure that the lagoons would be filled with brackish water, rotting vegetation and putrescence. That is not the case. Rough-hewn houses dot a swath of grassy savannah where large mango trees, breadfruit and palms offer shade along the margins. Our room on the second floor of the *hospedaje* is in a perfect position to catch a brisk breeze blowing across the lagoon from the southwest. And, until dusk, we encounter neither mosquitoes nor sandflies.

Don Felix is Palacios' de facto *jefe* (chief); business transactions are completed through him. He runs the Isleña Airlines concession, the eight-room boarding house, a *comedor* and the gasoline distributorship. He's a diminutive sage who's always around and always seems to have enough time and information to solve everyone's problems.

At dusk, we sit on the second-story porch, watching our first day here wind down. The breeze blows itself out by late afternoon and the choppy, brown surface of the lagoon becomes a mirror reflecting both the verdant mangrove foliage on the far shore and the shifting hues of the sunset. Hand-carved canoes and the homeward-bound motor launches, powered by blatting two-stroke engines, ferry people to outlying villages. Sparrows and small shore birds dart and flit around, feeding on nocturnal insects.

These fringe towns on the coast seem to have it easy, I think to myself as I settle into bed. This is a relaxed way to start off, but I know that it won't last.

↑

Jean-Philippe, 4 September 1999

On our first day out of Palacios, after paddling four miles through a natural canal to enter the large fresh-water mass of Laguna Ibans, I stop on the shore at a local settlement named Coyote. Waiting for Luke, I am surrounded by local Miskito children. Curious adults also come to catch a glimpse of my strange *cayuco*; a few men take turns trying to paddle my kayak, to the great amusement of the crowd. When Luke arrives, we resume paddling to Raista, the goal for today. Our friend Derek had told us to look up Eddie Bodden, a Miskito man, who is running the butterfly farm, an ecotourism project initiated by the Peace Corps and entomologists from the States. Eddie greets us with a strong handshake and warm smile. He is the type of man you trust from the first moment you meet him and we become instant friends. We fall in love with the inhabitants of this settlement and spend a few days relaxing and exchanging culture and adventure tales with Eddie, his wife and their extended family.

✳

Jean-Philippe, 9 September 1999

Five days later, we paddle out of Laguna Ibans on a reconnaissance mission that takes us down a long and monotonous hand-dug canal through alternating tracts of thick mangroves and cattle-grazed savannah. The canal opens into a small lagoon by the village of Kuri, where we stop for a short break. Miskito kids playing in the water work up the courage to approach us and, within minutes, they are climbing all over the decks of the kayaks, four or five at a time, asking to go for a ride. In the late morning, we navigate the last canal, which will lead us out into the Platano River. Less than a mile long, it is the most beautiful one we have seen. A study in varying shades of green, it is less than four feet wide in spots as it curls its way between the roots of giant tropical trees. The canopy above is often so dense that it feels as if we are paddling through a tunnel. Tangles of serpentine vines hang from trees and vibrant flowering epiphytes cling to branches all around us. A few rays of golden light, like concentrated beams, pierce the canopy creating a lace-patterned contrast of light and dark throughout the forest's magical understory. I am so absorbed by my surroundings that I forget to maneuver my kayak through the narrow canal and I continually bump into the roots that are sprouting everywhere. As we pull out into the open sky and wide brown flow of the Rio Platano, we are witness to a fine mist that kisses the treetops and adds yet another air of mystery to our surroundings. I resent having to leave such a magical corridor behind but, our reconnaissance complete, we backtrack to the village of Kuri. Tomorrow morning we'll arise early to paddle up the Rio Platano.

↑

Jean-Philippe, 10 September 1999

The Rio Platano is the most famous river in Honduran La Moskitia. In 1980 UNESCO assured its fame—and survival—when it declared the entire river and the surrounding jungle a Biosphere Reserve and World Heritage Site. The reserve is home to many Indigenous Miskito communities as well as the last Pech tribe in the Mosquito Coast. Las Marias, located upriver on the Rio Platano in the heart of the biosphere, is a community composed of both ethnic groups, a perfect place for a documentary.

For us, the Rio Platano is our first jungle adventure. A year into the expedition, we are now well prepared to handle most coastal situations. We understand the waves and currents; we know about sharks and dangerous marine life. We can climb coconut trees and use other techniques to survive. We are familiar with the Belizean forest and some of its secrets. Yet none of that will help us here in the Platano Biosphere: we are entering a new world. Flora and fauna are different from one rainforest to another. During our solo ascent of the river, we may encounter some potentially dangerous plants that we will not be able to identify. Unlike the outgoing coastal fishermen, the people who live along these rivers tend to be more wary and shy, but this is a secondary challenge; the strong current of the Rio Platano is the primary obstacle for us to overcome. Most people that we've talked to down on the coast don't think that we will get very far. Local Miskitos and Pechs only paddle halfway up the Platano and then they switch to poling to push their long dugout canoes up through the rapids. We are taking our chances with the weather, as well. September is a month with a lot of rain and the river can surge and rise five feet over the course of a very few hours.

Have we paddled 2,000 kilometers of ocean through windstorms, high swells, breaking surf, deadly heat and electrical storms just to get to this point and turn around? we wonder. No way! If the Miskitos and Pech do it, so will we. Optimistic in spite of the ominous warnings, general pessimism and our ignorance, we begin to paddle.

Near the mouth, the river is wide and deep with a mild, steady current and, initially, we cruise along at a good pace. A few motor canoes ferrying passengers to villages higher up go by and we wave. For the moment, we feel up to the challenge.

In the early afternoon, we find ourselves kayaking against a much stronger current and our progress becomes slow and painful. We reach a bend in the river and an old man on the bank calls out to me. We decide to stop. A squatter and slash-and-burn farmer, he lives with his family in a small cabin on one side of the river. Five other families live on the other side. He offers us coffee and we politely accept; Luke sips his contentedly but I don't like coffee so I discretely dump most of it out when he isn't looking. While relaxing in hammocks, we talk for an hour and he eventually invites us to stay for the night. He offers us his children's beds, but we respectfully decline, telling him that we will be fine in our tent. His daughter prepares us a meal of rice, fried tortillas and orange juice and we set up the tent amidst piles of dung, snorting pigs, quacking ducks and clucking chickens.

According to our GPS we have only progressed seven and a half miles in six hours. During the paddle, I watched the compass move in a range of up to 160 degrees through the many turns in the river. We may have actually paddled over fifteen miles. The old Miskito man tells us that we have covered half the distance to Las Marias, the easy half, and that tomorrow we will start paddling against the current. We ask him to be more specific so he tells us that the water in front of his house is as still as a lagoon compared to what lies ahead. Luke looks at me with concern.

†

Jean-Philippe, 11 September 1999

Our alarm is set for 4:00 a.m. but the screaming pigs wake us up long before that. After a breakfast of oatmeal and ibuprofen, we load our boats while under torturous assault by thousands of no-see-ums. They are slightly bigger than the sandflies we encountered on the beach and much more painful; they leave large welts that seem to itch more with each passing hours and spots of blood all over the surface of our skin. We thought we had experienced the worst during our beach camping in Belize and Honduras—little did we know. Our host greets us with more coffee as we are about to leave, so we delay our launch until 5:45 a.m.

The current is indeed much stronger; we'll have to change our tactics entirely. We stick to the sides where the current flows more slowly and try to paddle up into the eddies and counter currents created by sub-merged obstacles. Every time the river curves sharply, we have to cross over to the bank on the inside of the turn; the flow around the outside is just too strong. As soon as our bows enter the main flow, the rushing water pushes the kayak sideways and we have to paddle full force to avoid being swept downstream. Once in the turn, it requires a tremen-dous amount of energy to move forward mere inches at a time; I estimate the current at six to seven knots in some of the curves. In a kayak, those sections are like paddling on a treadmill. Lots of wasted energy that gets us nowhere. Late in the morning, I stop on a gravel bar from which I can see far downriver. There is no sign of Luke.

Five minutes later Luke appears, and he's not paddling. He is walking through the shallow rapids and pulling his kayak with a rope! Before he can re-enter his kayak and cross the river, I see an old Miskito man standing in his *cayuco*, poling at a steady pace along the margin of the river. As he gets closer, I realize that it is our host from the night before and his wife. He leans on the pole, using his body weight as leverage, while his wife sits in the rear steering with a large wooden paddle. Together, they are remarkably efficient. They departed an hour and a half after us and they have already caught up. They easily pass Luke, who is struggling to paddle through the rapid. Luke is inspired to try a similar technique by pushing on the bottom with his paddle but fails miserably; sitting down in the kayak, he has no leverage. He looks dejected at the prospect of continuing on.

My biggest fear in these murky brown rapids is running into submerged sharp objects; our hypalon fabric hulls cannot withstand collisions with sharp bamboo or rocks. At one point, I am paddling strongly between two trees when I suddenly feel something against the bottom of my hull but it is already too late for me to react. My kayak gets stuck on top of a submerged branch from one of the trees and the current immediately turns me sideways. If I let it continue, I will be stuck broadside against the tree and, since I'm not wearing my spray skirt because of the heat, the open cockpit will surely flood and the kayak will sink. I need to do something quickly. I stroke hard on the downstream side to realign the boat upstream and into the current. Then, I paddle as hard as I can while bouncing up and down in my seat to try to dislodge the hull. I feel the branch slowly release the hull and I'm free. Almost totally exhausted now, I slow my pace and try to recover.

The sights and sounds of this section higher up on the river are surreal. Lime green parakeets, in pairs and larger groups, fly overhead in a regular stream. Their cacophonic squawking fills the air in joyous sound. Iguanas, startled by the noisy splashing of our paddles, drop from the low-hanging branches where they are soaking in the sun and dash for the water. I come across a few families loading their enormous dugout canoes with mountains of plantain and *supa* fruits to sell down in Barra Platano.

Eventually I ask a family how much longer they think it will take us to reach Las Marias. Without hesitation, they tell me two and a half hours. It's not the distance, they tell me, it's the current—from here it gets stronger. Their words destroy my morale. I've been paddling as hard as I can; Luke has spent half his time walking and towing. And it's going to get worse? The only encouraging thing about the entire day is the weather. It has been overcast and cooler all day and now a soothing rain begins to fall.

After an hour, I pull over to the riverbank by a small house to wait for Luke. At that moment, I realize that I am starving. It is very rare that I have food hallucinations, but I find myself dreaming of a well-done Camembert smeared on crusty, fresh-baked bread, though at this point, any food would be wonderful. When Luke arrives, we start talking to the owner, who has descended to greet us. This conversation with Sylvio quickly evolves into a proposition for a meal. A few minutes later, we step into the small thatched-roof house and meet Sylvio's brother, wife and children. The young woman prepares us some fried plantains with beans and river fish.

After the meal, we reboard the boats and, rejuvenated, it only takes us forty-five minutes of hard paddling before we pull up next to a large dugout at the base of steep banks below Las Marias. Kids swimming in the river help us unload and carry the bags up the muddy incline and over to a small *hospedaje* set in a wide clearing.

"Where are we?" Luke asks from behind, seemingly confused. We had heard that Las Marias is a settlement of about 600 people. All we see are six or seven huts set in a grassy savannah full of cows, pigs and chickens. Olvidio, the *hospedaje* owner, tells us that we are in *el centro*, the heart of the town of Las Marias. The village is spread out into several small groups of houses that cover a few kilometers along the river. We are too tired to socialize for long and we're not in the mood to find the beauty in our surroundings. All we can focus on for the moment are the negatives: endless rapids, pig shit and biting flies. I'm quite sure that in the morning we will see the town in a different light.

†

Las Marias

Jean-Philippe, 18 September 1999

The oral history of the Pech is a collection of fantastical and factual stories where, at times, it is difficult to draw clear lines between the two. Ironically, it seems like the more educated and assimilated Pechs are the ones working hardest in an effort to preserve their culture, but much of their knowledge of the history of their own people comes from books published by missionaries and anthropologists rather than the oral tradition of their ancestors. I wonder if the truth of Pech history can really be found in the books written by outsiders who have interacted with them or in the stories from the elders whose histories were told to them by their grandfathers?

In Las Marias we spend most of our time with the village elders, some of whom were living here decades before it was even an established village. Many of them believe that their true history is in the words passed down from one generation to the next. As we listen, we begin to realize that what is considered "history" among the elders is seen as "legends" by the younger generation. According to the youth, history began only with their conquest by the Spanish. We meet with village elder and tribal council president Don Divio Ramos Torres and his sister, Dona Catalina Ramos, the two oldest Pech people in La Moskitia. Bernardo, age forty-nine, a member of the Pech council and one of the most educated people in Las Marias, also joins us. He tells us: "About five hundred years ago, five or six thousand Pech people moved to the Rio Platano area. We are not sure where they came from; we are told from South America, but we don't know. They first settled in a place we call Chilmeca, located close to Casa Blanca." When I ask about Casa Blanca, Don Divio answers me: "This is where my grandparents were born. When I was a child, my grandfather told me he grew up in a city carved in white stones. They called it Casa Blanca."

In Honduras many people talk about a mysterious lost city they call Ciudad Blanca; an ancient metropolis rumored to have been swallowed by the jungle, it has recently become the focus of numerous international archaeological and treasure-hunting expeditions.

I ask if this is the Casa Blanca of his story and we listen with keen interest as Don Divio goes on: "Yes, it is the same place. The gods made it. Giant stones were carved in various shapes, wild animals and giant grinding stones." I ask, "Why did people abandon a city made by the gods? Why can't we find it today?" Don Divio replies, "My grandfather told me that at that time, a Tawaka man lived among the Pech people. He left the Ciudad Blanca after being mistreated by the community and cursed the place. Thereafter, terrible diseases and catastrophes happened. The Pech people understood that they could no longer live there. They had to move."

Their search for a more prosperous place took them downriver, he says, to a place they call "Sakorska Uya" (big written stone), the site of a large petroglyph that can still be seen today. They lived there for some time and evidence of their more modern habitation can be seen in the numerous fruit trees still found in that area.

Seventy or eighty years ago for unknown reasons, the Rio Platano Pech moved downriver from Sakorska Uya, their oldest "historical" dwelling, and founded the settlement of Buena Vista, where Don Divio, his sister and some other elders of Las Marias were born. From Buena Vista, they continued to move downriver to a place they call Quiaquimina but returned to Buena Vista a few years later. Finally, about forty years ago, they settled in Las Marias.

Las Marias' settlement and growth has occurred during the period in which the Pech culture has been most affected by outside influences. After a terrible hurricane, starving Miskito people paddled upriver and stole the food from the Pech. The Pech retreated to Buena Vista for a few years before resettling permanently in Las Marias. Miskito people, mainly men, started to move to Las Marias where the land is much richer than on the coast. There, they inter-married with the Pech and today their culture and language prevail in Las Marias.

Thirteen years after our jungle exploration, archeologists would discover the site in May 2012, thus proving the myth to be reality. Excavations wouldn't start until 2015, when famous author Douglas Preston was invited to join. The expedition would become the subject of a *National Geographic* feature and be narrated in Preston's remarkable book *The Lost City of the Monkey God*, where he brilliantly describes many of the dangers we were facing but were never aware of during our weeks there. So it wasn't Don Divio's father who lived in the Ciudad Blanca but his ancestors—a word that may have been lost in translation, as Indigenous people often refer to their ancestors as their defunct fathers. But the myth that young people didn't believe in, even though distorted through generations, was real verbal history. What would shock me when reading Preston's book was that the conclusion the scientists had agreed upon about the possible reason people abandoned the lost city was the same as the one Don Divio had told us in person years before. At the time, we wouldn't know where to draw the line between myth and history, but it all was fascinating.

To learn more about the Pech culture, we also spend hours talking with Don Divio's son, Ubense Ramos Torres. He is an exuberant teacher and we learn much about the Pech culture and lifestyle by following him around during his daily routine. Don Ubense is the president of the *Consejo de Tribu Pech* (Pech Tribal Council). Along with Bernardo and Francisco, he works to preserve Pech heritage, traditions and language. Although of small stature, he is an impressive man. At fifty years old, he is full of energy and impossibly strong. We spend a day with him tromping around the forest gathering huge bales of *suita* leaves to repair his roof. The 120-pound giant outworks us, carries heavier loads and, more impressively, out-talks me in conversation (a difficult task I must admit). In the high heat and humidity, after four hours of non-stop labor, Luke and I are exhausted and dehydrated. Ubense hasn't stopped once to eat, drink or rest. His life is a balance between the daily necessities of a poor Indigenous man living a subsistence lifestyle with his family, and the political fight he wages with the Honduran government for rights he believes his people have yet to obtain.

Don Ubense's school was the rainforest and his curriculum, the Pech culture. He is outspoken and eloquent in denouncing the politicians who have closed their eyes to his people. Although he can count on little support outside his village, without hesitation he has entered the political game. He converses with both great tact and powerful rhetoric. "The Pech culture needs to be revived, the language saved and the people need to receive titles for the land that their ancestors have always occupied."

We learn that fewer than twenty people in the community speak the Pech language fluently and it has become clear that here in Las Marias, we are witnessing a culture on the verge of extinction. If current trends continue, the Pech culture and the people themselves may fade into the jungle like Ciudad Blanca and be forgotten, despite the efforts of the remaining tribal leaders.

Don Ubense is one of the last surviving Pech and one of the few who still speaks his native tongue. The sad thing to him is that although his children understand Pech, they prefer to speak Miskito or Spanish, the languages they learn in school and use with their friends. Unless the government funds the Pech bilingual school project, Ubense's generation could very well be the last of the Pech. In his words, "There is no culture without a language."

Another significant threat to the Pech culture is the work of the missionaries; Indigenous cultures all over the world are threatened by their misguided intentions. In Honduras the church has had a dramatic influence. In Las Marias alone, there are three churches: a Moravian Evangelical Church (an English denomination), a Catholic church and one called La Cruz; all of the congregations are very devoted.

I meet a twelve-year-old girl who asks me if I am afraid of the year 2000. Perplexed, I stare at her. She can't be talking about the Y2K computer glitch! She's never seen a computer in her life. When I ask for clarification, she tells me that she is terrified that the apocalypse is upon us, that

January 1, 2000, will be Judgment Day and she is afraid that she and all her family will die. It turns out that the pastor has preached to them for months about the end of the world and it has never occurred to her or anyone else that he could possibly be wrong. He announced that he had received a message from God and that people were running out of time to show their faith. I smile at her and try to explain that sometimes people, even pastors, make mistakes, that if God had spent all his time creating all the beautiful things we can see, he would certainly not destroy them all in a day but my speech fails to reassure the girl. I am no match for a preacher who stands in the pulpit every week and makes a living from his words. It's a shame that he uses them to control people's thoughts starting so young.

Many villagers have been so brainwashed that they turn their backs on their traditions and their culture. Their interpretation of the Bible puts taboos on alcohol, music and dances. "One shall not drink." That includes the traditional Pech drinks like *chicha de maiz*, a concoction of fermented sugar cane juice and corn, and *chicha de yucca*, the original Pech drink made from chewed and fermented yucca root. Pastors have told them that, in the words of God, dancing is a sin. It is no wonder the traditional Pech dances have almost entirely disappeared. And if nobody is going to dance, why should people learn the traditional music? Few of them have any knowledge of the traditional bamboo flutes and snakeskin drums that we had hoped to see.

After a fascinating week in Las Marias learning about the culture, it is time to experience it firsthand. To do this, we want to spend time with a native family in a remote spot and Bernardo and his brother, Francisco, offer us a golden opportunity. They invite us to come up to their private compound, Weiknatara. The name literally means Little Big Man, symbolic of the proud spirit with which they have carved their riverside farm from out of the jungle. Located four hours upriver in the heart of the biosphere, it sounds promising.

†

Jean-Philippe, 19 September 1999

We accept Bernardo's generous invitation to visit Weiknatara and leave our kayaks in Las Marias to head upriver with him in a dugout canoe because the rain-swollen river is too fast for us to paddle. As we make our way up, the scenery along the riverbank starts to change. Lower down, we were disappointed to see so many clear-cut, cattle-grazed gaps in the forest but here, the uninterrupted greenery is a spectacular utopia of color and wildlife. Gravel bars at the turns in the river are covered with flowering trees and foliage rather than steaming piles of dung. Red cedar and mahogany trees, 125 feet high, loom over the narrowing flow of the river, like towering sentries guarding nature's masterpiece. Vines cascade from the top of the ten-story-high canopy all the way to the jungle floor. It's a magical playground for monkeys and birds rather than grazing land for livestock.

At Bernardo's cottage, we're both awestruck and humbled by the setting and its natural surroundings. The house is perched on the upper bank, overlooking the confluence of four streams that form the main branch of the Rio Platano. Around the perimeter of the house is their own personal orchard of oranges, lemons, avocados, coconuts, *supa* fruit and *jicaro* gourds, and a medley of fresh, verdant scents fill the air. Their environmentally integrated farm is planted with coffee, cacao, plantain, bananas, beans and rice and a spice garden of lemon grass, chilies and cilantro grows around the house. The soil looks rich and black and nourishing, and the weather is sunny and humid, ideal conditions for agricultural bounty.

If not for the sandflies, I'd say that they have found paradise. Their kids like the place so much that they don't ever intend to leave. The older sons, who recently got married, live there, too. They tell us that, when their wives go downriver to visit their families in Las Marias, the two of them often choose to stay here.

The highlight of our time there is the food processing. We press sugar cane juice and boil it into *miel* (syrup). The mother leads us through the entire process of coffee production: we harvest coffee cherries, mill the beans, dry, roast, grind and finally steep them to produce a robust brew that we sweeten with the *miel* we made. We also learn how to make *chicha de maiz* by fermenting the cane juice with corn. The fermentation process is so fast that the sweet beverage we make in the morning is strong enough to make my head spin by evening and we quickly develop a taste for it. Bernardo and his family usually drink one or two glasses with each meal, "for energy," of course. We ask them about the religious taboo. According to them, religion is a good thing; they attend church but the traditional *chicha* is an important part of their culture that they will not give up.

Bernardo takes us into the jungle for a tutorial on edible and poisonous plants. My first lesson is a hard one: I'm shooting photos when it begins to pour, so I look for some large leaves to drape over my backpack and shield the photographic equipment. Luke points to a plant with wide leaves and I rip off a couple to put over my head and camera gear. Bernardo sees me, but it's too late. "That's *puerco*," he says, "very poisonous to the skin, as you'll soon find out." Five minutes later, my hands, forearms and neck, which had all been in contact with the sap, start to burn. He tells me that only two things can be done to relieve the deep burning pain. The first thing is to urinate on the affected skin. But there is no way I am going to touch myself with my hands full of sap and I'm not going to ask Luke or Bernardo to pee on my head and neck so the other alternative is mud. The alkalinity of the mud soothes the inflammation so I cover my arms and hands with it and patch some on my neck. This is one plant I will never forget.

Our most enduring and humbling lesson comes not from Bernardo and his strapping sons, but from his young daughters. Since we are among local people, living with them, sharing in their work and eating like them, it's only right that we should learn how to travel like them and get accustomed to poling a dugout. Two days later, the two giggling daughters lead us down the riverbank toward the canoes.

↑

Jean-Philippe, 21 September 1999

Networks of rivers drain the rainforest from frequent tropical storms. These rivers are the lifelines of the Indigenous people living along their banks, providing fish to eat and water for consumption and crop irrigation. Curving their way through thick vegetation, they are the sole means of travel and transportation and traditional people have adapted their entire lifestyle to the water's flow. The canoes they use to travel, fish and transport cargo are carved out of a single tree. When operated with skill, these dugout canoes are surprisingly efficient at navigating the waterways. On a wide and deep river like the Amazon, people paddle their canoes, while on fast and shallow rivers they stand and propel them with long poles.

Seven-year-old Lilian is an expert at maneuvering a *pipante*, as the dugouts are called here in La Moskitia. She is growing up on the Rio Platano, swimming, poling and paddling the strong currents and seems to use little effort to send the *pipante* wherever she wants to go. On one particular occasion, she was taking me up to a shallow but very fast confluence where I could sit in the narrow dugout with my camera and take action photos. When I asked her if there was a risk of capsizing, she smiled and said, "No problem." She quickly gave a few orders to her six-year-old sister, Bernarda, who was standing at the front and poling. With amazing balance and a natural understanding of hydrodynamics, she quickly switched back and forth between a large wooden paddle and a long stick. She alternated pushing and paddling on both sides in order to keep the boat aimed at the right angle against the raging current.

At the confluence, I lay down on my back, shooting photo after photo. The water started pouring into the boat from the upstream side; Lilian smiled as I got wet and then saw an expression of worry on my face as I tried to protect my camera. She was in control and made corrections in mere seconds. Immediately, she directed her sister to shift her weight. The flooding stopped and the boat kept its place hovering in the rapid.

When I indicated that I had shot enough photos, she steered back into the current and let the boat drift at an angle back to shore while she sprayed water over her face to refresh herself after the intense workout.

"Well done, Lilian and Bernarda. Now it's my turn," I said. We stopped and left both my camera and Bernarda along the shore; the day before I had flipped the boat a few times when she was in it and she didn't want a repeat. Bernarda isn't afraid of falling in the middle of the deep river's strong current but she prefers swimming on the side, where she can return to shore quickly. Lilian, on the other hand, enjoys being the one in charge and if my clumsiness sends her into the water as well, it just adds to the fun. Besides, I couldn't go without her anyway. I need her to sit in the rear of the boat and steer with the paddle, or should I say counter-steer, to compensate for my mistakes. It was my third practice and, this time, I stood up in the narrow canoe without any problems. With years of skiing and other demanding sports under my belt, I have developed good balance and coordination—or so I thought—but even the Pech children in Las Marias have skills far superior to mine.

When done well, the technique looks easy—but it isn't. You stab your pole into the bottom, lean forward on it and use your weight to move the *pipante* forward; your pole ends up toward the stern. In strong currents, using the pole is a little more difficult. You need to have good balance and apply a lot of power to stop the stick from skidding along the rolling rocks of the bottom. It is especially tough when you have missed your entry into a fast stream and the canoe is moving backwards, then it takes even more power and skill to stop the momentum of the heavy dugout. Sometimes the water is so deep you have to hunch down to push, your hands inches away from the surface and the pole fully submerged. When it becomes too deep to pole, the person at the rear paddles. It can be exhausting, but with skill you avoid mistakes and keep efficient control of the *pipante*.

I started poling next to the riverbank where the water was hardly moving. Then we steered away from a rock and faced the current of the first confluence. The boat swung from side to side. I lost my balance, swayed back and forth and tried to stab my pole into the river bottom. I felt like a clown: my poling was completely ineffectual and we lost ground rapidly against the current. With the help of Lilian's remarkable steering, we maneuvered over to the other side where I could again attempt to be "useful" in the boat. I poled three times and we were ready to enter the second, faster branch of the river. Again, I poled hard and we gained a few feet. Once in the current, however, the bottom dropped away to a depth where I could no longer touch. The stick lost its purchase on the bottom of the river, slipped out of my hands and was carried away from the boat by the current. Shortly thereafter, I tumbled over the side and ended up following my pole downstream before recovering it. In the middle of a rapid while standing on a *pipante*, mistakes are not allowed, unless of course you're looking for a big, beautiful laugh from the seven-year-old captain. Lilian steered the canoe back to a neutral position in an eddy while I was breaking the surface and I swam back and climbed in. I tried for a while longer and fell into the water countless times more for my effort.

When we returned to shore, I asked Bernarda if she wanted to come with us the next time. She answered, "*Tengo miedo con tigo,*" "I'm afraid with you." I had to appreciate her point of view. If I were her size and sitting in a dugout next to a giant, unbalanced standing gringo, I wouldn't give him another chance to tip me over into the stream, either. I was relieved to watch Luke take his turn to practice: the skiing champion couldn't stay upright either! The river was wonderfully refreshing and we ended our practice session by playing with the girls in the water where we redeemed ourselves, at least partially, with our swimming ability.

Every day I went out with Lilian to practice in the small *pipante* and, with time, I improved a great deal at standing and poling, but that was relative only to my original inability. Now only fast rapids caused me to fall and I could stand and pole but still did not instill much confidence in my passengers. Bernarda was the ultimate judge and, to her, the dugout was still swinging too much from side to side and this gringo still looked like an uncoordinated marionette. Lilian thought I had improved enough that she challenged me to a race. I had to turn my seven-year-old competitor down. I would have no chance of winning and, after all, a man has his pride!

I was also interested in learning the traditional fishing techniques and asked Lilian's two older brothers, Maxi, twenty, and Elias, twenty-two, to show me. The grace and power of two strong men is best seen when they go fishing with the traditional long harpoon. The harpoon can be fifteen to twenty-five feet in length and is used in the shallow rapids where the fish can be seen more easily. One person steers and paddles at the rear while the fisherman stands in the bow where he uses the backside of his harpoon to pole when necessary.

Elias steered one of the larger dugout canoes into the strong current and Maxi stood watching the water for fish while holding his harpoon in position. The boat didn't swing an inch; with no visible effort, the two men were perfectly synchronized with the movement of the water. The water visibility was poor that day because of the heavy rains of the previous week so we left the *pipante* on a gravel bar on the side and followed Maxi into the shallower rapids where he stood thigh-deep in the current, searching for fish. He missed the rare ones he was able to see but he had already told me that with such poor visibility we would be very lucky to get anything at all. Even when the water is clear, he sometimes spends more than an hour before returning home with fish, but a few delicious *cuyamels* (prized river fish) for the family makes the effort well worthwhile. Needless to say, I haven't yet tried to fish standing in a *pipante*. I will keep practicing poling and I will try to spear a *cuyamel* from a dugout before we paddle out of La Moskitia. The Pech have been doing it forever; I have hundreds of years of tradition backing me up so how can I possibly fail?

After a wonderful week with Bernardo's family, we left Weiknatara to return to Las Marias.

↑

Luke, 28 September 1999

With the rains picking up for the last two days here in Las Marias, I have been anticipating our descent of the Platano. Now the river is up, the flow is fast and it is time to head down; it should be easy just bouncing through a few rain-swollen rapids. Just after dawn, we lug all our gear to the riverbank with the help of two of Olvidio's sons and say our goodbyes. By 9:30 a.m., we are off and running—our average speed is nearly eight knots, a new record by far. *What goes up must go down. Piece of cake*, I think to myself, smiling.

The first fifteen miles are very relaxing. The water level is much higher, the current is stronger and all the sand bars, logs and other obstacles pass smoothly below us. What had taken us six hours when coming up four weeks ago, we do in two and a half going down.

From this point, the river widens, the current slows and my heavy, wide-blade paddle slowly works my shoulder muscles into oblivion. We have been traveling at such a terrific rate of speed that we don't want to slow down. In a slower current, the only way to make the scenery pass as quickly as before is to pull on the paddle harder but I am used to the slim profile of the touring blade. Imagining rapids, we had stowed our fragile touring paddles out of reach and this clunky spare one is much more labor-intensive. After two more hours at a good clip, my shoulders finally cramp and threaten to quit working completely. I try every trick in the book to keep them moving. I pick out land formations and make miniature goals for myself. I try rhythmic breathing to get into a meditative state. I sing songs in my head to distract myself from the pain.

I stop regularly for breaks to drink and peel oranges to eat, hoping that the liquid and fructose will re-energize me. Late in the afternoon, I pause to take off my sunglasses and watch an afternoon squall roll in from the mountains. Thunder booms from low-lying clouds and just next to us, on the riverbank, lightning strikes a tree, splitting the trunk down the middle. I am so tired I don't even flinch.

By the time I reach the canal to Raista, I am barely putting the paddle in the water. Jean-Philippe has arrived forty-five minutes before me and is wet and impatient. He gets back in his boat and pulls in behind me as we enter the canal; I dictate a very leisurely pace. I chug a liter of double-strength Tang for the last push and we arrive in Raista at 5:00 p.m. after seven and a half hours and forty-five miles in the boats. We need to renew our visa every two months to stay in Honduras, so tomorrow we will collapse our kayaks, store them in Eddie's house and then catch a *colectivo*, the local water taxi, to Palacios and fly back to La Ceiba. From there we'll return to Puerto Cortes by bus and take advantage of Richard's hospitality, spending a few weeks writing the first pages of the Pech cultural documentary for Jean-Philippe to add to our website.

↑

The Deluge

Luke, 25 October 1999

The first three weeks of October were not fun. We gradually realized that the structure of the website was not what we wanted. The bottom line was that the site was becoming very difficult to navigate and the information that we wanted people to see was getting buried, so we re-did it entirely. It took a seemingly endless series of grueling days and the credit lies entirely with Jean-Philippe: he was superhuman. Eighteen-hour days on the computer were interrupted only briefly for meals, showers and sleep—even a malaria attack set him back only a day and a half. Jean-Philippe's drive is a miracle of nature.

It's the rainy season and we've just flown from La Ceiba back to Palacios, the entrance to the Rio Platano Biosphere; we're on our way to finish the documentary that we began in Las Marias last month. This time, we will leave our kayaks in Raista and walk up to Las Marias because the rain-swollen current of the Rio Platano is just too strong for us to paddle against. To travel upriver in a motorboat from the coastal town of Platano would take all day and we would have to pay for all the gas, which would cost us at least $100, so we choose the adventure of trekking by foot instead.

↑

Luke, 26 October 1999

It's just after dawn and there's still a chill in the air. I hunch down into the wind shadow of Bernardo, our friend and guide from Las Marias, as we blast through the short motorboat trip across Laguna de Ibans. We're heading from Raista to the trailhead where we will begin our trek, which is on the other side of the water. The boat is a twenty-foot-long, narrow craft, with high gunwales and wooden chairs with backrests set in a single row from bow to stern. It is pretty to look at but the worst hull design ever for high speeds in choppy water. At speeds over ten knots, the bow wake curls up in a steep arc and the wind blows it straight into the boat. By the time we disembark, all our gear is completely soaked.

As we get out of the boat, I see nothing but thick vegetation and mud. I don't need to see the insects, I can already feel them—I'm simultaneously shivering, itching and scratching. We need to get moving quickly before I go insane. "It usually takes eight or nine hours," Bernardo says to us. And with a wink and a smile, he adds, "but you are not normal tourists."

For the first two hours, we follow Bernardo through a pasty mud bog; the entire area is a flood plain for the Rio Platano. We slog through alternating tracts of eight-foot reeds and thirty-foot secondary-growth forest with its feet snarled in roots and ground vegetation. Saw grass and spiky young bamboo claw equally enthusiastically at exposed flesh, loose folds of clothing or pack straps. Vines, fallen trees and low branches force us to duck, high step and protect our faces. The one constant is the viscous layer of decaying biomass that sucks and swallows our shoes and disgorges foul putrescence with every step.

It takes me half an hour of adjustment before I learn how to walk in this stuff. Standard heel-toe walking motion gives the heel too long a contact time with the mud: the heel sinks and creates a vacuum that holds the shoe fast and you walk right out of it. The only way to go is with the ballet step: Point the toe and insert, preferably into an existing cavity. Use the hamstring to pull back and up to extract the foot. After ten minutes of concentration on this technique, it becomes automatic.

After three hours, the scenery shifts and the trail becomes more solid. We move out of the flood plain and secondary forest into high-canopy, prime-growth forest. Here, less ground water makes for firmer earth and faster progress. With so little sunlight able to penetrate to the understory, the underbrush is thinner and the temperature is also cooler. We come across numerous creeks twisting their way through the forest. We ford them by stepping gingerly across on greasy fallen trees. At one point, Jean-Philippe almost steps on a brown and red speckled fer-de-lance snake lying camouflaged in the fallen leaves. The fer-de-lance's venom will quickly stop even the heart of a human and thus they are greatly feared. Until now, we have been so focused on keeping the pace that dangers such as this had not yet registered in our consciousness.

We cross many slash-and-burn farms along the route. We'll be slogging through thick brush and fifty-foot canopy, then suddenly find ourselves in a thicket of sugar cane or a grove of plantain trees. Crude, thatched-roofed, open-walled shelters usually stand at one end of the clearings, some are occupied, others abandoned. All are in the middle of nowhere, surprisingly far from river access.

Last night, we told Bernardo that we weren't "tourists" and I think he has decided to test us. Today's pace, brisk from the start, has never slowed down a beat. At the four-hour mark, my legs are protesting; this is a rude awakening for muscles long underworked during months of paddling. After five hours, when we reach the distant outskirts of Las Marias, I am glad to see the forest open up into a wide, well-trodden path along the river. We exchange hearty greetings with people we met last month, giving us second wind for the final steps of the trip. We arrive much earlier than Bernardo's original prediction. "We Pech are strong," he says. "It comes from our lifestyle. You gringos do okay, too. I have been up and down this trail only two times in ten years. This was my fastest."

I look at my supply of water and snacks. I've gone through two and a half liters of water and a bag of food. Bernardo, at age forty-nine, would have completed the whole trek without any food and water had we not stopped and insisted that he share some of ours. As we sit on the porch of the *hospedaje,* peeling sodden water booties from blistered feet, Bernardo skips off to do some work.

We wash off the grime, sweat and insect repellent in the river, stuff ourselves with rice and beans and settle in for a nap. Just as I lie down in a hammock, the sky barks and lets loose a deluge. "Great walk, great scenery, better timing," I say to Jean-Philippe, and to the muffled hush of rain on a hot thatched roof, we sleep.

†

Luke, 29 October 1999

We've been waiting here in the center of Las Marias for four days now. We have a list of things we want to accomplish and document, but the weather is killing us. It has been raining constantly both day and night since we got here.

The radio reports that there is a hurricane with 250-mile-per-hour winds further south over the Mosquito Coast of Nicaragua. People speculate that the coastal towns of Bluefields and Puerto Cabezas are now being pummeled. We hear one account of fishing boats failing to make it back to port; even at full throttle, they couldn't make any headway against the winds. The announcers fear that much of the region's Nicaraguan lobster fleet may be lost. Without access to broadcast news, we never found out how many people were lost, but having experienced smaller storms on the ocean we could imagine the danger they were in.

Here in Las Marias, twenty miles inland, it is quite safe. The winds may pick up a bit but the only real effect of the hurricane is rain. The river has already gone up five feet in the last twenty-four hours. The village lies on the high banks above the river and is in no danger of flooding and, for the people here, life just comes to a standstill until the rain diminishes. The trails are too wet and muddy to navigate and the fields of corn, rice and beans are sodden and unmanageable. The only thing to do is sit in the hammock and fiddle with crafts like whittling and basket weaving. People say that the end of October to the end of November is their most productive month for the crafts that they make to sell. Now I understand why. I am bored to the point of stupor and Jean-Philippe is so frustrated that he is ready to lose it. Irritated by the rain, we decide we want to get downriver and back to La Ceiba as soon as possible since at least there, we can do some computer work while we wait for the rains to abate. But there is no way to get back; for now, the river dictates all. Even motor boats can't reach the village. Entering the water in a slowly swirling eddy by an indentation on the riverbank, we go for a brief swim to get a feel for the current. Jean-Philippe swims out into the main flow and is immediately swept downstream. Angling back toward shore and stroking as hard as he can, he reaches shore seventy-five yards down. Just then, a pair of logs floats by. We look at each other and nod. We've just discovered our ride down to the mouth of the river.

↑

Jean-Philippe, 1 November 1999

It's raining as hard as ever when we wake up, but it no longer bothers me. I'm looking forward to today: we have a major activity planned. With two machetes and an axe, we head off into the woods with our new friend and guide, Mariano. Today we're going to build a balsa raft and tomorrow we'll float it down the raging river.

First, we collect some strong vines by pulling them down from the trees. The challenge is to find the perfect vines, ones with the right balance of thickness, strength and pliability. We will need to be able to wrap them around the logs and tie secure knots that will hold the raft together. Once we have enough vines, we hop in the dugout to go and find the most important material: balsa trees.

We pole and paddle upstream along the margins of the river for twenty minutes before Mariano spies the first balsa and tries to point it out. To us, in the low light and pouring rain, the *wano* (balsa) tree is indistinguishable from any other tree so we leave the canoe, hacking our way through the dense vegetation toward a tree that only Mariano can see. Suddenly he runs back toward us, slapping his head with his hat. While cutting his way through the foliage, he had stumbled into a wasps' nest. A few times, I switch places with Mariano to cut trail and learn the hard way how painful their stings can be.

Wasps are not the only insect menace. Fire ants are everywhere. While we are felling the trees and cutting a path through the underbrush, they find their way up our soaked pant legs and inside our shoes. Despite the rain, mosquitoes buzz around our heads, too. It is almost impossible to focus on the work at hand.

The *wano* tree is tall and straight with few branches and the wood is yellow-white, tender and remarkably light. We cut the tree into three ten-foot logs and remove the bark easily by scoring strips and peeling them off. As a finishing touch, Mariano trims one end of each log into a point, and says, "This is so you'll be more hydrodynamic and go faster." We will remember these words on the river.

When the logs are ready, we cut our way out through the underbrush to make the shortest path for carrying the logs to the river. Once again, wasps are waiting for us in the thick vegetation. Slapping and cursing, we carry the logs to the canoe. While loading the second one, Luke loses his grip and drops his end of the log into the canoe. I am in the middle in an odd position and find my left middle finger crushed between the log and the edge of the gunwale. Although I doubt that it is broken, it swells up, turns purple and will be useless for the rest of the day. When we have felled one more tree and are back in Las Marias with all of our materials, Mariano begins the building clinic. He stands in waist-deep water and shows us how to make the vines more pliable by twisting them. We tie five logs together and use two smaller logs as crossbeams and are surprised at the buoyancy of this small raft. After a long day of work in the jungle, we anchor the finished raft to a tree and return to the lodge, completely waterlogged. A good cup of hot lemongrass tea is the treat of the day.

In the evening, Luke gets sick with a fever. We wonder if he has caught a cold, as half the village seems to be suffering from one since it is impossible to stay dry during the rainy season. We stuff him with ibuprofen, hoping he will recover enough for our departure the next day. With my injured finger, I know I will have trouble getting a good grip on one of the heavy wooden paddles we carved out yesterday with our machetes. I need Luke to be in shape since I'm not, but we are both a mess.

⚊

Jean-Philippe, 2 November 1999

We wake up at 4:15 a.m., and my finger has doubled in size and can't be bent, Luke's fever has receded, but he looks pale and exhausted. Not a promising start.

We walk out to our raft and load it with coconuts to drink during the trip. People tell us that the river is fast and that it should take us ten hours to reach the coast. At 6:00 a.m., we cut the vine holding our raft and start drifting—it is buoyant but surprisingly sluggish. For the first few minutes, we have no control. We're ducking under branches and obstacles on the riverbank and can't figure out how to compensate for the weight and lack of maneuverability. After ten minutes, we figure it out and begin to progress smoothly. We focus our attention on reading the river to stay in the fastest part of the flow. The first couple of hours are fun, but then the river widens and the current slows to a crawl. We have a load of coconuts, so we drink and eat and try to focus our minds on other things. I spend the next two hours trimming weight off my wood paddle with a machete.

It takes us five and a half hours to descend the first and supposedly fastest third of the river. Now, the current has grown weak, the raft is too heavy to paddle and we are fighting a headwind. We are no longer moving. Our estimate of travel time is upped to twenty hours, meaning that we will sit in the pouring rain for another fifteen hours and then arrive in the middle of the night in Barra Platano. From there, we'll have to trek another eight miles on the sand in the dark to reach Raista. A few weeks before our return, a drunken Barra Platano man had slit the throat of one of his Kuri neighbors to steal less than two dollars. The villagers did not report him to the police; instead they took the matter into their own hands. Though justice was ultimately served, the last thing we want is a midnight encounter with a drunken townie.

We stop in a small settlement on the riverbank to buy bananas and the locals all come out to see our raft. It is the first time they have ever seen foreigners rafting down the river! We are lucky and pull up to the dock at the same time as a *colectivo* boat, which has dropped off its passengers and is now preparing to return to the coast. We jump at the opportunity to ride in style. For thirteen dollars, we buy two seats and then donate our raft to the kids of the village. Three hours later, we are walking along the beach toward our Miskito friends in the lagoon-side villages of Kuri and Raista. We find Raista flooded. The level of Laguna Ibans is very high, approaching that reached during Hurricane Mitch. People are anxious.

↑

Jean-Philippe, 3 November 1999

We spend one day in Raista packing our gear and kayaks that had been stored in Eddie's house for more than a month. The rains never stop. The water level is rising by the hour and the lowest houses have already started to flood. People have dug a trench to drain the water from their fields, but it is proving inadequate. After another sodden day in Raista, our friend Eddie offers us a boat ride back through the lagoon and canals to Palacios. It is a good time to get out, as the villages of Raista, Cocobila and Ibans are in danger of becoming inundated. People fear that, if the weather continues, they will find themselves in the same condition as they had the previous year: they'll lose their houses, crops, livestock and some maybe even their lives. Several people comment that it is raining harder now than it did during Hurricane Mitch. A lobster diving boat has not returned to port and the word is already going around. We can feel anxiety mounting.

↑

Jean-Philippe, 5 November 1999

We fly back to La Ceiba in the morning. We found out later in the day that we were lucky: our flight was the last one out. They shut the Palacios runway after we took off and, from what we hear, it may not re-open again for two months. La Ceiba is flooded as well. We walk in the streets and spend some time taking photos and videos of people struggling through knee-deep water. Some even try to fight their way through on bicycles. Shopkeepers prepare themselves for the worst as sewers back up and the water levels come within inches of their doors. It's déjà vu; they lost much of their merchandise during Hurricane Mitch a year ago. Luckily, the rain stops for a few hours in the afternoon, long enough to allow the streets to drain. We decide to leave La Ceiba immediately so we jump on a bus to Puerto Cortes, 160 miles north, where we intend to settle in at the house of our friend Richard James. Well-protected, there will be nothing for us to do there but to work on our website and wait for the storm to pass.

The weather doesn't change. After we arrive in Puerto Cortes, we learn that we were on one of the last buses to get out of La Ceiba before two of the main bridges were washed out to sea. Honduras is once again in a state of emergency. Roads are sinking, houses are flooded and crops and livestock are being lost. We can hear people in the streets shouting, "Mitch is back, Mitch is back!" We're all helpless. All we can do is watch and wait.

⭐

Luke, 17 November 1999

Nearly two weeks after our narrow escape from La Ceiba, we are still holed up in Richard's house in Puerto Cortes. Richard, a U.S. expatriate who has called Honduras home for more than thirty years, is our patron saint in Honduras and has already helped us many times. By profession, he is a consultant on sustainable forestry and is the country's leading expert on the operation and calibration of drying kilns (warehouse-sized hot rooms that accelerate the drying and curing process of raw lumber). On the side, he's a political and environmental advocate and Internet junkie. As fellow members of the Honduras mailing list, he, Derek Parent and Jean-Philippe exchanged emails and, at some point, he agreed to help us out upon our arrival in Honduras. I'm quite sure he never envisioned the current scenario.

Just two days after settling into Richard's house, the monsoons of La Moskitia and the floods of La Ceiba are behind me but I still feel burdened and ill at ease. It's as if the murky waters flowed through me and left heavy deposits of silt behind in my body and brain. Jean-Philippe has asked me for my input and given me a list of writing projects: educational texts on the history and mythology of the Pech and Miskito people, traditional agriculture, religion, music and cuisine. As always, both his to-do list and his ambition exceed my wildest imagination. With all the photos and video that we've taken in La Moskitia, the journals and educational texts we've written and the mental images that we've filed, we have a massive amount of work to be done. I should be excited, fired up for the challenge yet, mentally and physically, I can barely get myself off the sofa. Battling a constant high-grade fever, I alternately lie in an easy chair or on a mattress up in a loft in the rafters, popping Advil and swabbing my forehead with wet cloths. At this point, he realizes that asking anything of me would be like trying to squeeze blood from a stone.

In marked contrast, except for a few hours of sleep and short breaks to eat, Jean-Philippe has been on the computer non-stop for the past thirty-six hours. At night, while Richard, his Honduran wife, their two daughters and son sleep, Jean-Philippe works quietly. Sound travels easily here. In this house, made of cement with zinc roofing and a wide-open floor plan, nearly every activity is a public forum. I am uncomfortable and sleepless so I hear everything. At 2:00 a.m. when he connects to the 'net, I can hear him trying to muffle the modem's dialing sound by wrapping a wadded-up shirt around the computer's speaker.

At 3:30 a.m. Jean-Philippe finally goes to bed, but I still can't sleep. What the hell is wrong with me? It's been forty-eight hours since we arrived at Richard's and my fever is getting progressively worse. I'm nauseated, my lower back is throbbing, my joints ache, I have a headache and I can't seem to retain any fluids. I drink liters of water and they run right through my kidneys and into my bladder. I'm peeing constantly. During my third trip to the toilet during the night, I am so dizzy that I have to sit. When I try to stand up, I black out. Ten minutes later I wake up, clammy and dazed, on the concrete floor of the bathroom; a tennis-ball sized lump has already emerged from my forehead.

Jean-Philippe thinks I have malaria, but I don't have the classic symptoms. Usually there are cycles that start with severe chills, progress into bursts of high fever and end with ever-shorter periods of calm. I have a constant fever and a headache that just won't go away. In the late morning, I'm sitting in an armchair trying to dab my forehead with a wet cloth to keep my temperature down. Within the span of a few minutes, my fever spikes, cresting 106 degrees. My vision begins to darken around the edges and quickly fades to total blackness. My breathing is labored and I feel like I'm suffocating; with my last reserves of energy I yell for Jean-Philippe to come and help me. I can faintly hear Jean-Philippe say to the others, "Holy shit, he's burning up! Give me all the ice you've got in the freezer." Somebody comments that they can see sweat pearling on my skin as soon as they wipe me down. They immediately douse me with water and cover me with bags of ice. I'm blabbering incoherently, "You gotta call my folks and tell them I'm dying. Gotta call, gotta call." Fortunately, in a few minutes the fever comes down, my vision is restored and my breathing returns to normal. I am worried this could be dengue fever or worse; just to be "safe" I take a loading dose of six chloroquine tablets for malaria and they take me to the hospital.

At the hospital, the malaria test is inconclusive because I have taken chloroquine, which masks the presence of the parasite. Thus, the only thing the doctors can say with certainty is that I have a fever of 104.5 and that I am severely dehydrated. They immediately hook me up to an IV drip and pack me with ice. Over the next twenty-four hours, my temperature finally stabilizes and they release me but the chemical side effects of the chloroquine are so powerful that I am too woozy and dizzy to walk unassisted. Richard and Jean-Philippe have to support me on both sides in order for me to walk to the car.

⊤

Malaria

Jean-Philippe

My first malaria attack in Central America (though certainly not my first attack) came in early October during our first break from La Moskitia. It struck while on a visit to Richard's Puerto Cortes home, a full month before Luke got sick there. This was just the beginning though, as both Luke and I had numerous recurrences of malaria as well as other infections during the rest of the expedition. Most travelers we met were surprisingly misinformed about this deadly disease and often asked us what it feels like to suffer from malaria and why we had not taken preventive medicines. Although very different from Luke's experience, my symptoms were fairly typical of the disease.

The first discomfort I noticed was a slight headache, which worsened within ten minutes until all the muscles around my spine, from my lower back to the top of my neck, cramped with excruciating pain. Although I was wrapped in blankets and sleeping bags in a room the temperature of a sauna, I was so cold my teeth were chattering. The pain was unbearable. All I could do was shiver and cry. In a desperate effort, I called for help and when Luke appeared, I could read the worry on his face when he said, "Geez, you look terrible! What can I do?"

I knew without a doubt that I had been re-infected with malaria during our stay in La Moskitia. This was my fourteenth attack in seven years and I recognized the symptoms well—I needed blankets and clothes for warmth and I needed medicine immediately. Although he could barely stand the heat and didn't understand how I could be so cold on the second floor under a tin roof baked by the midday Honduran sun, Luke willingly brought me a hat, socks and more blankets. My hands were freezing cold and numb and I had to stick them in a pair of wool socks under the blankets to warm them up.

Luke was alarmed at the speed with which the symptoms hit: ten minutes earlier, I had been sitting in the room we used for an office, working on the computer. I felt tired and had just a slight headache when I told him I needed to go lie down for a few minutes. It is not unusual for a malaria attack to come on that quickly. The parasites take refuge in the liver and reproduce after entering the blood stream via a mosquito bite. When they break out of the liver, they hit hard and fast. This case was no different, and even though I felt and probably looked like I was going to die, I knew I would be fine. We carried all the most potent FDA-approved medicines (Larium, chloroquine and pri-maquine) in our first aid kit.

Years ago, when I first read about malaria to prepare for my jungle travels in Indonesia, it struck me as an exotic disease that is easily warded off by taking preventive medicine. I took my prophylactic medicine religiously. Much to my surprise, a year later when I returned to the States, I was hospitalized in a coma from a malaria attack. The doctors put me on an IV and treated me with high dosages of Larium and primaquine. Other tropical diseases and the preventive medicine I had been taking had masked the symptoms of a rare and virulent strain of malaria until I nearly died. Doctors said I was lucky to be alive since it was a vivax strain resistant to most known medicines that I had caught in the jungles of Irian Jaya. I was told to expect relapses and that I would have to be retreated each time with a high dosage of the harsh drug, Larium. Whenever I took it, I would suffer the pounding migraines and complete weakness that are the drug's terrible toxic side effects. Primaquine, which is supposed to kill the malaria in the liver to prevent relapses, was ineffective against this strain. Specialists told me that I would probably have to live with malaria all my life but the good news was that I survived the first attack, so it probably wouldn't kill me if I always carried the harsh treatment of Larium and primaquine.

After that experience, malaria was no longer distant, exotic or mysterious. It became a part of my life. I paid the price for my blind trust in modern medicine and for my ignorance of one of the deadliest diseases in the world. Every three months, painful chills followed by high fevers and pounding migraines kept me in bed for a couple of days and incapacitated me for two more weeks I had so little strength I could barely walk to the supermarket down the street. After each attack, I spent three days in a zombie-like state as a result of the side effects of the Larium, which remains the most effective, yet toxic, FDA-approved medicine to fight malaria. Then, I'd spend the next two and half months before the next relapse trying to get back in shape. I consulted many tropical disease specialists from the States, France and Japan and all of them told me the same thing: there is no hope.

I did a lot of research on the disease and eventually decided that my next step would have to be to go to China to seek treatment using a plant compound called artemisinin. The Chinese have used the artemisia plant for over 2,000 years to treat migraines, fevers, heart problems and malaria. During the three-year period after I first contracted the disease I radically changed my diet, continued rigorous physical training and maintained both a positive attitude and a staunch belief that I would someday experience a full recovery. Fortunately, my relapses faded so I didn't need to seek treatment in China.

Although the attacks ceased, I continued to do research, knowing that one day I would return to tropical rainforests and be exposed to malaria again. To my great surprise, I have since learned that malaria is not only the most widespread disease worldwide but also one of the leading causes of death. The World Health Organization estimates that 270 million new malaria infections occur annually and twenty-five percent of the childhood deaths in Africa are attributed to it. The mosquito-borne protozoal disease is endemic to most tropical and semi-tropical regions of the world. Transmission occurs in an estimated 100 countries where two billion people are at risk of infection. The numbers are staggering and, today, the situation is made worse by the appearance of virulent new strains. Some of these strains even reappear in countries that have been free from the disease for decades and scientists believe that even the United States may be susceptible to infection.

The techniques for eradicating malaria are simple but accomplishing them on a large scale is a monumental task. Many countries have achieved it by spraying with an insecticide that kills the carrier, the female of the genus *Anopheles*. There are problems, however, if the mosquitoes aren't killed in all the surrounding malaria-infected countries as well. The infectious species will continue to return to the areas that have been treated and, once there, begin building resistance to insecticides. Spraying costs remain too high for many developing countries, which also prohibits comprehensive eradication.

In her article "Resurgence of a Deadly Disease" published in *The Atlantic Monthly* in August 1997, Ellen Rippel Shell best described why and how science is losing the war against the spread of malaria. An excerpt from her conclusion states:

"...in the West early success in controlling infectious disease has bred arrogance and a belief in whopping big solutions—vaccines and antibiotics that wipe out rather than contain. We know successful pathogens to be highly evolved and clever creatures, but we bluster about, attacking them as though

they were the dumb, plodding aggressors that perhaps we ourselves are. When a microbe mutates around our onslaught, we go off in search of a bigger weapon with which to blast it. But like all re-emerging diseases, malaria has managed not only to dodge the bullets but also to turn the revolver back at us. Our attacks have made the parasite not weaker and less certain but more virulent. Controlling this disease requires vigilance, patience, and, to a certain degree, sacrifice—there are places we might have to avoid. There are tradeoffs to be made, but so far we've shown ourselves reluctant to make them. Scientists pursue their quest for an effective vaccine or a more powerful drug while treasure hunters of another kind [miners mentioned previously in the article] in Thailand and Brazil help the disease find a new foothold. Whether the scientific adventures will eventually pay off is uncertain, but for now there's no question that a price is being paid. Malaria, an ancient disease, a controllable disease, is spreading."

The spread of malaria has led to heated controversy over prevention. People traveling through malarial areas who take prophylactic drugs to preserve their health only compound the problem for the locals. They encourage mutation of the malaria plasmodium by exposing the mosquitoes to diluted concentrations of the drugs in their blood. In that way, the new strains become resistant to known medicines. For that reason, neither chloroquine nor Fansidar protected me in Irian Jaya. For the same reason, primaquine is becoming less effective every day. Curbing the development of new strains is necessary but it requires a major change in prevention policy from a body of people and governments who currently choose to disregard these issues. The people suffering most are the poor Indigenous or local inhabitants who rely on chloroquine as the only available medicine. During our entire three-year expedition in the jungles of Central America, neither Luke nor I took any prophylactic drugs. Other travelers were often shocked to hear that and, when asked why, I told them the truth: that prophylactics put local people at risk; there are bad side effects, especially if taken over a long period of time and there is no guarantee that they will protect completely. Most people responded with puzzled disbelief. They never knew, they had just followed the advice of their doctor back home. Ultimately, we as travelers have a responsibility to do research and educate ourselves. The decision to take or not to take preventive medicine is up to each of us. Malaria is a painful disease but it is curable. The media often publishes breaking news on cancer, diabetes or AIDS research but malaria is usually ignored. There is little research in western countries, as it is considered a medical issue pertinent only to the developing world.

In the mid-1990s there was a discovery that may revolutionize malaria treatment worldwide, a medicine called Artenam. Because it is not FDA-approved and thus not available in the States, it has received little media coverage. Derived from the artemisia plant (Artemisia annua L.), known in the west as sweet wormwood or annual wormwood, the Chinese call it *Qing Hao* and have been using it in its natural form to combat malaria for 2,000 years. A Belgian company called Arenco produces a pure distillate of the plant in pill form.

Because of FDA regulations and the French government, it took me more than a year to obtain any Artenam. Although we received it too late to treat our first attacks during the expedition, I used it during those subsequent and was surprised by its efficacy. It stopped the major symptoms of the attack in half the time normally required by mefloquine and by the next day I was active, felt healthy again and suffered none of the secondary effects that I had become accustomed to with other drugs. This has made me a strong believer in Artenam's value. Unlike the other medicines available, it doesn't just kill the parasite in the bloodstream, it is also one-hundred-percent efficient in cleansing the liver to prevent relapses. Recent studies also suggest that artemisinin is effective against a wide variety of cancers.

Once you have had malaria, it is easy to identify the early symptoms and treat yourself. Two of the many usual symptoms of malaria are nausea and vomiting so I ended up vomiting up the initial dose of Artenam the first time I tried it. Unless you travel with a large quantity of the medication, you ought not waste more than one dose this way. My friend Snakeman, the natural healer living in Belize, advised me to crush the pills into powder, mix them with a little bit of butter or water and use them as a suppository. This alternative route for ingestion is a good thing to remember if nausea prohibits oral consumption.

People often asked us what we feared most during our odyssey through Central America. It's not the sharks, crocodiles, guerrillas, storms or big waves. Rather, it is disease, and malaria is on the top of that list. It is a painful reminder that we are both human and very vulnerable.

↑

The Biggest Challenge: Documenting the CASKE2000 Expedition from Central America

Jean-Philippe, December 1999 – March 2000

After being chased away from La Moskitia by non-stop rains and then contracting malaria, Luke was ready for a long break. I, too, needed time off from kayaking to concentrate on producing the online documentaries I had envisioned. So Luke returned to the U.S. to spend Christmas with his family, while I spent the next four months anchored to my mini-computer.

Of what social benefit are the dozens of high-profile "extreme" expeditions that, with the assistance of sponsors and professional marketing teams, are splashed across the pages of popular media? I planned CASKE2000 in the belief that such an expedition should produce more than mere photographs of sporting acumen, that there is a responsibility to educate and inspire as well. We, as adventurers, are passing through remote lands and interacting with those people who call them home. They should feature prominently in what we present to the public. I began this expedition committed to that goal and remain so, however I soon realized that some of the physical challenges of this adventure were easier to overcome than the mental and logistical obstacles of trying to produce a multimedia website on-location in the wilds of the developing world.

One of the toughest lessons I have learned is that fame dictates who will be chosen to educate and inspire people. Recognition seems an arbitrary, haphazard confluence of chance, politics and economics and it seems unfair that an average professional basketball player will be better known and better paid than the best athletes in some extreme sports. The same is true for expeditions: media coverage seems to determine the "success" of any adventure. Sadly, without media exposure, it's impossible to procure sponsorship or funding and, without such support, it is next to impossible to stage a large-scale expedition. Even completed, an expedition is still worthless without publicity and the real message can only be delivered after aggressively marketing the physical accomplishments of the expedition: two guys, two kayaks, 3,000 miles, three years, Mexico to Panama.

When I started to plan the CASKE2000 expedition, the sporting challenges were only part of the project. I designed the expedition to document the lifestyles of Indigenous peoples in Central America and to make people aware of the beauty and importance of cultures and lands threatened by development and our voracious consumer habits.

In order to realize my goals, I knew that some fame would help tremendously. I needed publicity to get my message out. The problem is that recognition comes predominantly to people participating in activities more trendy than ours. We were not planning to sail a million-dollar racing yacht around the world or climb Mount Everest or traverse Antarctica solo and unassisted. We were planning to paddle rivers in unknown rainforests to meet Indigenous peoples forgotten by the rest of the world. It was during the early stages of preparation that we tried to break into the cliquish world of extreme sports marketing.

Luke loved the idea of the expedition, but he did not realize the amount of work it would involve. We spent our final eight months in Japan chasing this dream five to ten hours a day in addition to our full-time jobs. We earnestly looked for equipment sponsors and media contacts but they wouldn't take us seriously. We contacted notable names in adventure and travel publishing and the most encouraging responses we received were polite brush-offs telling us to stay in touch. If we let them know when we were on the water, maybe they could do something with us then.

This reality was hard to accept. However much we believed in our project and its educational mission, we didn't yet have the compelling material of Jon Krakauer (*Into Thin Air*) or the marquee name of Peter Hillary (Sir Edmund's son). Even specialty paddling magazines showed little interest in our project. We struggled to pull in the dozen small sponsors who provided us with less than twenty percent of the equipment we needed. We expected that the duration of the expedition, from planning through follow-up, would be over four years. That's four years without a salary so even if we lived cheaply and received most of our equipment from sponsors, we estimated our costs at over $150,000.

We started the expedition with nothing more than our own savings and now, more than a year and a half later, we are nearing the red zone. Finding sponsorship and media coverage becomes more important every month. Trying to make contacts was frustrating before our departure; it is virtually impossible while paddling through the most remote regions of Central America!

This lack of success is disappointing, so I have begun to focus more energy on the documentation. I have put the magazines aside and have given priority to my website. But there, too, I have been put to a test. After the first six months of hard work and sleepless nights, the site was only recording 100 visitors a month—it was demoralizing. Yet, I continue to believe that the website remains the best and most important way to document what CASKE2000 is all about.

During each paddling leg, our focus is on the expedition. We fight big storms, heat and bugs. We experience nature at its best and its worst and work hard to adapt as well as we can. That is the part that most people can imagine; that's the aspect of our expedition that they understand. What our followers don't see is the stuff behind the scenes: all the work that goes into producing the website as we move along. We take notes out in the field and wait until we're in town to do the computer work.

Although our journals describe the challenges of the expedition, they fail to relate what happens when we spend time in town. I think that most people imagine that we sleep, rest and enjoy life for a while after roughing it. In actuality, I usually spend eighteen hours a day anchored to the frustratingly tiny keyboard and six-inch screen of one of the world's smallest, fully functional palmtop PCs. We take turns typing all the journal entries and cultural notes and then I start the web production. There is nobody to help us. I do everything from page layout, photo editing, cross-linking and programming to fine-tuning the site, adding meta-tags and registering with search engines. And when that's all done, I continue to tinker with the design and content organization to accommodate future additions. It would ordinarily be a full-time job for a team of three or four people.

Computing in Central America is nothing like computing in the developed world. Even with the occasional access to a cooling fan, in minutes, my hands sweat profusely. My fingers slip across the keys, my palms slide along the base of the keyboard. I have to wipe the drops from my forehead every few minutes so they don't fall on the computer and the acidity of my perspiration has eaten through the rubber knob of the embedded mouse button until it barely functions. To top it all off, after a few days of computing, my chronic carpal tunnel syndrome returns with a vengeance.

Our ability to upload content to the site varies depending on the phone line and local service providers. I have yet to see anything faster than an 18.8k connection speed. The connection often crashes in the middle of transmission, forcing us to resend everything. And, in addition to the frustration, prices for phone line time are usually significantly more expensive than in the States.

The website requires dedication. I give it all my free time because I believe in the final result; my reward comes when I hear that I have touched people. Feedback is great. A little media recognition would be even better. It just cheapens everything to have to scrounge around and beg for it.

A year ago, I envisioned an adventure-education website, a supplementary resource for people wanting to learn about Indigenous ethnic groups. Now, I realize that it could be so much more. I envision a site that will become not only an archive of the information that we produce, but also a vehicle for contributions from Indigenous people themselves, a way to allow them to preserve their culture in their own words. The site could develop into a forum where knowledge, difficulties, solutions and ideas could be shared with other Indigenous groups. The site could be a virtual library, a place where, in the future, the young people of the tribes who are raised in a more modern society can learn about their heritage.

The website is becoming an obsession. I can be paddling in the middle of nowhere and suddenly think about it. Sometimes I wake up at night with new ideas. Sometimes I'm not sure in which arena I am more challenged, in the field or online. I engage in both with the same intensity and am sometimes surprised when I find it hard to dissociate one from the other.

Luke likes to say that I'm not normal, not human. Luckily for me, he is and it is often due to his efforts that I actually eat. If not for the plates of food he serves me while I work, I would starve. He also likes to say that I'm contagious. When I first asked him what he meant by that, he replied, "Through inspiration and shame, people around you always work harder!" I hope my enthusiasm becomes an epidemic! In spite of its present size, the CASKE2000 website is still in its infancy. I wouldn't be surprised if we end up with more than 3,000 pages by the end of the expedition. The possibilities for expansion are endless. At times, when he is overwhelmed by the list of things to do for the site, Luke rolls his eyes and groans, "Man, you've created a monster!" I see that. And it's a hungry one, too.

ↈ

April Fools: La Ceiba

Jean-Philippe, 1 April 2000

After finishing our long documentary work in Las Marias, and spending a few months out of the kayaks writing stories and producing our website, we restart the expedition from La Ceiba, where we had first landed last August. This stage will take us southeast along Honduras, through the Mosquito Coast to a spot just north of the border of Nicaragua. On April 1st, our second day out from town, we wake at 4:00 a.m. and struggle to paddle sixteen nautical miles against a light current and a headwind. Our time away from the kayaks always makes us soft and already our hands are shredded and our bodies feel pummeled. We are miserable and feel like the biggest fools this month.

Drained, we are in bed less than an hour after sunset, our alarms set for 1:00 a.m. Tomorrow we are looking at a seventeen-mile paddle to reach the town of Trujillo. The weather won't allow us to leave any later in the morning: in addition to the oppressive heat of the day, the seasonal headwinds escalate steadily until early afternoon every day. This completely alters our sleep schedule, forcing us to paddle in the middle of the night when it's calm, In Trujillo, we will check into a cheap hotel on the beach for a rest day. Our muscle spasms, cramped fingers and blisters need relief. We also realize that, in spite of the difficulties of these first few days, we have seen nothing compared to what awaits us in the next few weeks. Although it doesn't feel like it, we are still in the Bay of Trujillo, protected from the open swell of the Caribbean by the long arm of a cape. After Trujillo, we will be fighting bigger waves and stronger currents and it will take us four days of hellish paddling to reach the next protected lagoons and canals at the northern fringe of the Mosquito Coast. We are scared to leave.

↑

The New Rush: Kayak-Surfing at Night

Jean-Philippe, 6 April 2000

After a day's rest in Trujillo, we leave the protected bay and paddle west-ward for three days along the rough coast to La Moskitia. Launching through eight- to twelve-foot waves is something we often have to do; after a year and a half it has almost become routine. Occasionally we worry about not being able to see the waves at night, but launching is usually easy. After paddling seven and a half hours, we find a nice grad-ual sand beach, the best kind to land on and launch from. Shore breaks can be dangerous on steep beaches but on long flat ones, the surf zone is much wider and the waves are usually easier to handle. So, we land on that beautiful beach with the intention of doing the next day what we have done every day before: get up at 1:00 a.m., pack our gear, pull the kayaks to the water, load them after eating a quick breakfast and enjoy the night-paddling before the wind and sun become too strong. The hardest time is usually the few minutes it takes us to remove our pants, fold them into a dry bag, don shorts and kayak shoes, close the bag and lash it on deck and then get into our kayaks. We dread these few min-utes because of the hundreds of painful bites we get on our legs from the terrible sandflies. We never thought we had a reason to fear anything else on this beach.

We set up our tent above what looks like the high tide line, pull the kayaks up on the beach, tying them to the tent, just in case. After dinner, a strong onshore wind picks up and we decide to move the tent higher up the beach. By 7:00 p.m. we are ready to go to sleep in our wind-blasted tent. We have been warned that when the wind starts blowing from the north, it brings dangerous sea conditions, the worst effects being on the third and final day. With the wind at our backs, we cover good distances the first two days. After enjoying this small *norte* storm, we aren't at all prepared for the third day.

At 11:00 p.m., we wake up instantly to the feel of water rushing beneath us and the kayak ropes pulling at the tent pole next to my head. We jump out of the tent and grab the kayaks to prevent them from drifting back with the wave, pulling them up a few feet and quickly tossing all the bags higher up onto dry sand. We aren't quick enough, though, for our tarp and tent and another wave submerges both, so we lift the flooded tent up with its entire contents still inside and carry it away. The sky is dark, the waves sound big and the wind isn't showing any signs of letting up. We decide to reset our alarms for 3:30 a.m., giving us two more hours of sleep.

At 5:00 a.m., we're ready to launch. The waves still sound big but, in a total darkness under a moonless starless sky, they don't really seem TOO large. After all, we're on a gradual beach, how bad can they be? I walk into the water to try to get a feel for the waves. There is a strong side current and they are hitting the beach straight on in a succession of white foamy trails, anything but regular, some small and others quite large. One follows the next with very little gap between, but they don't seem overwhelmingly powerful—I still think they look manageable. Two other wave patterns are also hitting the beach at sharp angles, refractions of the main waves from the opposite sides of the large bay: where those two meet, they explode with eight-foot vertical splashes. For five minutes, I stand in the water observing the sea but none of these collisions ever happens in the same spot twice. Everything is irregular today. I anticipate that the first step of the launch will be tricky but that, once paddling, we will be all right.

Because of the frequency of the waves, I can't pull my kayak out too far. I wait for a big wave to float it, then pull it forward, run to the back and use both hands to keep it facing straight into the waves. I have already learned from sad experience that holding the boat from the bow when there are horizontal currents or waves is a guaranteed disaster as the kayak instantly goes sideways and gets hit by the principal waves that come in straight and fill it up or flip it. So, I jump into it and, as soon as my butt touches the seat, I rush to throw my legs over the deck, fold them into the cockpit and extend them inside the sea sock. After the next wave hits me, I find my kayak sitting on the sand parallel to shore—not a good position to be in—so as the next wave lifts me, I use my hands on the sand to partially reorient my kayak before settling back. When the next one comes in, I paddle hard at a quarter angle into it, pass the wave without taking on too much water and quickly let go of my paddle to put my spray skirt on. It isn't easy to quickly position the skirt behind me, stretch it to the front of the cockpit rim and put each side into the groove while being buffeted by the surf and trying to hold on to my paddle but, until I do so, my kayak continues to fill with water from each wave. Although I am hit by another wave and again put in a position parallel to the shore, this time I'm still floating and almost ready to go. All I have to do now is to reposition my boat and get some speed which I do with a few power strokes; I easily pass the first big roller, then number two and number three. That's it! I've done it! I'm through the difficult passage and will soon be waiting for Luke outside the surf zone.

But this beautiful flat beach has not yet revealed all its tricks. The fifth breaker is a monster; going full speed, I barely make it through. I almost stall on top of the wave but I put all the energy I have into my strokes and quickly regain speed, passing the sixth breaker with nothing more than a big splash in the face. Now I am racing out of the surf zone with powerful strokes and nothing can stop me!

There are only three more breaks to go. The huge seventh wave explodes six feet in front of me, but with a heavily loaded kayak moving into it at four knots, I never doubt that I'll make it. At the last second, I tuck my paddle to the side and bend my upper body forward to break through. To my great surprise, I find myself entirely submerged and catapulting backwards. Fast. When the foam finally recedes down to my chest level, I realize that I am actually surfing backward at great speed and, as I raise my head, my kayak almost backflips, the stern pitched down underwater and the bow pointed up toward the sky. Leaning forward, I keep on surfing backwards in this mass of white foam until it reforms into a swell and rebreaks, instantly enveloping me in its curl.

All I can think about is not capsizing. I was a long way from shore when that first wave hit and it is still very dark; capsizing would be disastrous. At best, I would lose everything I have on deck, maybe even the full kayak. I do everything possible to keep my weight forward and my kayak straight; if I go sideways, I might end up upside down. My first reflex is to put my paddle on the wrong side of my bow but I'm going backward and this movement almost throws me sideways. I instantly switch sides and am able to keep the boat surfing straight—I can hear the hull slashing into the wave. After this second backward surf set, I am going too fast and the wave is still too powerful to hope to paddle out of it. My kayak suddenly jerks to a stop as the stern slams into the sandy beach, bending my rudder and sending me sprawling. At least I'm safe on shore—or so I think!

Before I even realize what is happening, one of the side waves, determined to crush me down onto the sand, sets me parallel to the main wave. In a final burst of effort, I throw my body into the wave in a heavy brace stroke but end up leaning too much and capsize into it. I find myself face down with my hands against the sandy bottom, trying to protect my head and neck, while still holding my paddle with one of the blades sticking out of the water on the sea side. Before I have time to think, the next wave catches my paddle blade and puts me back right side up. It isn't really an Eskimo roll, it's more an "I have no idea where I am anymore" roll but it works. I open my spray skirt, jump out and pull on the bow of the kayak; I am entirely worn out but back on shore, safe. As I pull my kayak out of the waves, I scream to Luke, "Don't go. We can't make it in the dark. It's crazy out there!"

Luke is still on the beach and very surprised to see me on shore. Minutes ago, he had lost sight of me and thought I was already out of the surf zone waiting for him. He never made it past the first waves. As soon as he put in, wave after wave dumped on him, completely filling up his kayak before he could even put his spray skirt on.

The night launch is not going to happen today; as we wait for the day to break, we check my kayak for missing equipment. Miraculously, the deck bag, bilge pump, GPS and spare paddle are still on my bow deck, and my dry bag, fins, rope, and paddle float still on my stern deck. All I lost was a watermelon that I had lashed under a spider net near my dry bag. Luke calls my attention to the bent rudder, which I am able to straighten with my knee. I am all right and considering what has happened, even the equipment came out of it without much wear and tear. I was very lucky.

There isn't much to do when you are wet and stuck on the beach at 5:30 a.m., so we go body surfing in waves that frequently shake us around as if we are in a washing machine. The more we can see of the waves, the more we realize that we have tempted fate by trying to launch: attempting it at night was just plain suicidal. There are days that the sea doesn't want us and the best thing to do then is to respect her wishes and wait until she's in a better mood.

We rest all day in the shade of a sea grape tree, staring at the angry ocean. By 3:00 p.m., I notice that, at low tide, there are fewer breakers to pass, and more space between each one. The wind has stopped blowing and the surf appears easier to handle. I wake Luke up and we get ready to go because we don't want to be stuck on this tricky beach for another day if the wind picks up again. I think we have a good chance to get out so we take it. Luke nervously launches first while I take photos of him. A couple of times, I think he is going to end up in a backflip as he catches some air, but he makes a clean exit out of the surf zone.

I follow after packing up my camera gear but with the experience of the morning still vivid in my mind, I am apprehensive, too. With good timing between the waves and vigorous back-paddling to avoid the explosions of the second set of rollers, I have just enough time to gain adequate speed to break through. One close call throws me in the air just as I clear a curling wave that has dropped off right under the stern of my kayak but a few minutes later, I'm out and it takes me five minutes to catch my breath from the effort. A sharp pain is throbbing between my left shoulder blade and spine—I must have torn a muscle on the last violent paddle stroke I made to pass the final wave.

Luke is waiting, recuperating from his launch, and it is 4:00 p.m. before we actually start paddling south. We know we have two hours of light and need to find a better beach to land on and, after forty-five minutes, a beautiful beach appears. The surf looks very big but, from the sea, we can't really judge its size or the shape of the waves. All we know is that there is large swell breaking on the beach in a curl of light blue water: we can't tell if the surf is smooth or dumping. We have never landed our foldable kayaks through a twelve-foot shore break and never want to try—not only would the kayaks break, we'd be crushed as well.

We decide to push on until dusk. The beach becomes steep with dunes and the farther we travel, the less appealing the beach becomes. At 5:30, as the sun dips close to the ocean, we decide that we must land without delay. Just as Luke approaches the surf zone, we notice a jeep going full speed on the beach. It is followed a minute later by a slower pickup truck. It seems odd to us that private four-wheel drive vehicles are patrolling the beach in the evening in such a remote place. We recall the stories we have heard about drug traffickers along this coast and remember the armed drug guards who had forbidden us access to a beach north of La Ceiba. We don't want to deal with that type of situation, but our only alternative—spending the full night in our kayaks paddling—isn't much more appealing. Discouraged, we resign ourselves to a long uncomfortable night on the ocean. At 6:00 p.m., the jeeps have long since passed and the wind and surf are getting stronger. Luke makes the call, "It's almost dark. If we land and quickly haul the kayaks and hide them in the bushes, nobody will see us."

I am still nervous about the landing but there is no time to waste: soon we won't be able to see the waves forming behind us. I take the lead and Luke follows two waves behind. I wait for four large waves to pass and let the last one break a couple of feet in front of my bow, then paddle hard behind the lip of the wave so as not to be caught by the next large set. Then I stop and back-paddle into the second set as it is breaking and as soon as it goes by, I paddle as hard as I can. Closer to the beach now, I surf down the smaller third set and end up bracing and side-surfing the last set onto the beach. Luke follows a few seconds later and we quickly haul our kayaks up the beach. It is a faultless landing for both of us. Our timing is perfect, both in the waves and with the light: five more minutes and we would have been landing blind.

The beach is very steep and narrow and the high tide line goes up to the very edge of thick vegetation. We find a small patch of dry sand hidden behind some trees and hurry to unload our kayaks. As I return to my boat, I see people walking toward us. Our secrecy hasn't lasted long. All I can see are the shadows of two people: the one behind is holding something that looks like a rifle and the man in the front is holding a machete whose sharp edge flashes in the night. Less than two minutes on the beach and already we're in trouble! I start closing my hatches, trying to hide my concern, but then I see a third silhouette, that of a child. Reassured, I walked toward the couple with their little daughter and greet them. They had been working in their yucca field and what I thought was a rifle was just a machete the woman carried with the blade resting in the crook of her arm.

They are surprised to learn that we have been on the ocean in these conditions: none of the local people ever go to sea during *nortes*. They cannot believe that we have come all the way from La Ceiba in our little *cayucos*. They reassure us that there are no bad people around but tell us we have to move our kayaks off of the beach as it is the main road between Limon and the last Garifuna villages of Punto Cabo Camaron. We have covered barely six and a half nautical miles today, a meager distance compared to the 25.5 miles of the day before, but it has been a day full of emotion and challenges. Not knowing the sea conditions we'll have tomorrow, we decide to enjoy a good night's sleep. We have earned it. Waking up at 4:00 a.m. should be enough to be ready to go at daybreak.

🕇

Herbs, Hooch, Healed!
Guifiti: The Best of Garifuna Bush Medicine

Luke, 8 April 2000

In the past few days, we had paddled through the last Garifuna villages of the Caribbean Coast, stopping in places such as Santa Rosa de Agua, which had been almost entirely wiped out by Hurricane Mitch, then Limon and today Plapaya, which we had already visited during our first trip to La Moskitia.

"Jicaco negro, ajo, pimienta gorda, clavos de olor y los dos ingredientes mas importante, hombre grande y hombre muerto. Ah tambien, casi olvide, una botella grande de Ron Plata!"

The well-traveled Garifuna *marinero* behind the bar of his beachside eatery listed the roots and herbs sealed in the bottle. He smiled and winked as he poured us each a mouthful.

"Para todos los enfermedades, amigo. Me entiende." (For all illnesses. If you know what I mean.)

Guifiti, the magic elixir of the *Garifuna* people, is a strong brew. The whole cocktail is built upon the foundation of a bottle of white or silver rum. The magic happens when you add the herbs. A few you may know: garlic, cloves and allspice. The rest, well, the names alone give you a sense that you're getting bush medicine at its best: roots of the jicaco negro tree, dead man bush and big man bush.

In each region of Honduras, people like to think that they possess the only legitimate recipe. From Limon down to Plaplaya—the last Garifuna village in Honduras—the communities of the Cabo De Camaron region on the northern fringe of the Mosquito Coast swear by their *guifiti*. As the largest, most traditional, true-to-their-heritage enclave of Garifuna communities in the Caribbean, it is a matter of pride that they produce the best.

I had sampled *guifiti* before, further north in Belize and northern Honduras. My recollection was of the harsh bite of cheap rum and everlasting bitterness. Gag! In that case—rather than a spoonful of sugar—a glass of water and an Altoid made the medicine go down.

It wasn't until we paddled into the picturesque bay of San Jose de la Punta and landed on the beach south of Limon that I tasted the real thing, or so the proud locals told me. As I mentioned, the proprietor of the beachside eatery pulled a bottle off the shelf. Suspended in cane spirits the color of the harvest moon were the pure fruits: the wisdom of more than 400 years of Garifuna shamanism and healing art. He let a few cc's trickle into a plastic Dixie cup and I quaffed it in a straight shot. What came to mind was the fecund, peaty nose of twenty-year-old scotch, the lingering anise whiff of French Pastis, and an overwhelming swampy bitterness that made me want to pull at my uvula. Think Jaegermeister mixed with potting soil with half the viscosity and twice the alcohol.

I walked into the village *tienda* fifteen minutes later and saw the owner administering *guifiti* to her sick four-year-old daughter. She poured a dram of the stuff from a similar-looking bottle down the throat of the sniffling, colicky child. Miraculously, the child's whimpering stopped and she ran off. To play with her friends? To retch in the bushes? To escape Mom, the evil witch doctor?

I've come to the conclusion that *guifiti* is merely an acquired taste (ask a European what he/she thinks about Dr. Pepper sometime). All adult Garifuna whom I meet smack their lips and sing its praises. Can 75,000 people be wrong?

The Fine Print:

For the trippers and stoners and/or old-school literary types looking for a substitute for absinthe, sorry, *guifiti* is not psychotropic.

BUT, for budding ethno-botanists and herbal remedy buffs, get a load of the medicinal properties. I won't bore you too much with the standard ones. Garlic is a natural immune-system booster and good for mucus membranes. Allspice is a blood tonic. Cloves are a flavor agent. Nothing too sexy there.

Now for the good stuff:

1. Yo ho ho and a bottle of rum! The cathartic effects of alcohol should be familiar to you: vasodilator, circulation enhancer… you know the rest.

2. *Jicaco negro.* Ever had the shakes and jitters from a three-day binge of liquor and late nights? Ever had fried nerves from stress, shock or too much excitement? *Jicaco negro* is a black nut-bearing tree found on the sandy, breezy margins of tropical beaches. An infusion of its dried roots is an effective nerve tonic.

3. Big Man. The name says it all. A long, narrow root the color of mahogany, it'll make you strong. Regular consumption of this root and you may wind up with a basketball scholarship. Although not big by American or European standards, the Garifuna are the tallest Indigenous people in Central America.

4. Dead Man. A Rasta islander who laughed at all the rich whities stumbling over themselves to buy Viagra first told me of its properties. With graphic gestures he explained: "When yer little man down der ees dehhhd, ya got ta wehhhk 'im up wid dis."

Many of the smaller Garifuna communities don't have any sort of clinic. In a real emergency, they enlist one of the few owners of an outboard motor to ferry the patient to the nearest community with a clinic or to a radio to call for an airlift. Otherwise, it's the bottle. They will accept ibuprofen tablets for a headache or fever but, as the giver, you must know that they won't be washing them down with water.

The Garifuna are a robust, healthy group. The young adults are blessed with incredible physiques. And even though the old men begin to wither away and the older women become quite stout, they can still outdo you in most pursuits. I have been humbled by many an old man walking down the beach, miles from home carrying giant burlap bags of crops and tools. No Powerbars or water bottles either. And the grand old dames of the village will put you to shame when they get together for a Punta dancing festival. One night, a corpulent sixty-five-year-old matriarch took me out on to the dance floor for a furious session of Punta. Never have I been so outdanced in my life. Twenty minutes later I was taking a break while she and her compatriots were out on the floor, gyrating and chanting to the contrapuntal drum rhythms, for hours on end. There must be something potent in that *guifiti*!

Herbal remedies are currently enjoying a wave of commercial success and popularity in developed nations. Rainforest remedies of Mayan origin, herbs from Asia and infusions from the Amazon are readily available and the subject of much public discourse. The validity of many is undisputed and, due to their organic make-up, there are fewer toxic side effects than the potent chemical medicines we get from the pharmacy. Unfortunately, the efficacy of Mother Nature's medicines aside, the names are bad and the tastes are worse. You just gotta know that something called "jackass bitters" or "tincture of wormwood" is not going to taste like a cherry cough drop.

How about *guifiti*? It starts out as *Ron Bacardi* or *Flor de Cana*—the nectar from cane fields in the Caribbean—and becomes an infusion of Garifuna heritage, a blend of African and Carib Indian cultures. It's deliciously exotic. And I'll say it again: "Eets good fer ya, mahn!"

↑

Outposts in the Jungle

Luke, 10 April 2000

Beginning in Plaplaya and down most of the rest of the Honduran Mosquito Coast, we paddled through the maze of canals and inside lagoons that were the prime hideouts of pirates. We reached the town of Barra Platano at the mouth of the Platano River. We've been here once before and we felt a bad vibe about the place. Nothing has changed: garbage still lies strewn on the banks amidst a jumble of motorboats and empty shipping crates. We are on our way again in less than five minutes.

The passage through the canal to Brus Lagoon is an infinitely long, hot chore. There is no jungle foliage or wildlife like the Kuri canal, just endless stretches of flat, open savannah. I play mind games—singing, counting, and reminiscing—to distract myself from the boredom, heat and discomfort. Eventually the stagnant canal opens up onto the feathery chop of the lagoon. With renewed vigor, we strike out across it in anticipation of bedding down in the village of Brus and taking a rest day to explore the town.

The back of the lagoon is latticed with estuaries and murky shallows; sandbars rise up suddenly in places. Jean-Philippe grounds out twice and has to exit and pull his boat to deeper water. Numerous small settlements dot the shoreline. They confuse us and we have to ask three times for the proper route through the proper estuary to find the actual town center of Brus.

Rarely have I been so disappointed after a period of such anticipation. The landing in Brus is a cesspool. A dozen houses that mark the edge of town hang out over the water on stilts. The ground beneath them is a morass of decomposing garbage, sewage, rusting cans and pieces of metal. Yet the slew of *cayucos, pipante* dugouts, brightly colored motor launches and their captains and passengers bustle about: they step out of the boats and tread through the stinking pollution without batting an eye.

Surprisingly, the newly built hotel is pleasant and clean with concrete walls, bright paint and a fan. Unfortunately, the generator only comes on at dusk. We swelter through the afternoon, attempting to nap.

We awaken for dinner to find the eatery across the way filled with people downing Pepsi and watching a fuzzy TV broadcast of a soccer match between Honduras and Mexico. We eat dinner in the back room with a view into the living room of the hotel owner, whose two daughters sit on a ragged sofa, eating cookies and staring, engrossed, at a *telenovela* on their TV.

No rest day here!

↑

Dining on Iguana with the Most Hospitable Bandits: Rio Patuca

Jean-Philippe, 12 April 2000

From Brus Laguna, we left the protected inside waters and returned to coastal navigation. Launching from the bay was nearly impossible. After a few failed attempts, we spent most of the day waiting for calmer wave sets to let us through and even then, barely made it. So far, the physical demands of paddling the Mosquito Coast have exceeded our expectations. We knew it would be one of the most difficult legs of the journey but there was no way to predict the ferocity of the waves and the insects. Unfortunately, there is another evil element in the region that has made us even more wary: *bandidos*.

When we left Brus, people warned us to be very careful further south in Patuca. "The people in Patuca all have guns," they said. "They wait for other people to pass by, then chase them with their powerful motorboats and attack without mercy. They kill you before they rob you."

As we paddle toward Patuca in the early morning, these words echo in our heads. I hear a motorboat and I look up to see it coming right at us bouncing violently up and down in the swell. A nervous shock passes through me, but the smiling face of the captain instantly puts me at ease. He shouts a few words of encouragement and tells us that he is bringing passengers to Brus and that he will return. An hour later he is back, just as we are approaching the mouth of the Patuca River.

"Where are you going?" he asks.

"South to Puerto Lempira, but we'll stop in Patuca to rest," I reply.

"I'm going to Patuca, I can give you a lift," he shouts.

I explain that we want to paddle in and he frowns, worried that the waves at the river's entrance are too big for us. I am confident we can handle them. People always underestimate our ability to handle big seas in our small kayaks. Concerned, he says he will come to meet us just outside of the surf zone when we get closer in. An hour later, we arrive at the river mouth and, rather than the motorboats full of bandits our Brus friends had warned us about we meet only our new friend who, true to his word, has come out to see if we are all right.

We are very glad to see him. From our vantage point, the exact river entrance is obscured by bouncy five-foot chop and lost amidst a long, low sandbar on shore. We would not have known where to aim had he not appeared in his boat. After politely refusing his offer of a lift one more time, we follow him through the waves into the mouth of the river. Once on shore, Feliceando, our new Miskito friend, offers us breakfast with his brother's family.

As usual, once in town we are the main attraction for curious locals. People come from all over to see the two little boats that the crazy gringos have paddled from La Ceiba. Feliceando's brother, Felimon, shows us wonderful hospitality and his wife prepares a delicious meal of stewed iguana and rice. They were so gracious that we decide to call it a day and sleep here. With our hosts' assistance, we carry all our gear into their front yard and set up camp.

Our host is much better off than most people we have met in La Moskitia. At first, we wonder if he is one of the local drug barons in the burgeoning Caribbean cocaine trade. Our impression is reinforced when his wife picks up a .45-caliber automatic handgun that has been sitting on the living room table and takes it into the back room to hide it. However, Felimon is friendly and knowledgeable and we talk for hours. We learn that he is the captain of a large foreign-owned fishing boat. This explains his social status. As for the gun, like everybody else in La Moskitia, owning one is necessary to protect his family and wealth.

Watching us eat the local food amuses the family. They were sure that gringos had never eaten iguana before. They are surprised to hear us say that we find iguana meat delightful and that it's not our first time. They laugh when we tell them that, to us, the taste and texture is like a cross between chicken and white fish.

According to our hosts, this month is the best time of year to eat iguana: there's an extra surprise to go along with the meat. It's mating season and the females are full of eggs. Mixed in with tender morsels of meat swimming in a thick sauce are pale yellow orbs that look like deflated ping-pong balls. Luke tries to stick his fork in one. The thick rubbery skin, unlike any eggshell I've ever seen, repels the fork and the egg rolls to the side out of his plate. Frustrated, he grabs it and shoves it in his mouth. I'm curious about the taste but hesitant about the shell, so I wait for a facial expression of approval or disgust. He chews on it repeatedly, at first determined then confused. Luckily at that moment a neighbor calls our host outside and Luke discretely spits the egg out onto the plate and tells me: "Man, this thing is impossible to eat! Are they teasing us?"

We are trying to be discrete but we must look like a couple of kids chewing on giant wads of bubble gum. Our host has left his eggs in his plate and is talking outside. This can't be a joke. Everywhere we've gone in La Moskitia we have heard that iguana eggs are a prized delicacy. People will prod the stomach of female iguanas with their fingers to check for eggs. When they find them, their faces light up with joy.

I ate many bizarre-looking things in my jungle explorations through Indonesia and Thailand: worms, giant rats, dogs, bats and snakes. They were, at least, edible and there was no mystery about how to eat them. Yet here we are, clueless as to how we should attack these things. There is no way I will swallow one whole. I'll choke. And it doesn't look like it will digest well. But we can't just leave them on our plates and offend our host. I'm just about to throw them to the dogs when Felimon returns to the table.

He sits down, grabs an egg and asks us, "You don't like the eggs?" Then holding the rubber ball in his right hand, he punctures the skin with his two front teeth, tears the skin off and squeezes the cooked yolk into his mouth. With a satisfied grin, he drops the empty skin on the plate. We feel like total idiots. "Oh, we were just saving the best for last," we reply. We finish our meal (the yolk is richer than any egg I have ever had), laughing at our mistakes.

After our meal, I lie down in a hammock and review in my mind our paddling trip of the Honduran Mosquito Coast up to this point. We had prepared ourselves for encounters with dangerous bandits, drug dealers, inhospitable locals and malnutrition. Yet here we are, in the house of locals, being fed and treated like royal emissaries.

†

The Fear of Nicaragua

Jean-Philippe, 1 May 2000

As we approach the border of Nicaragua, we are hearing more terrible and more specific stories about the dangers that lie ahead. We've always known that the northeast coast of Nicaragua is a notorious place that has long been a hideout for opposition guerrillas. We are familiar with the political history of the region and know of the violence that ensued when the States intervened in the 1980s, so we are afraid to introduce ourselves as or even be taken for Americans as we travel through.

This remote jungle is also a favorite place for bandits. Unlike most places, where small-time crooks operate with knives, machetes or bare hands, the bandits in Nicaragua are well armed. After the Contra war, there was a large surplus of automatic weapons. They are sold for ridiculously low prices throughout the Nicaraguan Mosquito Coast: anybody can get an AK-47 for chump change. In another recent twist, La Moskitia is increasingly used as a stopover point for Colombian drug boats on their way to the States.

When we left La Ceiba, we were not fully briefed on the situation in Nicaragua. We assumed that we would be okay if we took precautions and planned intelligently.

Since leaving Trujillo, we have met many Garifuna and Miskito people with horror stories. They often travel to Nicaragua to visit family members. It seems everyone has a family member or friend who has been killed or robbed. After leaving Belize, we heard countless tales of this nature. And, as we never encountered any threats, we became numb; all the stories seemed overstated, overdramatic. We ignored the first warnings here in La Moskitia but now the people seem more agitated, more nervous as they tell their stories. Little by little, these tales are weighing on us and making their way into our minds; that is why we imagined the worst a few days ago when we saw cars patrolling the beach at dusk. To make things worse, the closer we get to the border, the more specific the stories become. People here use real names of people, places and landmarks. The danger is becoming much more real and palpable.

The most distressing recent news we have heard is that Honduran troops are moving toward the border for a possible confrontation with Nicaraguan troops in the heart of La Moskitia. In the last few weeks, the tension has been building over a maritime territorial conflict between the two countries.

Although we think it is unlikely that we will find ourselves in the middle of a war, we are aware that nervous soldiers and locals alike could have itchy trigger fingers. Considering this, we have decided to better investigate the situation when we reach Puerto Lempira, the last town in Honduras before the border. If the risk of military action is high, it isn't worth putting ourselves in a position where we would be easy targets. In such a scenario, mere robbery would be the best we could hope for. We may have to delay or cancel the Nicaraguan leg to Costa Rica altogether. There is one hard and fast rule that past expeditions have taught us: compromise your itinerary before you compromise your life.

A Miskito friend told me that Jacinto Molina, one of the most famous Miskito leaders and a political activist, lives in Puerto Lempira. We stay in town for a couple of weeks waiting for his return from the capital. This time allows us to rest and catch up on writing. When we finally meet Jacinto, he is fascinated by our project and, though worried about our safety, he willingly agrees to help us plan the next stage of our expedition into Nicaragua. We receive letters of recommendation from Jacinto to his friends Brooklyn Rivera and Avelino Cox Molina, powerful political leaders of the Nicaraguan Miskitos. In spite of their reputation, the immigration officers of Puerto Lempira were equally friendly and, after trying to change our minds worrying about our safety, stamped our passports with letters of recommendations explaining our possible delays before reaching the immigration office of Puerto Cabezas, Nicaragua. The danger we have heard of over the last few weeks is now real, but we have tools to negotiate our way out. Three weeks after our arrival in Puerto Lempira, more scared than ever, we start paddling, leaving behind us the last town of Honduras.

↑

Point of No Return:
Benk to the Nicaraguan Border

Luke, 4 May 2000

Despite all the warnings to the contrary, our gear and souls are secure here in Benk because we have expended a lot of effort to make it so. After exiting the river mouth this afternoon, we paddled another half-mile down the beach to the only house along the shore, ferried the gear 250 yards back inside a friendly fisherman's barbed-wire compound and set up camp. Everything is piled around the tent and all tied together. At the first sign of movement or sound, we can be up and ready to confront a would-be thief. The alarm is set for 1:30 a.m. and once again we will rest only briefly.

↑

Luke, 5 May 2000

The Nicaraguan border has loomed large and menacing in front of us for months. Today is the day we cross it. There will be no phones and few radios for more than 100 miles, until we reach the first town, Puerto Cabezas. Not wanting to dwell on our worries, we rouse ourselves and pack up the tent without delay. After wolfing down our breakfast of cookies and dry granola, we carry the gear a long 200 yards to the shore. By 3:00 a.m. we are ready to launch.

Contrary to the expected seasonal wind patterns, a strong headwind plagues us from the start. It plants another seed of doubt in minds already well fertilized with fear. Although the main purpose for the night launches is to minimize encounters with rough characters, we also hope to take advantage of the usual pre-dawn calm. These conditions are disheartening. With thirteen miles remaining to the border, we are worried we won't make it before daylight. Our plan is to discretely cross the frontier and situate ourselves in a hidden campsite off the beach. We will rest until 10:00 p.m. and then launch again for an all-night, thirty-mile paddle through dangerous territory to the safe town of Sandy Bay, where we have a contact. This slow pace may throw everything off.

Although we make decent progress, we encounter one final obstacle that we had not anticipated. The mouth of the Rio Coco (aka Rio Segovia, the river that forms the border between Nicaragua and Honduras) is much wider and wilder than we anticipated. Blocking our path is a half-mile-wide zone of roiling six-foot surf and standing waves that pop up suddenly and without pattern to bounce the kayaks around uncontrollably. For twenty minutes, we paddle at maximum exertion, brace-stroking for balance the entire time, in order to reach the far side. We pull around into the lee of a sharp point and our headwind becomes a quartering tailwind that pushes us southwestward. In our exhausted state, we paddle lazily and look for a spot to pull onto the beach and hide. We can't make it to a safe town in one day, so we'll have to risk camping on the beach for one night.

The shoreline presents us with few options so we choose randomly and land on a stretch of open beach with a thicket of low-lying brush. We haul the boats up over a small bank and lug the gear into the shadows of the foliage. It's a miserable spot to hide out: hot, filled with insects and so exposed that we can't set up a sun shade for risk of being seen from the water by passing boats but we have no choice. It's too late in the morning and we risk being seen if we continue on.

While Jean-Philippe hacks out a shelter from the bushes, I cook lunch in the sweltering heat and fend off doctor flies and stinging ants. We eat quickly and nestle into our shelter by mid-afternoon, wearing long pants and long sleeves to protect ourselves from insects. Unfortunately, not even the faintest breeze cools our shelter and we lie, unmoving, while rivulets of sweat pool beneath us and stealthy doctor flies leave swollen welts on our exposed fingers, wrists and ankles. We pray for respite and for a few minutes of sleep. I have to remind myself that I am doing this by choice; I am here in Nicaragua of my own volition. It is beginning to dawn on me that this leg of our journey may stretch me to my physical and mental limits.

CHAPTER 5

NICARAGUA

The Wild North Coast

Jean-Philippe, 5 May 2000

WE HAVE SURVIVED storms at sea, malaria, tropical rain and heat, insects and terrifying shark encounters. We have camped in areas notorious for bandits and drug dealers. Though we have made the best of every situation so far, we know that Nicaragua will be the most dangerous part of the CASKE2000 expedition. Although decades of civil war have ended recently, out in the remote Caribbean there is still a large quantity of military hardware remaining in the hands of very poor people for whom life has come to have little value. We are easy targets in our kayaks so, for safety, we have decided to paddle long distances and camp out in the open as little as possible.

Paddling to Nicaragua will become a nightmare if we encounter both bad weather and hostile people; what little culture we can document during our dash down the coast will come at a high cost. To survive Nicaragua, we will have to push ourselves to the limit every day.

↑

Jean-Philippe, 5 May 2000

I have never understood self-flagellation. What emotion could possibly consume people to the point where they abuse themselves? I was intrigued by the remarkable movie *Fight Club*, in which a character, suffering from violent multiple personality disorder, is shown punching himself in the face. At the time, I thought to myself, *That is true insanity.* Yet here I am, in the Caribbean on my way from Honduras to Nicaragua, paddling a kayak in the middle of the night. We are entering Nicaragua as the *narco-traficantes* do, stealthily at night. We are in bandit and guerrilla territory now and there is no official presence to protect us here, so we can't risk spending a night on this coast. After a brief day camp five miles past the Honduran border, we must now paddle the thirty-six miles to the first settlement of Sandy Bay in one stretch. As the night drags on, I remind myself that I am here by choice—that alone would be considered by most as proof of my masochism. The meditative rhythm of the paddling and my profound fatigue are pushing me to the brink of unconsciousness. All I can think about is sleep. I'm slapping, pinching and biting myself, doing anything I can think of to stay awake but no matter what, in the back of my mind, I am still afraid for my life. There is no way we are going to stop and sleep out in the open on this notorious stretch of coast.

It is now 2:30 a.m. and we have been paddling since 10:00 p.m. last night on less than four hours of sleep. This is our fourth long, tough day in a row, perhaps the longest day of the entire expedition and twenty-one miles still separate us from Sandy Bay, reputedly a place where we will be able to sleep soundly without fearing for our lives. I don't know how many more of these days our bodies can take but we have no other option. We choose self-imposed physical ruin over physical harm at the hands of drug runners, *bandidos* or guerillas.

Due to the overcast weather, star navigation requires my full concentration. My reference stars keep disappearing behind clouds so I am paddling with my head perpetually tilted back, face up, staring intensely at the black sky, trying to guess where they will reappear. Even the pain from my stiff neck and aching body is not enough to keep me awake. I want to paddle faster, hard enough that I hurt more, so that my body will produce endorphins to keep me awake. Nauseated, Luke is bouncing around in the darkness without any visual reference points: he just can't paddle any faster.

By 3:00 a.m., after five hours of intense concentration, there is nothing I can do to keep my eyes open. For a few seconds I have some stars in sight and then they disappear behind clouds or behind my drooping eyelids. I am paddling longer periods of time with my eyes closed. I bite my fingers at the base of the nails, which awakens me, but then the pain fades to a dull throb. I start biting the tip of my tongue and my lips, but that gains me only a few more minutes of alertness.

After more than six hours in the kayaks, we search the pre-dawn blackness in vain for a beach to land on. We need a quick break. Luke attempts to land on one stretch of dark shore and his kayak bumps into a massive pile of driftwood caught up in a snarl of tree roots right on the shoreline. There is no beach: the forest runs all the way to the water's edge. We have no choice but to keep going and I am forced to keep navigating. Usually, I'm up to the task despite the weather, even in zero visibility. But, with my mind wandering into the world of sleep, I am afraid that we will end up on our way to Africa. I splash water over my head often but it isn't cool enough to be refreshing. My last alternative is to slap myself. These aren't little taps; gentle slaps would have no more lasting effect than biting my fingers had. Every five minutes, I put my paddle down and plaster my cheeks, forehead and neck with blows so hard that the sting takes minutes to dissipate. At one point Luke sees me. "What are you doing?" he shouts. From his tone of voice, I can tell that he is afraid that I'm losing it; he thinks that perhaps I have finally gone mad. By the time the sun rises, I look like a lobster and, for once, it isn't from sunburn.

Along the shore, the forest is so dense that we can barely see past the second layer of trees. This is the Mosquito Coast I had pictured a year ago, before we entered Honduras. Hurricane Mitch consumed the entire beach: left behind is a mess of rotting logs, and the exposed, half-submerged root systems of high-canopy trees.

Finally, an hour after dawn, I see a small patch of sand we can land on. It could be the only stretch of open beach in the whole thirty-five miles, so we pull our kayaks up on shore and collapse next to them. An hour and a half passes before we are able to move a limb and, after a two-hour break, we resume paddling. Sleepiness gives way to deep body fatigue and aching joints.

Three hours later, we look for another landing spot where we can stretch our legs and backs. I paddle close to shore to scout out the landing, accidentally misjudge the surf and a sudden high breaker curls over me while I'm broadside. I brace, lean into it with all my weight, but it's too late, the bow of my kayak has already been taken by the wave and I start to tip. As I capsize, the surf is pushing me rapidly toward dead logs lying in the shore wash. I start an Eskimo roll and pop out on the backside of the wave. Before the next one can crush me into shore, I back-paddle out. Luke arrives a few seconds later and is depressed to see me retreating. "No landing here," I yell. We eventually find a small black sand opening between the trees that is barely wide enough to hold both kayaks. We sit on a log and rest for a few minutes. Neither of us speaks. We sit in silence for twenty minutes, dripping and slapping lazily at biting flies.

When we start paddling again, I calculate that we have another two hours to the village of Sandy Bay. Unfortunately, our large-scale map of the entire Mosquito Coast from Honduras to Nicaragua isn't sufficiently detailed. After two hours we discover that the village is located beside a large lagoon whose entrance lies five miles further south than the actual latitude of the village. Luke looks as if he's going to cry.

More than two hours of paddling later, there is still no sign of the canal leading to the lagoon and village. My back muscles are screaming with each stroke. Luke is far enough behind that I can't see him. I know that if I stop and wait for him, once he catches up he will paddle no further and in spite of the danger, we will be forced to camp here. I refuse to give up so close to our destination. We've already been moving for thirteen straight hours and I am determined to keep going until I find the entrance to the *laguna*.

A few minutes later, I find it and land on the beach to wait for Luke as I stretch out my cramping shoulder and back muscles. Ten minutes later, I can see Luke moving along on painstakingly slow autopilot. The village is not even in sight, so we start paddling into the maze of canals leading through the mangroves, asking directions from several passing motorboats. After more than fourteen hours on the water, we arrive in the small village of Sandy Bay *Norte*. A sympathetic Miskito man invites us to stay under his roof. As he helps carry our gear into his house, we pass beneath the curious gaze of dozens of villagers. None of these people have ever seen kayaks before.

"*De donde vienen?*" someone asks.

"*De Canada,*" I lie, not wanting to give away that we're Americans.

"*No, no, ahorita?*" no, no, now, someone asks again.

"*De la frontera,*" I answer.

"*Cuantos dias?*" How many days?

"*Hoy mismo.*" Just today, I say.

I can hear them chattering among themselves. They can't believe it.

I hear someone say, "*Puro remo? Madre de Dios!*" Just by paddling? Mother of God!

A large, older woman dispatches her daughters to get us some fresh coconuts and food. I hope I have enough energy left to eat.

The people of Sandy Bay are overwhelmingly friendly. When our hosts offer us their own bed, at first we refuse, but when they insist, we go to sleep without even seeing the village. We sleep all afternoon and through until the next morning. When we finally awaken, we realize that despite its remote location on the poorest Central American coast, Sandy Bay looks surprisingly upscale. All the houses are on stilts and painted in vivid reds, blues, and yellows. Mango and coconut trees line the lagoon side of the village. All of the houses are even linked with a winding concrete pathway. At first glance, these people seem well-off compared to villages we saw in Honduras, but a closer look raises doubts in my mind, especially when I notice the remains of an electrical station, a litter of wrecked fishing boats and useless motors, and a decaying saw mill.

Villagers tell us that five decades ago, Sandy Bay was an active and prosperous town but the glory days of the fishing and timber industries are long past and conditions have now regressed fifty years. The end of the last brutal civil war brought peace to the region but little else. The Caribbean Coast of Nicaragua is a forgotten land, standing low on the priority list of the recently installed democratic government. This area has fewer towns with electricity and clean water sources now than it did half a century ago; the better-established villages here subsist while the poorest marginalized settlements can only struggle.

During the 1960s, the Sandinistas used Russian and Cuban aid to recruit soldiers in the Mosquito Coast and then armed them heavily to fight against the U.S.-backed Somoza regime. After a brief breakout of peace following the successful revolution in the late 1970s, war came again to the region when Contra forces supported by the U.S. coerced many locals into the fight. The extensive graveyard found on the outskirts of this village reminds us just how recent that war was.

Most Nicaraguans resumed their poverty-stricken existence peacefully after the war, but for some, armed with leftover AK-47s and handguns, the war continued. Today the best-organized groups espousing ideals are known as guerillas, while those with neither organization nor ideals left have become just plain bandits. Unfortunately, with no one else to fight, they have come to prey upon their own people. The last decade has also brought a new threat to the poverty-stricken villagers from Nicaragua to

Belize: the lure of violence-soaked cash from the Columbian drug cartels' cocaine trafficking operations to the United States.

Sandy Bay was a living lesson about how modernization creates needs, depletes natural resources to meet them and then disappears in a blink, leaving assimilated villagers with nothing and nothing to return to. Most people on the Mosquito Coast have long ago lost their cultures and traditions to evangelization and assimilation and are left only with the desire to attain a modern lifestyle, an aspiration they can never achieve. Because we found no traditional culture left to document, this is clearly a lesson that needs to be learned. Later we will document their plight on the website but first Luke and I must paddle one of the most notorious stretches of coast on the way to the government town of Puerto Cabezas.

†

Jean-Philippe, 7 May 2000

After a day of rest, at 1:00 a.m. on our second day, our hosts arise with us to help us carry our gear to the lagoon. Many of the neighbors come to see us off, too. In the faint moonlight, all that is visible of our route is the dark outline of a wall of mangrove swamp a mile and a half across on the far side. We were too tired coming in the other day to think of marking the GPS coordinates for the canal that connects the lagoon to the ocean. That mistake will hurt us now. Someone in the group points us in the general direction and we push off toward where we think we might find the canal entrance. To keep my heading, I use the stars as reference; they are a better choice than land features, which change as we get closer.

The canal is a maze of intersections to which we paid little attention when entering. After an hour of navigation by guesswork in the dark, I hear the dull distant sound of the surf and slight undulations in the water bounce my kayak. These are comforting signs that we are on the right course toward the sandbar and the opening onto the ocean.

Half an hour later we are stretching on the beach, preparing for yet another long paddle. We estimate that we will have to paddle at least twenty miles to reach another safe harbor. Fortunately, tonight's navigation will be simple. The coastline is straight with no major bays to cross—all we need to do is keep the shore in sight and follow it.

In the dim light just before dawn, we hear a strange sound.

"What the hell was that?"

I turn back toward Luke but I'm afraid I already know all too well. During my time in the army I had heard that sound thousands of times: the pop of a rifle shot muffled by distance. A second shot soon follows. On the beach, I can see a man waving his arms wildly, after shooting at us he is now signaling us to come in. I hope we are far enough out that he can't see me turn to look at him. We have to ignore him; I force the pace and we now paddle further out from shore.

After an hour, we edge closer to shore to see if he has followed us. He's nowhere in sight. Before we reach a point of land visible on the horizon, two friendly fishermen launch a canoe and come to meet us out on the water. They issue us a kindly warning about passing by this point. According to them, thirty armed bandits use it as a base from which to attack passing boats. They appear to be amicable, God-fearing men and they insist that, for our safety and for the salvation of their own souls, they cannot let us go by the point unaided. They invite us to come ashore for a rest. Once on the beach, they advise us to wait for the speedboat water taxi that runs several times a week between Sandy Bay and the town of Puerto Cabezas, saying that it's the only way for us to get through that dangerous zone safely. The bandits are ex-guerillas, they continue, who will not hesitate to kill us for our gear as they have killed others before.

The men are very convincing. Luke and I discuss our options. They seem harmless and, other than machetes for work, they are unarmed. If they are telling the truth, then we should consider taking their advice. Luke is inclined to listen to them, but something doesn't feel right to me. It's as if they are trying to stall us. One of the fishermen tells us that an "official" armed guard from the village is coming to check out the situation. At that moment, I see a man in tattered clothes walking down the beach carrying an old assault rifle, an AK-47 submachine gun, across his shoulder. My heart skips a beat. It's the same man we passed earlier and who had shot twice in our direction.

The fishermen are now more worked up, almost eager. They tell us that we should wait on the beach while they walk to the point and "check out the situation" with the *bandidos*. They start off up the beach and then return less than five minutes later after having walked only a small fraction of the distance to the point, conversing frantically among themselves the entire time. Something is definitely not right here.

When they return, they ask for a *derecho de pasaje*, a "toll fee." They say that they will convey it to the *piratos* on the point and use it to negotiate our safe passage. When I ask them how much, they reply, "Very little, just a hundred dollars." We scoff at their price, nervously explaining that we never travel with that much cash. In reality, we have about $200 tucked away in our bags but it's not the money I'm worried about. Although these men are not aware of it, our gear is worth $40,000.

I search my mind, groping about for any piece of information or a name that might help us. We spent some time with an important Miskito leader, Jacinto Molina, back in Puerto Lempira in Honduras. He told us that if we ever got into trouble along the northern coast of Nicaragua we should mention a couple of names: Brooklyn Rivera and Avelino Cox Molina, so I lie and say that those men, two of the most powerful Miskito leaders in the region, are waiting for us in Puerto Cabezas. And, if we don't arrive there today by 4:00 p.m., they will come out with the police and the coast guard to look for us. The fishermen and the gunman are taken aback at the mention of these names. They talk rapidly among themselves in Miskito and we hear the names Molina and Rivera repeatedly.

They soften their demands but continue negotiating with us. After twenty minutes, one of them, a zealous, muscular little man, starts to lose his temper. Excitedly, he waves a large knife around and, at one point, he looks at the fabric skins of our collapsible kayaks and suggests that bandits could very easily rip our boats to shreds with knives.

The man with the AK-47 remains calm but rigidly reiterates their request. He is trying to mask his tension but I can see one hand repeatedly gripping and un-gripping the stock of his rifle. "So, what are you going to do?" he asks. "We will take them your money so they let you go and I will ensure your protection with my gun. Give us the money now."

Suddenly, a motorboat comes within range of shore; the men exchange excited words in Miskito. All we can understand is "*policia, policia, policia.*" They are afraid it is the coast guard and our so-called "official" runs to hide himself and his AK-47in the bushes. It's a false alarm. The boat turns out to be a water taxi on its way to Sandy Bay.

Now we have no more doubts that they themselves are the only thieves. Although they've been trying to scam us in a friendly way, it is clear that they're starting to lose patience. They don't threaten us directly, but we know that they are not willing to go home empty-handed. We need to do something.

The tension is rising. My training in the French Special Forces comes back to me in a blink. I have a vision of how easily I could take away the stocky little man's knife and plunge it in the throat of the tall guy with the AK-47standing next to him. In less than five seconds I could have the machine gun in my hands—or we could be shot. It's only a brief, passing thought and then reason returns and I realize these people aren't a real threat; they just want some money.

Now everyone is anxious and nervous, they want money, yet clearly fear the name of the Miskito leaders we mentioned. I tell Luke, who is carrying our small stash of Nicaraguan *cordobas*, to pull out a 100, the equivalent of eight dollars. Surprised, he asks me if I am serious. "Do it!" I reply. I repeat again that Brooklyn Rivera is expecting us and hand over the money.

Even though they know that I have seen through their ruse, they can't back down. Yet I sense that they want a peaceful resolution to this confrontation. I play along with them and tell them that we are grateful for their help in negotiating our safe passage with the bad guys out on the point. They accept the donation and, as a peace offering, I pass around one of my water bottles full of Tang. We shake hands all around and they help us carry our loaded kayaks back to the water. They are still too proud to admit their scam and they send us off with a thoroughly inauthentic display of good will: a Christian blessing.

Once out from the coast a short distance we laugh, still a bit nervous. In retrospect, the conclusion of the situation was funny: eight dollars was the appropriate price to pay to such amateur armed robbers. As I paddle on, thinking more and more about their actions, I recall that one of the silent men with a machete was high on drugs. We had received numerous warnings about the increasing prevalence of cocaine in this region. Life in these countries is already cheap; drugs only cheapen it further. Those guys were just poor, opportunistic fishermen who saw us as a free meal. Next time, high on coke, they might just kill us without even bothering to attempt a scam.

Our original plan was to camp on the beach tonight but I feel increasingly uneasy about stopping. I wait for Luke to catch up and we confer. "We need to paddle all the way into Puerto Cabezas today," I say. I can see his face drop as he does the calculations: "Fourteen more miles... that's another thirty-five-mile day!" he groans.

Nearly seven hours later, we drag our boats onto the dirty beach in front of the first beachside restaurant we see. Filthy, dripping wet and stinking of sweat, we sit down for a meal; as we dig into our fried fish and plantains like starving dogs, other diners notice us. After the requisite questions about where we've come from and what we're doing, someone comments that we ought to check in with the captain of the port and with immigration. "We'll go after we eat," I reply. That will make it official, I think to myself, but I know that we've already paid our dues to get into the country.

†

Jean-Philippe, 15 May 2000

My minor stomach problems from yesterday have developed into strong cramps and bloody diarrhea. Unfortunately, we have twenty miles ahead of us today. I'm not sure if I am capable of it but I have no choice. We can't risk camping here in the open, exposed to any passersby. I relieve myself in the bushes one more time and spend a few minutes doing controlled breathing exercises to calm the cramps before getting in my kayak to launch.

The first three hours through the pre-dawn blackness are manageable. I lack energy and feel nauseated the entire time but I am okay if I paddle slowly. I can't bring myself to drink any fluids, even though I know I am severely dehydrated: the Tang drink I have in one bottle is too acidic for my sensitive stomach and the water in the other bottle smells and tastes like chlorine. The odor alone makes me want to heave. By this point, we have covered half the distance so we stop for our first break. As soon as we land, I have to run to the bushes. I want to lie down in the shade of a coconut tree and die.

Back on the water, Luke takes the lead and I try to follow as best I can. It's a strange role reversal, my being behind him struggling to maintain a three-knot speed; reading the pain and fatigue on my face, he offers to tow me. How could I let my friend tow me for ten miles and three and a half more hours? His muscles must be as sore as mine. I can't accept his offer.

I can only imagine one scenario worse than this: a malaria attack. I don't know what we would do if one of us got that sick out here in the middle of nowhere; it is what I fear the most. With no shelter other than a hot sticky tent and limited water supplies, getting malaria out here could be deadly, even with the proper medicine. Despite my misery, I feel fortunate in only suffering from stomach problems and dehydration. I have experienced worse. I know I can paddle through it.

When we arrive in the village of Tasbapounie, Luke looks at me with pity. "Don't think I could've done it," he says. He has no idea. The truth is, I feel more miserable than I look. It is time for me to dig into our first aid kit, begin a course of Flagyl (an antibiotic), and then restrict my diet to bland foods: plain rice, bread and Coke.

My timing is terrible: we have just landed in a village that serves the best food yet in Nicaragua. Tasbapounie is a village of turtle hunters (our political and environmental concerns aside, on this trip we eat what the locals eat). It's torture watching Luke feast on succulent morsels of stewed meat as I force myself to finish my plate of plain boiled rice. He then finishes his meal with a delicious cassava cake.

This village, situated on the sandy *barra* between a large lagoon and the ocean, is one of the nicest we have seen in Nicaragua and one of our favorites all-around. Although still very poor by western standards, compared to the Miskitos living in the north, this Creole community is well off. On their land, they grow a multitude of fruits and vegetables and raise some livestock and horses. But their most important source of food and their meager earnings come from the water. On the lagoon side they pull in bushels of shrimp, and a few miles out to sea, islands yield fish, conch, and lobster. But this time of the year, the bounty comes in the form of sea turtles.

Westerners often cringe and avert their eyes in disapproval at the thought of eating a protected marine species. It is a good thing that more people have not discovered green sea turtle meat because it's absolutely fabulous. Turtle liver is divine—French and Japanese people with a taste for foie gras and monkfish liver would adore it. Most of the turtle organs are edible and even the fat, which I usually avoid in other meats, is a pleasure to the palate, like a briny, smooth gelatin.

To the villagers' credit, they do not hunt turtles commercially; they catch only what they will consume. Infinitely greater numbers of turtles are killed and thrown away by commercial fishing boats as by-catch from drag netting.

The butchering process is morbidly fascinating. The butcher kills the turtle by stunning it on the head with a log. The procedure is quick, and far more humane than the pig or cattle slaughter I have witnessed in Europe. Then the expert butcher works quickly. He cuts out the front fins first, then inserts a sharp knife along the edge of the carapace and cuts around the circumference of the soft ventral shell, opening the turtle as if it were a can of food. A huge can of food indeed: a 200-pound turtle yields more than 120 pounds of meat. The only parts that are discarded are the abdominal lining, spleen and intestines, and alert dogs and vultures await these handouts. The ventral shell is cleaned of its contents and all the meat is then piled back into the main shell to be doled out to "shoppers." Women arrive with plastic bags, buckets and cooking pots and point out the parts they want: lung, leg meat, liver, heart, etc. They even scoop out all the blood, which is fried into a thick sauce as a topping for rice. Nothing goes to waste.

Having witnessed this kind of sustainable harvest, I can't agree with activists who want to impose a complete ban on turtle hunting. We should differentiate between the large-scale commercial fishermen, most of whose catch goes directly to the States and Japan, and the poor native communities, which consume the turtles they catch from the waters around their villages. As one of the villagers told us, "This is our beef." Supporters of a total ban on turtle hunting should visit a poor Creole, Garifuna or Miskito village and witness the need, living conditions and conscious consumption of these peoples before voicing their condemnation of traditional practices.

↑

Jean-Philippe, 17 May 2000

When we started our Mosquito Coast paddle in La Ceiba, Honduras on April 1st, it was the height of the dry season. We didn't see a drop of rain for weeks. One of the main reasons we paddled at night was to avoid the midday heat and direct sunlight. The few times we were forced to paddle during the day, the sun dehydrated us and burned our skin despite sunscreen and long sleeve shirts. The dry season is the only time that it is possible to paddle the Atlantic Coast because once the rain starts, it never stops. And the rain has now started. It causes more problems than just the downpours: floods, insect infestations, diseases and infections occur. The sandflies, always bad, become much worse and stagnant pools of groundwater hatch millions of new malaria-carrying mosquitoes and many other pests. Unable to tend to their fields, travel safely or do much of anything, locals spend most of their time in their hammocks, patiently waiting for windows of clear weather.

Under constantly damp conditions, additional health problems arise. Skin rashes and infections are unavoidable. Cuts and abrasions are never dry, so they take forever to heal. Even under a dry roof, it's so humid that there is no such thing as "dry clothes."

In these conditions, camping a single night is a nightmare. Roughing it two nights is masochism and going for a week becomes purely an ordeal of survival. For us, the wet weather combined with strenuous hours of paddling and perpetual discomfort is a recipe for insanity. When we lose patience with the conditions, we lose patience with each other and we end up yelling and fighting.

We were told that the rainy season starts in mid-June, so we started paddling the Nicaraguan coast without worries. Since leaving Puerto Cabezas we have encountered thick cloud cover; it looks like the weather is changing a month ahead of schedule this year. Three days ago in Tasbapounie we got our first storm of the season. I have rarely seen rain come down so hard; the roar on the zinc roof was so loud we couldn't hold a conversation. The visibility out our front door was less than 100 feet.

Now, fifty miles separate us from the town of Bluefields, the capital of South Nicaragua. Another storm has been brewing and I'm afraid we will be caught out in it because we'll need two days to cover that distance. Today we will try to do twenty-five miles.

In a steady downpour, we land at Punta de Perlas after seventeen miles. The sky doesn't show any sign of clearing. We have two options: we can paddle for another hour or two, set up camp in the rain and wake up wet and miserable at midnight for a thirty-mile all-nighter, or we can keep going until late afternoon, sleep all night and have a shorter day tomorrow. We decide to go for it.

Aided by a northerly tail wind, we finally head for shore an hour before sunset after a total of thirty-four miles. We find refuge in a tiny cove and set up camp in a drizzle, a few hundred feet away from a *palapa* fishing hut. Our muscles are so sore and we are so exhausted that we are confident even a monsoon will not prevent us from sleeping.

In the little bay, protected from the wind, nightmare sandflies force us into the tent. The rain cover that we normally never use transforms our normally breezy mesh tent into a steam room. Perspiration drips down our sides and pools beneath us on our mats. The smell of our unwashed bodies and moldy clothing is overpowering and the air is almost unbreathable. The drizzle stops, permanently we hope, and we remove the rain cover. If we don't, I know we won't be able to sleep at all.

The rain starts again just as I drift off. We rush outside to re-cover the tent and again lie down inside, sweating in misery. We go through the same cycle half a dozen times. At 3:00 a.m., with less than an hour of sleep, we give up, get up for good, randomly shove the soaked gear into dry bags and pack up the kayaks.

We are twelve miles from El Bluff, the commercial harbor at the entrance to the wide bay where Bluefields lies another five miles toward the back. Three and a half hours later, we enter the bay through heavy surf and choppy seas and land on the wharf of a Navy base.

Luke has a look on his face that I've seen before. His skin is gray and he is shaking with the chills; above and beyond exhaustion, there's definitely something wrong with him. He tells me that his muscles ache and that he has a headache. I can see that he has nothing left in him. He tries to spit and it lands on his shoulder. Without the energy to wipe it off, he leaves it there. I pull the towrope out from under my deck straps and clip it to his kayak. I think I know what's happening to him and we need to put an end to this day from hell.

I had towed Luke before, but never after such a long day. For forty-five minutes, I make an all-out assault on the last two miles to town. I have Bluefields in sight and as we creep through the flat protected water, I concentrate on the docked ships in the distance: with each paddle stroke, I imagine them appearing bigger and bigger. I dig deeper. There is not even a puff of wind and, in spite of the rain, I have to splash my head with water every few minutes. While I am overheating, Luke is freezing. He looks like a ghost lying in his kayak. There is no doubt that he has malaria.

The harbor is shocking. The surface is thick with floating garbage and shimmering pools of gasoline and oil. Most of the boats look like they've been through a war. Some are floating. Some are partially submerged and resting on the bottom. Amidst a mess of wharfs, jetties, docks, and sagging buildings, I can see nothing that even looks like a hotel. Luke stays with our gear while I go and look around. A zealous local offers to help: he leads me from one whorehouse to another. Some rooms are so bad that they don't even have a window, just a hole in the wall looking out onto the chaos of the harbor. I excuse myself from my guide. Luke is laying down in his kayak under the rain, suffering. I have to hurry and find us a decent place close to the waterfront.

Half an hour later we unload onto the dock of a hotel down the beach. It's still raining. Luke can barely stand: he's too weak to carry anything so I send him off to the room.

When I get to our room, he is lying in bed, delirious with fever; fortunately we have medicine that should decrease it quickly. I go in search of vital liquids; dehydration causes many malarial deaths and water alone cannot replenish body fluids. In a small filthy market, I purchase a few green coconuts and some limes—mixed with a soupcon of salt, they'll be perfect. When I return to our hotel room, the stench from our equipment assaults my senses; I open the window and then can see Luke, high on chloroquine. He is moaning and tossing endlessly in a pool of sweat and I spend the rest of the night checking on him as he has nightmare after nightmare without ever regaining consciousness. I don't want to think about what could have happened if we had been a day or two slower in reaching Bluefields.

Nicaragua has been a nightmare, and we have already done more than our share of tempting death. Over the next couple of days, as Luke slowly recovers, I consider our situation and think seriously about our planned itinerary to Costa Rica.

↑

Bluefields To the Border

Jean-Philippe, 20 May 2000

The immigration officers and port captain urge us not to paddle to the Nicaragua-Costa Rica border town of San Juan. "There are many pirates and poor people down by Punta Mono and Rio Maiz," they say. "There is no way to pass in secret and they will kill you first, no questions asked." Until now, we have never altered our course to heed the warnings of locals and officials; they always inflate the level of danger for foreigners. Of course we are careful, but we have always gone where we were planning to go. But here something feels different—and wrong. Our passage to Bluefields has already been too difficult; although we have avoided any major mishap, the past couple of weeks have been an endless series of steadily escalating mental and physical trials. Luke is too weak to paddle long distances, and we found Bluefields appalling. Our first total failure could be fatal. So, we will go around by land, the long way. Although we are not afraid of physical challenges, the mental strain of worrying about the human threat is getting to us. It is a wise decision.

↑

Jean-Philippe, 21 May 2000

The six-hour boat ride upriver from Bluefields to Rama is described as "unique" in the Lonely Planet guidebook, "a good reason to make the 12-hour trip from the capital to Bluefields." We find the boat ride painfully slow, long and very boring; it is less scenic than most rivers we have seen elsewhere in Central America. However, the ride that follows will be enough of an adventure to make up for it.

The old, converted school bus we travel in is now reduced to wreckage. The seats have no padding, few of the windows work and the bus is completely without suspension. The radio speakers are blown but the driver has the music cranked full blast anyway; the resulting racket sounds like the roar of a jet engine with a tiny hint of melody.

The condition of the bus is so bad it is comical. The mixed asphalt and dirt road ahead of us looks—and rides—like a minefield, and the heavy rain pools in dents on the roof and spills over whenever we hit a bump. The windows long ago lost their rubber seals and steady cascades of water stream down the interior walls. The wet floor reeks: covering it is a layer of ooze that smells of oil and rotting food.

My favorite feature is the windshield wiper. The motor for the wiper burned out so the driver rigged up a manual system. The wiper blade is attached to a bungee cord that runs across the windshield all the way to the broken passenger-side mirror. This adds tension to the wiper arm. On the driver's side there is a blue plastic rope that snakes out the window along the base of the windshield and attaches to the blade. Wiping is simple: the driver opens his window and reaches around to yank on the blue rope and the wiper squeegees the windshield. It's rudimentary but effective. Each time the driver opens his window to clear the windshield, we all get a shower.

The young ticket collector doubles as onboard mechanic. Hearing a strange clicking noise, the driver stops the bus. The boy grabs a big wrench and runs outside into the rain. He sets wood blocks under the wheels and gives the signal to passengers who are lining up to get off. It's an opportunity to go to the bathroom; if not for the breakdown, we would have to hold it for hours. The women take just a few steps from the bus to squat in plain view.

Great clouds of steam pour from the engine compartment but, in just a few minutes, the boy drops the hood and climbs back in. Fixed! All of the passengers are now completely soaked but, without complaining, they just sit back in their sticky clothes, squeezed against each other for the remaining few hours it will take to reach our destination.

Although happy and relieved to finally get off the bus in Managua, I am overwhelmed by what I see. This capital city has a higher standard of living than the big cities of Tegucigalpa and San Pedro in Honduras or Guatemala City. It's as if we have landed on a different planet. There is little architecture to be found in downtown Managua; the entire center was flattened by an earthquake in 1972 and has languished vacant to this day. Just a few isolated, earthquake-proof structures survived intact; the square tower of the Bank of America breaks through the skyline among a few skeletons and shells of buildings. A renewed economy supported by foreign aid has brought American symbols such as McDonald's and Pizza Hut as well as movie theaters and even new fashion boutiques. Bursting with people fighting their way through heavy traffic, Managua strikes me as a sterile and soulless capital. How can wild forests of the remote Atlantic Coast and the slums of Bluefields coexist in the same country with a metropolis teeming with icons of prosperity? Appalled, Luke and I catch the next bus to the colonial city of Granada. From there, we plan to catch a ferryboat across the lake and then another boat back to San Juan on the Caribbean Coast.

Granada is everything the guidebook claims: "enchanting, charming, friendly, rich in history..." Set on the shore of Lake Nicaragua, the largest body of fresh water in Central America, it offers views beyond compare. The water itself is mercurial, seeming to change from seaglass green to cerulean blue, depending on the position of the sun.

Concepcion, a volcano so majestic that Zeus himself wouldn't appear out of place glowering from atop it, stands proudly on its own island in the middle of the lake. Granada's beautiful colonial architecture reminds me of Antigua, Guatemala, before it was overwhelmed with a constant flow of tourists. Quaint white porches and charming homes that could've been plucked from the English countryside. A few American expatriates have started to open hotels, guesthouses and bars, but the city has kept its laid-back atmosphere, minimal traffic and clean air. While waiting for the next ferry, we spend three days eating at local restaurants, uploading files to our website from Internet cafes and catching up on sleep.

↑

Luke, 23 May 2000

To get back out to the Caribbean from Granada, we will have to take a ferry across the lake and descend the Rio San Juan, the river that forms Nicaragua's border with Costa Rica.

Inversely proportional to my improving condition, the outlook for our itinerary continues to decline. The rainy season is a month early. It will make not just the paddling, but all of our travel, more difficult. It has been nice to spend a couple of days here in the colonial city of Granada, but we need to get moving; unfortunately, our battered kayaks would not survive an attempt to run the San Juan River, which is jammed with floating logs. We will need to reserve spots on the ferry to San Carlos, and from there, take a *colectivo* downriver and resume paddling from the town of San Juan.

I arrive at the ticket counter as soon as they begin selling at 10:00 a.m. It turns out that the four-hour hydrofoil ferry to San Carlos that was mentioned in the guidebook has been discontinued. The high-speed, Russian-made craft broke down a couple of years ago and was retired for lack of replacement parts. Our only option is an all-night slow boat that departs at 2:00 p.m., to arrive at 4:00 a.m.

We show up at 12:30, nice and early, to stow our gear and get a good spot on board. To our surprise, most of the passengers have already arrived and there is hardly an open space left. To make it worse, the people working in the cargo bay of the port are completely uncooperative and hostile. Nobody will let us borrow a dolly. The foreman wants to charge us extra money for our equipment. The hired porters with carts want more money to carry our gear 150 yards than we paid for the taxi ride bringing all of it from the hotel. It isn't a lot of money, but we are so angry that, on principle and out of stubbornness, we carry the 100-pound kayak bags and large dry bags of gear to the boat ourselves in the pouring rain. Once on board, we change clothes, find an unoccupied bench, unroll our air mats (to the envy of our neighbors) and settle in for the night. The rhythmic pinging and clunking of the diesel engine puts us to sleep.

In the pre-dawn darkness, we unload in San Carlos. The ticket salesman for the motor launch *colectivo* to San Juan tells us that it won't depart for another two and a half hours so we go back to sleep. Bustling on the dock awakens us before 6:00 a.m. and we rush to load our mountain of gear into the launch to be assured of a spot onboard. By 6:30a.m., the narrow thirty-five-foot boat with fifteen rows of seats designed for thirty passengers is listing to the side and low in the water with forty-three people and huge mountains of cargo. The zealous ticket salesman has oversold tickets. The port captain comes out for his inspection and shakes his head. "No way!" The boat driver and crew demand that some people disembark; with flustered crew, complaining passengers and the port captain holding fast to his decision, we sit in the boat for two hours waiting for a solution to materialize. Finally, at 8:00 a.m., we all move into a larger boat borrowed from another company as the engines from the smaller boat are also transferred. Not surprisingly, they don't provide enough power and what is usually a seven-hour ride looks to become much longer. After brief calculations, I realize that we will not arrive before dark. With a sinking feeling, I look to see if the boat is equipped with lights. There are none.

The most vocal defender of the passengers' rights is a black Creole family of four. The two young men and their sister, all in their twenties, have a lot to say to the captain and crew. Much to our amusement, they joke amongst themselves in Creole and then complain in Spanish to the delight of the rest of the passengers.

Once under way, our primary concerns are seating positions and the question: to drink or not to drink? The first issue, the seats, is a constant struggle. The hard, plastic, straight-backed seats are anchored to the fiberglass frame of the boat with little leg room in between and no cushioning. Some of the large Caribbean mamas with ample posteriors have no problems but for us it is miserable. My ass is killing me! I change position every ten minutes.

The second problem is hydration and excretion. It becomes very clear that the boat will not make many bathroom stops. Five hours into the trip we take our first break. We debate whether or not we should buy drinks from the one vendor on the boat. We split a can of viscous, warm apple nectar and endure the rest of the day dry-mouthed and dehydrated.

Morning haze changes into intermittent squalls, and by afternoon it's raining steadily. The boat is equipped with a roof and plastic side curtains that can be lowered during downpours, but once closed the boat becomes a steam room.

At dusk, we are still more than two hours away from San Juan. The crew is forced to navigate by flashlight as the wan light fades to total blackness. Some passengers look worried, others begin to grumble, "This never would have happened if we'd left on time!" The young ticket taker stands on the bow with the flashlight and yells directions to the captain who stands at the helm, thirty-five feet away. It looks to me like a recipe for disaster.

An hour after sunset, the pilot steers us into the left channel and around an island in the middle of the river. Some of the passengers, locals apparently, comment that it is the wrong way, too narrow and twisty. A shout from the front and a quick move from the pilot narrowly save us from running aground on the left bank. At that moment, it begins to pour. The pilot, now blinded by the rain, is unable to recover from his steering overcorrection and we plunge into the low-lying branches on the right bank. Like gunshots, the wooden posts holding up the roof snap and it caves in on top of us. The boat lists to the side, the right gunwale dangerously close to water level. People scream and flounder, trying to push the heavy canvas and wood awning away. A post gashes my forehead. And suddenly the roof is off. We're clear. In the aftermath, the boat goes silent for a few seconds as everyone waits to see if we are still afloat.

The four-man crew scrambles to assess the damage. The pilot is afraid to engage the engines. He passes long poles to the two deckhands to direct the boat as it drifts in the current. The passengers calm down and began to reach overboard to the partially submerged awning and dislodge the life vests tied to its underside.

After ten minutes of drifting, we approach the riverside shack of a homesteader. Dim candlelight guides us in. We pull up to the bank and once again the complaints begin. The two black guys, now unhappy about being rained upon, yell at the crew. "You almost killed us! If you don't have life vests for all of us and can't find the right way, we're staying here, man! You can send another boat for us in the morning! It's your fault, this accident! If you had any organization, we'd have left on time and we'd be there now!"

The homesteader tells us that we're close. Finally the rain lets up, our narrow branch rejoins the main flow and we continue on with no further incidents. The pilot keeps the engine on low throttle, the deck-hands navigate and, two hours later, we pull into the dock at San Juan. I have been sitting for hours wrapped in a plastic bag, shivering. At this point, I will pay anything for a dry hotel room and I see one 200 yards away. We carry the gear, dry off, choke down a warm meal and collapse into bed.

⸸

Jean-Philippe, 27 May 2000

Reluctantly, we had just skipped a sixty-mile stretch of coast separating Bluefields from San Juan, the last southern Nicaraguan outpost. When we had reached Bluefields, the combination of events—our lucky escape from Miskito bandits, the daily physical and mental exhaustion and the sudden onset of Luke's malaria—took its toll on us. We had lost both our self-confidence and the essential drive to finish this expedition. The final blows were the strong words from the Bluefield coast guards, "Paddling past the Punta Mono (fifteen miles south of Bluefields) is suicidal and we can't let you do that. Just last week bandits there killed locals to rob them of only a few *cordobas*." These last frightening words resonated in my head. Was our expedition really about paddling from point A to point B or was it about the experience we sought and a message we wanted to send? Risking our lives for nothing made no sense but after already skipping sixty miles of coast, I could not bear the thought of crossing the border of Costa Rica on a bus. San Juan stands on the delta, just a mile north of the main river of the same name that marks the border between Nicaragua and Costa Rica. It is the first and last government-protected settlement south of Bluefields. From there, we would only have to paddle sixteen miles to reach the Rio Colorado, the first large river on the northern coast of Costa Rica; Luke and I agreed that we would paddle our way into Costa Rica.

Many people have told us that the immigration office in San Juan will not stamp us out of the country unless we pay a bribe. Because of border problems with Costa Rica and narcotic trafficking, they don't like to let foreigners cross over from San Juan. In the morning under pouring rain, we knock on the door of the immigration officer's house. The man seems friendly and interested in our tale. He confirms all the stories we have heard about the coast from Bluefields to San Juan. Every time the coast guard or the police land on that coast, the bandits retreat into the bush and all that's left are poor fishermen and farmers who are too afraid of reprisals to denounce them.

The immigration officer has a hard time believing we have safely paddled the entire northern coast. In his words, "The Mosquito Coast is the most dangerous region of the country." Then he says that it will be a very long day for us to paddle the full network of canals and rivers up to the Costa Rican border town of Colorado. His jaw drops when I say that we intend to take the short route and paddle the ocean. Like all the locals, he says that it is crazy to paddle out through the mouth of the San Juan River; it's very dangerous even for small motorboats and no one can paddle through the strong current and enormous breakers that frequently kill fishermen. Going into the mouth of the Rio Colorado is even worse, he tells us. But we've heard these warnings dozens of times already. If storms or warnings had stopped us, we would probably never have left Belize.

There is, however, another very real threat: sharks. The mouth of the Rio San Juan has one of the world's largest concentrations of tiger and bull sharks. Bull sharks have even made their way upriver to Lake Nicaragua and marine biologists from around the world come to study the only species of shark that has adapted to fresh water. Known man-eaters, both tiger and bull sharks often prey on marine mammals on the surface of the water and in the waves. Their sight is poor and they are known to mistake kayaks and surfboards for food. The largest of these sharks can reach up to sixteen feet and our kayaks would crack in their jaws like peanuts. They are so notorious that the immigration officer doesn't even warn us about this threat. He just asks, "Aren't you afraid of sharks when you are in your little kayaks?" We smile at him but I can see my fear mirrored on Luke's face. Capsizing in a large breaking zone is one thing but capsizing in a large river mouth full of bull sharks, thought to be responsible for most coastal attacks on humans, is quite another. But we can't give up again. We have to paddle to Costa Rica.

The officer stamps our passports and shakes our hands while shaking his head, bemused. "Good luck, I'm proud to have met you," he says sincerely, but we can see on his face that he doesn't believe we'll live to see another day. By 11:00 a.m., we are on the last stretch of the Rio San Juan. The river is swollen from the strong rains of the past eight days and it's rushing headlong toward the mouth. We stop on the sandbar to observe the conditions. The waves are separated into three zones. The first one is a wide field of choppy clapotis, small irregular bouncy surf created by the current from the river confronting the incoming wave wash. The second set of breakers, much further away, looks much bigger, and the third, over a half-mile out, is barely distinguishable. It looks do-able but we can't judge the strength of the current or see any sharks from here on land.

Back in our kayaks, I take the lead and we clear the first breakers easily. *Too easily*, I think. I realize that the strength of this current has pushed us much faster than any we have ever been through. I reach the second breaking zone in no time and the waves are much bigger than I anticipated. They are nearly perfect ten-foot tubes and their crashing sound is intimidating. Like overconfident idiots, we had launched without wearing our life vests but, caught in the current, it is too late to do anything about it. There is no time to twist around and grab my vest from under the bungee net. Passing through large breaking surf is all about timing. When I see a ten-foot wave about to break, I stop paddling and wait for it to collapse ahead of me. Unfortunately, I have misjudged the strength of the outbound river current and it pushes me forward so hard it feels like I'm being sucked into the curl of the wave. It's too late to back-paddle and the curl lifts my bow, standing my kayak nearly vertical. I paddle hard on the crest and, just when I think I am through, the stern gets sucked back and to the side. It happens so quickly that I have no time to react and I find myself upside down.

The left is my weak side for rolling and I fail on my first try. Before I can make a second attempt, the following wave ejects me from my cockpit. My left foot becomes entangled in the seasock cockpit lining and the kayak drags me underwater. I am swallowing murky water and I'm in danger of drowning but all I can think about are sharks. I need to get my act together in order to free my ankle and get my head back to the surface. I have to reach inside the reversed cockpit to free my foot. The pushing force of the wave on the kayak is strong and it drags me along as if I were already a corpse. Swallowing more water, I no longer worry about the sharks. I need air. Quick.

When I finally surface, I grab a hold of the kayak but another wave rips it out of my hands. Just then, Luke paddles by, completely engaged in his own battle to crest the waves. I scream for help, but there is nothing he can do to help me. I'm in a dilemma. It is crucial that I keep holding my paddle because I won't be able to do anything with my kayak without it; however, it's impossible to swim with it in my hand. Each wave is carrying my boat further away.

Without a life jacket, I'm not as buoyant as the kayak and the waves are carrying it away further and faster than I can swim. At that moment, I realize that, if I can't get to my kayak, I could die here. I am in limbo, caught between the two powerful opposing forces of the current and the surf in murky, shark-infested water. I have already swallowed too much water, I'm exhausted and unable to swim and my shoes and clothing hamper my movement. I need to catch my kayak soon.

For fifteen minutes, I struggle just to keep my head above water. The waves are tossing me around so violently that survival is my only focus. I don't realize what is happening around me, that there is now a third force in play: a current running parallel to shore. In a brief moment of calm, I look up to see that I have drifted down the beach a couple of hundred yards. Fortunately, I'm no longer in front of the river mouth. The waves here are washing in toward the shore with less opposition.

I body surf a wave and nearly reach my kayak but I'm still a quarter-mile from shore when I manage to grab the deck riggings. Still holding my paddle in one hand, I hold on tightly, vowing not to let the kayak go, no matter what. As I continue to drift farther away from the river mouth, the waves slowly decline in size and power. I'm about to climb aboard when I see Luke paddling quickly toward me. I quickly swing my hips up into the cockpit and stuff my legs in. The boat is totally swamped and barely floating so I start pumping frantically with my back to the waves. Before I can empty even half of the water, Luke yells, "Put your spray skirt on, man, here comes a huge set!"

Quickly, I stow my bilge pump under the deck straps and stretch the neoprene skirt around the cockpit rim. With so much water still trapped inside, the boat is so heavy I can barely move it and I only have a few seconds to reorient it before the surf begins to pound me. Adrenaline rushes through my body. If I am still broadside when those waves hit, I am done for. Fortunately, when the first wave breaks on me, I am well positioned and have gained just enough forward momentum; I punch through like a big log and, five minutes later, we clear the last surf zone. I collapse over my deck, twitching with adrenaline and sick with exhaustion.

As we resume the paddle south, I am in a daze. The shock of nearly drowning sends my mind wandering, spinning through all sorts of hypothetical situations. Had one little thing gone differently, I might have died. I remember a quote from the Talmud that a friend sent me in an email a week ago, when we arrived in Bluefields:

"Every blade of grass has its angel that bends over it and whispers grow, grow."

Then she wrote:

"It is clear that you have been lucky on many of these occasions and that there has been more than one time when things certainly could have taken a turn for the worse. I guess there is really nothing that you can do about that. However, I trust that you are not taking any undue risks."

Who knows how far away the sharks were when I was struggling to stay afloat like an injured animal? The truth is that today, once again, my guardian angel was there for me.

↑

Lightning and thunder draw me out of my introspection. The sky has become so black it looks like the sun has just set. The clouds are low and close and the thunder sounds as if it's booming right in my ears. Our day is not yet over; we still have ten miles to go before reaching the mouth of the Rio Colorado. I don't care about thunder, lightning and rain but I do fear the wind. Within minutes a strong offshore breeze kicks up, the sea instantly grows very choppy and the swells grow to enormous proportions.

We consider paddling for the beach but it is too late; already the surf is more than we can safely handle. Luke is lucky to be nearsighted: he cannot see the huge swell curling up into a gigantic shore break. I can see water vapor hanging over the curls, a sure sign of collapsing tubes, and the breakers must be over ten or twelve feet high. Professional surfers dream of this, but for us it means we are stuck out here. Minute by minute, the swell grows larger. I have entirely ruled out the possibility of going ashore; our only chance is to get to the river mouth and hope it's not too wild. But then the words from the immigration officer return to haunt me: "The Rio Colorado mouth is even worse than that of the Rio San Juan." Worse? How could it possibly be worse? I've had it with this expedition. I want out. No more paddling, no more crazy seas, no more bandits, no more camping, no more beans, rice and noodles. I want out now! I look around—surrounded by full-sized tropical trees floating up and down with the breaking swell, we could be crushed at any time—and realize, to my dismay, that to be able to quit, I have to survive this day.

In these crazy seas, we are insignificant; we paddle another five hours against the current as the swells keep growing. It was ridiculous for us to come out here to start with. We are completely at the mercy of the ocean and the weather; we're Dancing with Death to the sound and rhythm of the giant breaking swell, and we have no control over the music. There is no choice but to wait offshore for the storm to end. It could take hours—or possibly days. We can't even call for help because our marine radio died long ago. It turned out to be much less waterproof than the manufacturer stated.

For the first time since leaving Honduras, I am happy when I see a speedboat change its course and come toward us. I become frightened when I see a man standing at the rail with a rifle in his hands but, when I see that there is a Costa Rican flag flying from the bridge and that the three men are in uniform, I breathe a sigh of relief. It's the coast guard! They shake their heads incredulously when we tell them where we paddled from and say that we need to stop and report in at their base located inside the river's mouth. When I ask them about the entrance, they reply that, because of the huge waves from the storm, it is really bad. At first, they drive their boat slowly alongside to reassure us but when they see that we seem to be doing okay on the now twelve-foot rolling swell, they roar away and leave us alone. Luke and I look at each other, shocked and confused. We thought they would stay with us to ensure our safety entering the Rio Colorado.

I can't believe my eyes when we arrive at the river mouth. From behind me, I hear Luke swear: "Holy shit, we're fucked!" The waves are breaking in irregular sets and in oddly spaced zones that extend over a mile out from shore. Coming from the north, we have to fight the current and enter the center zone from the side and then try to surf into the mouth. When I start in, I realize that I am drifting north too quickly and that I will miss the entrance. I quickly turn around and paddle out to sea to try again. If we don't align ourselves so that we surf right into the mouth, the shore break will pulverize us on the rocks. We will have to hit it just right. Technically, the waves don't seem to be too difficult. More dangerous are the numerous huge logs, bouncing around in the murky water.

We both know that we are on our own for this landing. There can be no mistakes here. This river is even stronger than the San Juan from which we launched this morning. We start surfing in but, despite constant paddling, we make little progress. The out-flowing current is turning the incoming surf into standing waves. If the current is this strong a quarter-mile out, we might not have the paddling power to get in.

After clearing the last zone, I paddle so hard my body overheats, but I don't seem to make any progress. It takes me fifteen minutes of all-out paddling to cover the few hundred feet separating me from the sandy south point flanking the river mouth. Finally, I pull my kayak up on to the beach, worn out and dehydrated. I look back at Luke. He is battling. I can see the power in his strokes but he might as well be on a treadmill. I scream words of encouragements and five minutes later he lands with a torrent of expletives, his exhaustion and frustration spilling out in a tirade.

From the river mouth we can see the coast guard base (a tiny shack, three people, a dog and one boat) and the village of Colorado—we just can't get there. The current must be well over six knots inside the river; we just can't make any headway against it. It seems that we might be stuck on this sand bar unless we want to try to walk through the elephant grass along the shoreline while pulling our kayaks in the water.

Just then, two charter-fishing boats arrive and offer to tow us to the coast guard base. "Did you come down the river?" asked the captains.

"No, we paddled over from Nicaragua," we reply. The captain of one of the boats looks me up and down. "That sea? Today? I don't believe you!" But he can tell we are not joking. "Really? You guys are crazy!" I agree with him. What we did really was insane.

They drop us off half a mile further up the river where the friendly coast guardsmen check our passports and look in a few bags. While their narcotics dog sniffs all our equipment, the guards offer us some lemonade and listen with great interest to our stories. They told us that they didn't stay with us because they were worried about the worsening conditions at the river mouth since their 200-horsepower engines seemed to quit at random.

They also tell us that we must go to the capital city, San José, to clear immigration because there is no office here on the coast for another fifty miles. We are not going that far; this is nearly the end of the line for us in the Caribbean. I am almost ready to bag it just now, fold up the boats and jump on the first plane to San José, but we are too close to our next goal to give up: Tortuguero National Park, a preservation model for the green sea turtle, lies only one day away, through a network of inland canals and lagoons. San José and the immigration officers must wait a few more days!

CHAPTER 6
COSTA RICA

Taking a Break

Luke, June 2000

AFTER A WEEK in the country, we're finally legal. Not surprisingly, there is no immigration office out on the Caribbean Coast of Costa Rica. The towns of Barra Colorado and Tortuguero are popular tourist destinations for turtle watching and charter fishing, but all visitors arrive by bush plane from San José. Except for us.

Yesterday morning, we went to immigration as soon as we flew into San José. The immigration officers were unimpressed with our efforts to be conscientious: they couldn't conceive of how it was possible that we were standing in their office in the capital city, nearly 200 miles from the border, without stamps in our passports. "Many tourists go kayaking in Costa Rica," they told us, "but they never paddle over from Nicaragua." According to them, the only people who pass through those waters are Miskitos, *narcotraficantes* and *pescadores*. They assumed we were lying and, only when they phoned over to the coast guard and had them call the Barra Colorado field station on short wave radio, were they able to confirm our arrival. Grudgingly, after four hours, they gave us visas.

Ironically, all I want to do right now is to get the hell out of this country; nothing is fun at the moment. I need a break from this expedition almost as much as Jean-Philippe does and we both need a break from each other. I can't take another night of camping in the close confines of our moldy tent. Jean-Philippe's body odor, after multiple shower-less days, reeks of rotting mushrooms, burnt sugar and rancid vinegar. He makes similar comments and particularly about the smell of the fungal bloom on my feet when I remove my water boots each day. I must have a chance to cleanse myself of the saturating stench and filth of this expedition. On alternating nights, both of us also develop gastrointestinal issues; any shifting of our bodies in our bedrolls releases trapped pockets of gas. When we wake up in the morning, our heads are usually congested until we can get outside and breathe some fresh air. The air is only marginally better when we stay in a cheap hotel room.

Our recent personality conflicts have become more virulent. I become increasingly passive-aggressive with prolonged exposure to Jean-Philippe's sustained intensity. My attitude becomes more blasé and I needlessly question every move he makes. I become the naysayer. For him, anything worth doing is worth doing well—and then double-checking. In the abstract, his thoroughness and attention to the minutiae of details is commendable but, in reality, as his partner dealing with it every day, I start to feel inadequate and defensive. After a while, I just lash out: "Screw it! It doesn't need to be done that way. If you feel so strongly about lashing all the dry bags, pelican boxes and loose gear to the poles of the tent so that they won't be stolen in the middle of the night way out here in the middle of fucking nowhere, do it by yourself!"

Jean-Philippe gave me a "come-to-Jesus" speech in which he beseeched me to examine my motives and dedication: "You know, Luke, I put my life into this project. When we are in town, I stay up nights planning, making contacts and designing the website. My soul goes into this expedition; I made you an equal partner yet you don't put in one-tenth of the effort. We have the chance to do something amazing with the website and the documentaries but you don't seem to give a shit! Why are you here, what do you care about?"

I didn't have the heart to tell him that, from the start, I'd really only wanted to be a role player. I never fully invested every ounce of heart and soul because I knew that the expedition was his baby. He was on a mission. The breadth and scope of my vision for the project was not nearly as profound. How could I possibly hope to be more proactive in its design? My mistake was that I never fully communicated at the start or at any time during the expedition that I often acted like a passenger because I felt like one.

Much of our miscommunication and misunderstanding has resulted from the disparity between the respective goals and limits that we set for ourselves. My tolerance for pain and discomfort is high, but nowhere in the same stratosphere as his. My ability to work and focus comes and goes in bursts. His is enduring and seemingly infinite. I look at the labyrinthine sprawl of the website and groan. He sees only its glorious potential. I tell him that if we branch out any more we are at risk of spreading ourselves too thin. He tells me that I possess neither vision nor work ethic. We go back and forth with concessions and compromises but inevitably we come to an impasse: there is a point at which I can no longer temper his fanaticism and he can no longer squeeze inspirational blood from my stone.

For extreme expeditions, success is defined by results; only the results determine how you are perceived in the public eye. A common problem is that the desired result dominates the process. Expedition leaders have to walk a fine line between being patronizingly particular and astoundingly inspirational.

Over the past two years, I think Jean-Philippe has come to the conflicted realization that all expedition leaders do: success requires a proprietary, iron-willed approach to leadership and a willingness to take responsibility for and pick up the slack of less-inspired members. Few people have that capacity. Few among us are willing to invest and risk everything for even the most righteous cause. Yet, in true leaders, that inclination is like a biological imperative, a mantra: Go Big or Go Home. When the rest of us don't put in commensurate effort, it burns them up inside; they don't understand why we're not trying harder. In every leader there must be an ember of resentment smoldering in the pit of his/her stomach at all times, no matter how hard he/she tries to control it.

Something else is now eating at Jean-Philippe: rather than his usual pre-occupation with the website, he's now concerned that we may have to retire our kayaks. At the moment, we're on a scouting mission to check out the Pacific waves. This morning, when we got off the bus at the popular surfing beach of Tamarindo and looked out to sea, the booming spectacle made my jaw drop. "Wow! I thought so," Jean-Philippe said to me. "We need new kayaks. Our leaky Feathercrafts will never stand up to that."

While Jean-Philippe wants to return to Guatemala to document its highland culture, I am planning to take a summer break in the States, so my job will be to arrange to get two new boats down to Costa Rica. We suspected a while ago that we'd need new ones, so we've been negotiating with Seaward, a Canadian company. Their reinforced fiberglass expedition boats are second to none, and they have agreed to customize ours with an extra layer of Kevlar. Unfortunately, I may have to bring them down myself. Expatriates down here tell us that they live by a few cardinal rules, one of which is never ship anything big and valuable to Central America. Inevitably, the items will be lost, damaged, impounded and/or heavily taxed. So it looks like I will be pulling my car out of storage and driving them down. It could turn out to be cheaper and faster, I just need to get used to the idea that my car may never make it back home afterward.

At this point, I don't know how I can afford my kayak. I may be guilty of restricting my investment of soul and effort in all aspects of our project, but not my money; my savings are gone. Before leaving Japan, I had nearly $40,000. Now I'm starting to fill up my first platinum credit card; I know that the expense is necessary so I will have to charge my new $4,000 kayak. We will be taking our paddling to a new level from here on out, however, apparently I will have to go home before I can go big.

↑

Nicoya Peninsula to Manuel Antonio

Luke, 10 September 2000

In August I drove my old SUV and our two new kayaks all the way back to Guatemala, where I met with Jean-Philippe and gave him the wheel to Costa Rica: it was an expedition in its own right. We're now back in Costa Rica and, after almost three months off the water, we're anxious and excited about paddling again.

There is no such thing as a tight schedule in Central America. In my time here, I have learned what it means to be flexible. We had hoped to be on the water by the sixth or seventh. Three days late, we are now en route to our planned put-in on the coast.

The northernmost section of the Pacific Coast in Costa Rica is one of the last sparsely developed and truly wild areas of the country. We are trying to go to Playa Blanca on the Santa Elena peninsula, the remote end of the Santa Rosa National Park. It is now dawning on us why these beaches remain so quiet and pristine: visitors really, really have to want to go there. It's not possible without a high-clearance 4X4.

We leave the asphalt and drive for five miles on a dirt road to the town of Cuajiniquil. From there, I would no longer classify it as a "road." We spin through mud bogs, ford two rivers and, four miles later, we drive up to the gate of the national park. The track deteriorates even more once inside the park. It's the onset of the rainy season and the park ranger is hesitant to even let us try!

Even with two kayaks strapped to the roof and a mountain of gear piled in back, we are confident that we have ample clearance on top and bottom to make it. Once through the gate, the view of the road smothers our optimism. The canopy of trees closes inward and downward. A two-foot-deep gorge off to the right, caused by runoff, forces us to the left side. Our speed is, at best, a fast walk.

We have convinced Jean-Philippe's new girlfriend, Yumi—whom he met in Guatemala during the break in the expedition—to be our chauffeur. She will accompany us out to the launch site and then bring the car back to a safe place. To give her a thrill, we let her drive this section. Less than a mile in, the car slides on a muddy embankment and we smack into a tree. The fender is now bent in far enough that it's nearly rubbing on the tire. Without question, we switch drivers. Even with Jean-Philippe at the helm, our progress remains slow. I have to get out every few hundred yards to lift overhanging branches above the kayaks.

Some sections require tricky maneuvers. In places, the track is badly eroded and canted down to the right. Steady rain has begun to fall, creating a slippery layer of mud on the surface. A gorge on the right edge drops away steeply. In order to stay on the road, we have to build up speed, hit the canted section on the far left side and slide, skid, spin and counter-steer to stay as high as possible. Even so, the rear end often comes within inches of dropping off the lip. Jean-Philippe doesn't seem worried, but Yumi cringes and I wonder.

After forty-five minutes, we have progressed only five miles. With only three more to go to the beach, we turn a corner and an obstacle stops us in our tracks. A 100-foot tree has snapped off halfway up and fallen across the road at a steep angle. On the high side, the car with the kayaks is clear. On the low side, even without the boats on top we can't pass. I get out and try to push the trunk high enough to allow the car to pass. It won't budge. We'd need a chainsaw to do anything with this tree.

Foiled by nature, we turn around. Just as we do, the light, steady rain erupts into a downpour. We close the windows and they fog. We turn on the heater and we swelter. Jean-Philippe has to drive with his head out the window, looking down at the road for holes, rocks, roots and slippery patches of clay. I lean out on my side and look for low overhanging branches. Every few minutes, I have to hop out to direct, lift branches or check the depth of a crossing, the stream suddenly brown and engorged from flash flooding. Wet, dirty and pumped up with adrenaline, we are shaking with both worries and laughter. "This is insaaaaane!" Jean-Philippe cackles from the driver's seat as he steers with one hand and wipes a dirty sock over the windshield with the other.

When we return to the ranger station, neither the car nor we are recognizable. Leaves, sticks and bark are twisted in and around the boats and roof rack. The hood is covered. On the lower half of the car, not a bit of the white or tan paint is visible through the red-gray-brown spackle of mud. Smears of clay, scratches, streaks of blood and odd little green Velcro-like balls, the rainforest equivalent of burdock, cover my legs. We are ecstatic to have made it back. So, we get out, give the car an appreciative slap on the hood for its performance, high-five each other and begin chanting its name, "Mon-te-ro! Mon-te-ro!" in front of the confused park ranger.

The jungle has forced us to abandon a small section of our itinerary, yet we are ecstatic. If only misadventure were always so entertaining.

We have yet to unwrap the new boats, let alone get in them and paddle. It is our mission for the day and we will not be denied. In the late afternoon, we reach Playa Flamingo. Hurriedly, we unload and rip the layers of plastic, brown paper and foam packing sheets from the hulls. Even under rainy dark skies, the glossy paint jobs on the boats shine. They're perfect. We paddle around for an hour in the encroaching darkness, getting used to the feel of the new craft. Jean-Philippe points out to the rolling hills of white foam peeling around the rocky point at the northern end of the cove. "I hope these babies are as bombproof as they look. We're gonna be putting them to the test."

↑

Leatherbacks and Strip Development: Playa Grande

Luke, September 2000

We didn't paddle much in September—my SUV broke down the first evening we tried our new kayaks. We barely made it back to the main town, where a mechanic promised to fix it in three days but ended up taking three weeks, requiring us to check on him every other day. So we spent much time hitchhiking and visiting the local surf beaches and national parks.

Development sweeps through Costa Rican coastal communities like tidal waves. The discoveries of tourist-magnetic natural phenomena or the zoning of large hotels in rugged, scenic places are the tectonic events that trigger it. Opportunists blow through tracts of undeveloped land, pulling down trees and eroding the beach to construct so-called "eco-tourism" resort hotels and "environmentally integrated" bungalows. To be fair, some of them are, but nothing is as lovely as virgin beach. Almost all of the land, even the protected national parks, has been taken over, managed, in some form or another.

That same attitude has defined the history of the country over the past century. Other than El Salvador, Costa Rica is the only country in Central America without a significant Indigenous population left. Most groups have been "developed," so to speak—acculturated into mainstream society. The only natives we will see and include in our documentaries here are animals. However, many of those species may no longer exist in a few decades, either.

Playa Grande on the popular Nicoya Peninsula is a perfect example of misguided development. In this case, the irony is that the main attraction may disappear before all the hotels are built. The beach is currently one of the most important nesting sites in the Western Hemisphere for the endangered leatherback turtle, yet over the past ten years, their numbers have been in steady decline.

Although they are the largest and most formidable species of sea turtle, leatherbacks are perhaps the most skittish and choosy. The population that arrives at Playa Grande every year originally chose the spot for several environmental reasons: they liked the shape of the beach and the composition of the sand and water. Those are the few characteristics that biologists have been able to determine with any certainty during thirty years of study. The turtles' behavior and habits have revealed a few other patterns that remain unexplained. There is talk about the turtles' sensitivity to lunar cycles, tides and water temperatures, but it is pure speculation. All will agree however, that they react strongly to light and to humans. The emergence of more hotels exposes them to more of both.

Playa Grande was supposed to be a no-development zone—that was the original law. In a compromise typical of Costa Rica, the allure of tourist dollars caused policy makers to reconsider (read: lucrative kick-backs). Now only the beach itself is a no-development zone. Less than 200 yards back from the beach, lots are selling quickly and more hotels are springing up every season.

In the past few years, the number of nesting turtles has decreased dramatically. It used to be common to see over 100 per night. Now, on a good night, there are only fifteen or twenty, most of which are repeat visitors. Each female turtle will revisit the beach to lay eggs as many as twelve times during the five-month nesting season. Biologists speculate that the overall population of this nesting site may now be less than 100.

Fortunately, the park rangers and police try to compensate for the poor land-use practices. So as not to frighten or disturb the turtles, they strictly limit beach access at night. A licensed guide must accompany all visitors. No more than sixty people may be on the beach at one time and group size is limited to fifteen. At the peak of the season, tourists wait for up to two hours to be admitted and, at the end of the night, all they can take home are memories. Flash photography is strictly prohibited.

Although it is very early in the nesting season and there are few other tourists about, two vigilant policemen yelled at us the other night for using a low-emission, infra-red flash. Initially taken aback at their aggressive reprimand, we realized later that they were right to have made their point so strongly. It is not just the hotels that affect the landscape and the rhythms of Mother Nature; we as tourists can do more harm.

Historically, the biggest threat to turtles has been egg poachers. The "*hueveros*," egg collectors, have a long history of stealing turtle eggs. The traditional markets for the eggs are bars and restaurants in the capital. In Central America, they are considered to be a powerful aphrodisiac. Customers swallow them raw with a dash of Tabasco and/or steak sauce.

Most bars now serve legally harvested ridley turtle eggs from the managed, sustainable harvest program in Ostional, further south. However, leatherback eggs still appear on the black market. The owner of the hotel/bar where we stayed at Playa Grande told us that illegal vendors approach him every week. He tries to make a statement by loudly kicking all of them out, but others inevitably arrive.

For an intimate and moving experience with the leatherbacks, the only time to go is in October and November, before the start of the high season. The Christmas and January crowds are overwhelming. In October, the refuge is not even officially open, but the friendly rangers, unmolested by the hordes, are relaxed and will happily engage in long discussions as they lead you along the beach on a personal tour.

We stumbled out onto the beach to the main entrance at 10:00 p.m. During the high season, there are drink stands, a holding corral and ticket booth to keep crowds under control. On this night, we walked right onto the beach past the empty parking lot. Down the shore, we saw the faint glow of red lights. The only lights they allow on the beach are infra-red, in most cases a flashlight wrapped with a piece of red cellophane.

There is no way to accurately describe the feeling of having intimate contact with a massive animal at its most vulnerable and revealing moment. From a distance, we saw a small group of people surrounding a turtle. In the blackness, we could only see the dark mound of its body. I could hear it before I was able to see it clearly. From ten feet away a loud, geyser-like gasp of exhalation stopped me in my tracks. Once next to her, I was fully able to appreciate her dimensions: at six feet in length and 1,000 pounds in weight, she dwarfed me.

The shell was unlike any I had ever seen. Most turtles have hard chitinous shells, but the leatherback's is soft and pliable like leather, hence the name. Underneath, the thick skin is a frame of bony, longitudinal ribs. The whole carapace has an elongated, cylindrical shape. The flexibility of its body allows it to dive to depths of over 3,000 feet. The leatherback can withstand water pressure that would crush other marine life. Yet by far the most striking characteristics were the sheer size of her head and the texture of her gelatinous, fluid hindquarters. She looked like something from another planet and another time.

It may have been our first and last chance to see one. Marine biologists are in a frenzy, searching for ways to avert extinction. Twenty years ago, the estimated world population of leatherbacks was over 115,000. That figure has decreased by more than seventy percent. Healthy numbers remain in French Guiana and Suriname, but large populations in Malaysia, Sri Lanka, Thailand and some parts of Mexico have disappeared entirely. Playa Grande, even in its current depleted state, is still considered one of the top five nesting sites in the world. Numbers in the 1980s were estimated at over 1,600 females. Two years ago, the figure dropped to less than 220, and this year it may dip below 100.

Fishing, land development and egg poaching are the major factors that affect mortality rates worldwide. Gill nets without turtle-exclusion devices are still used by most of the fishing industry, the leading killer, which takes 1,500 turtles a year. Egg poachers continue to supply the underground market for the legendary aphrodisiac, even in "eco-enlightened" Costa Rica.

Serious studies and preservation efforts are underway but it may be too late. In Playa Grande, Drexel University coordinates with other researchers around the world to track females and protect eggs. I witnessed a group of students and researchers inject departing females with a tiny tracking device. Then they excavated the nests in order to relocate the eggs to managed hatcheries. The studies are producing excellent data on migratory habits and mortality rates. The managed hatcheries produce a much higher yield and the infant young have a higher chance of survival. Nonetheless, numbers continue to decline steadily.

We may be witnessing the last gasp of a species that has survived from the age of dinosaurs. All of its prehistoric peers were killed by the Ice Age or other epic natural disasters. Ironically, the leatherbacks may be swept into extinction by an epic disaster created by man. I would like to believe that what I saw on the beach was the birth of a new consciousness, of a conservation ethic. Yet even the fact that I was there made me part of the enduring problem. The leatherbacks want a quiet, dark beach lit only by the stars and marked only with the footprints of other animals. We humans want the same kind of beach when we go on vacation. That type of real estate is a limited resource these days—and, when it comes to leatherbacks versus greenbacks, we all know which wins.

↑

Playing Hide and Seek with Sea Turtles

Jean-Philippe, 27 October 2000

After launching from Tamarindo, the northernmost beach we could access, we paddled in a few days to a small settlement named Ostional. We stayed there for weeks waiting for a unique natural phenomenon. Although the surf here is spectacular, it is the sea turtles that we've been waiting for. Everyday we take our kayaks through the big surf and paddle just off the Ostional beach, looking for them. Today we saw a lot of reflection from shore, so we might get lucky. I tie my kayak to Luke's, don my freediving equipment and slowly enter the water.

The rainy season is early this year. The swollen rivers in the area discharge sediment into the ocean, turning it into a thick green soup. The water is so murky I can't see five feet ahead of me but I know I am not alone. I raise my head out of the water, wipe some of the algae from my diving mask and spot a dark mass floating sixty feet to my left. I fin over and glide in silently for the final few meters, holding my breath and keeping my legs still. When its two rear flippers are less than a foot ahead of me, I slowly extend my arms to try to make contact. It hasn't even noticed me, so I grab a hold of the shell. My new friend, an olive ridley sea turtle, takes me for a ride after first perusing my face with big, round, eyes. At only three feet long and a little over 100 pounds, it is surprisingly powerful. We swim together, diving and resurfacing for five minutes, and then she returns to her friends.

When I swim back and climb up into the cockpit of the kayak, I see the bobbing shells of turtles all around me. Some of them only come to the surface to breathe for a few seconds before diving again. Most likely, they are feeding on shrimp at the bottom. Others just lie there, floating and paddling lazily against the mild current. Finally, it looks like the major *arivada* might happen any day now.

Ostional is a little hamlet set on a long stretch of black sand beach on the southwest coast of the Nicoya Peninsula. Although not famous for its surf, there are world-class waves here. Amazingly, this place is a well-kept secret among a select few travelers.

In marine biology circles however, Ostional is world-renowned. It is the most important nesting site for olive ridley turtles in the Western Hemisphere. Once a month, throughout the rainy season, over a three-day period, dozens of thousands of turtles crawl ashore to lay their eggs here. The phenomenon is known as an *arivada* or *llegada*, an arrival. At night, the beach becomes so crowded that a person could walk for miles on the backs of turtles without touching sand.

For unknown reasons they have skipped a month. They were supposed to come ashore at this time four weeks ago. Some say that the stormy weather or the lunar cycle is to blame. We can see thousands of them going up and down into the breaking surf, but none are coming to shore. For us, it's yet another long delay. Costa Rica isn't famous for its Indigenous culture. The few groups that have not been exterminated were entirely assimilated and relocated from National Parks, as wildlife is believed to attract more foreign money than culture. The remaining Indigenous people were parked in tiny patches of land and the government made it difficult to get authorization to visit them. We resign ourselves to the fact that for us there would not be much culture to experience and document between the Mosquito Coast and the North of Panama. But the famous wildlife of Costa Rica was our reward and we didn't want to miss the opportunity to experience one of the world's largest sea turtle arrivals. So days became weeks, but we kept waiting, generally patiently and sometimes with frustration, as local biologists argued with old timers about the probable date and reasons for their lateness.

We've been out countless times at night over the past three weeks, waiting and anticipating. We've seen a few turtles on shore, nesting, but nothing that lives up to the hype. One of the old men in the village says that this is the week. He expects it to be the biggest of the season, with over 300,000 turtles flooding the beach.

In Ostional, villagers are usually knowledgeable about the arrival, and they should be, as more than eighty percent of them make a living from the turtles' eggs. In the past, poachers sold as many eggs as they could, without regulation. As a result, the ridley population declined rapidly. Since 1987, biologists have been working with a harvest cooperative. They organize villagers into groups that extract eggs only from the nests of the first two waves of turtles. The third wave they leave in peace. The managed harvest has been an economic boon for the village and the ridley population is stronger than ever.

All last week, we witnessed hatchlings from a previous, small *arivada* emerging from the nests. We were on the beach at dawn each day with our cameras. In the angular morning light, we watched the small, gray bodies dig upward and struggle out of the nest holes like an invasion of army ants. There were hundreds of thousands of them. Many villagers were out on the beach to give them a helping hand. They scared away vultures and dogs and collected bucketfuls of the babies and carried them down to the water's edge. According to biologists, the first few hours are the most crucial period in their lives. Unaided, less than one percent of the estimated fifteen million baby turtles that hatch on this beach each year will make it to adulthood.

This morning, after kayaking and swimming with the turtles for two hours, we return to shore. Since we're not paddling and because there is nothing else for us to do, we spend the rest of the afternoon working on the website. We're staying in the house of a new friend, a cheerful Italian woman, Sylvia. She's one of the few foreigners who live in the area and she's always happy for the company. From her brightly colored, open-walled adobe house high on the bluff overlooking the beach, we have an incredible view. At sunset, we can see the dark bodies of countless turtles suspended in the backlit waves.

Close to midnight as we are about to go to sleep, Louis, one of the group leaders from the harvest cooperative, knocks on the door. "*Ya estan!*" They're here, he says. "*Vamonos.*"

None of the stories we heard prepared us sufficiently for the sight that meets our eyes as we walk on to the beach. The turtles stormed the shores at dusk like an army, and they haven't stopped. There are thousands both coming and going. Onshore, they are writhing around, crawling over each other trying to find an open patch of sand in which to dig. We walk up behind one female to watch. With her rear flippers, she gouges out a two-foot deep hole in the black sand, hunches down over it, and in a series of convulsions, oozes out over 100 eggs. Once she's done, she refills up the hole and packs it down using her body weight. Then, regaining her bearings, she picks her way through the crowd and waddles down toward the water. For two hours we walk around, staring in awe.

We return in the morning when there is enough light to take photos. Although there are fewer turtles, the beach is still full of shells and flailing flippers as far as we can see. The smell is strong, a mix of reptile stench and the whiff of decay from thousands of eggs being upturned and smashed by the new arrivals.

The villagers are already at work extracting eggs. Men shuffle around, pushing into the beach with their heels to feel for less densely packed sand, the sign of a new nest. The women and children follow, digging up the holes and filling large burlap sacks with the eggs. Finally, the young men carry the large sacks to a waiting truck. They throw bags on top of each other without caution. The pliable eggshells can absorb shock and support heavy weight. Other workers then drive the trucks to a collection depot and transfer the bags into storage rooms to be cleaned and repacked over the next two days.

Villagers expect to harvest half a million eggs in two days, less than five percent of the total. The biologist-in-residence tells me that they could easily extract four times more without doing any harm to the turtle population. In great contrast to the leatherbacks at Playa Grande and the green turtles on the Caribbean Coast of Nicaragua, ridleys are thriving here. This program is a model of sustainable use of a resource, the result of a symbiosis of economic development and environmental ethic. It's a shame that we don't see more examples of that in the developing world.

†

Jean-Philippe, 11 – 12 November 2000

It took us less than two weeks—including a four-day break to return to San José, the capital to renew our visas and upload our site—to paddle the rest of the Nicoya Peninsula from Ostional to Manual Antonio, one of Costa Rica's most famous national parks.

After the natural spectacles of the Nicoya peninsula further north—massive turtle arrivals, baby turtles hatching, half-ton leatherbacks, etc.—paddling the rest of the Pacific Coast has been anticlimactic. The beaches and landscapes are less scenic. With more houses, resorts and people, the middle third of the coast is crowded, polluted and hazardous. I am totally unimpressed with the popular but dump-looking beach town of Jaco. Quepos, further south, is worse.

We are wary as we approach the rugged coast with plunging limestone cliffs and lush vegetation. We can't help frowning at the scars that development has left on some of the most spectacular scenery we have seen in Central America. In spite of the crowd, we decide to land on the main beach, and trust the guidebooks. We make our way through the mass of shiny red sunbathers, ferrying all our gear to the court of a luxurious looking hotel. Although we're stretching our budget, we make full use of all the amenities, spending hours showering, lounging at the bar, and calling it a day after gorging ourselves in one of the fancy tourist restaurants.

In the morning, we're the first people waiting in line to purchase our tickets to the park. Considering the experiences we've had over the last few years, we're not sure Manual Antonio will live up to its fame. Before we even walk 200 yards into the park, white capuchin monkeys scream at us as if to warn us we're trespassing. We take a few more steps and a raccoon crosses the trail right in front of us. We can't even walk—coatimundi and squirrel monkeys in the trees, foxes, giant lizards, birds, are everywhere. No cages, no fences—we're not in a zoo. The lush vegetation plays with the rugged coast to provide a perfect habitat for all these species. In spite of all the tourists arriving in the late morning, we can't leave the place and decide to skip lunch. After eight hours walking through and photographing this jewel park, we return to our hotel. Manuel Antonio, with its thickly forested little peninsula teeming with wildlife and its intimate pristine white sand coves hugging the turquoise waters, is a jewel. Our budget doesn't allow us to stay very long and we're looking forward to getting away from the tourist trail and the local hustlers. We move on to a place we know is going to be more challenging: the wild and remote Osa Peninsula.

†

The Osa Peninsula – No Way Out of Paradise

Jean-Philippe, 19 November 2000

A few paddling days from Manual Antonio, the approach to the Osa Peninsula begins on an ominous note. We pass a large river mouth and an outcropping of land called Punta Mala (Point of Evil). Seeing the broad zone of chaotic waves, I can't help but think about how I nearly drowned at the Nicaragua-Costa Rica border. I am tense and jittery for the twenty minutes it takes us to cross through.

For the next twenty miles, we paddle against the current the whole way. Fortunately, the coast is rugged and beautiful. Small patches of sand and clusters of coconut trees lie in the back of small bays encircled by jagged rock gardens and steep cliffs. The view takes our minds off our fatigue. We arrive in the sheltered bay of Punta Violin so tired that it takes us half an hour to realize that we are being eaten alive by mosquitoes.

†

Jean-Philippe, 20 November 2000

After an early start, we pull out around the point and see an uninterrupted, forest-lined coast stretching as far as the eye can see. The eastern shore of the Osa Peninsula is a forest preserve with absolutely no signs of civilization on it. By this evening, we will be two days away from help in any direction if something happens. That becomes more of a concern in the afternoon as we realize that we will not find a sheltered beach to land on. We have no choice but to land through a big shore break onto a steep beach.

Luke goes first while I wait outside the breaking zone. He makes it safely to the beach after some skillful back-paddling to avoid being pounded by two good-sized breakers. He has barely touched the sand when I look back and see a set of rogue waves, much bigger than anything we have seen in the last hour. I paddle out frantically and just clear the lip of the first wave before it breaks. Unfortunately, the next one coming at me is a fifteen-foot monster. I am in serious trouble; I have never been out in waves this size before. Shaped like a mountain, it rises quickly as it approaches. Adrenaline and fear make my heart pump. I know I have to make my arms move faster—it's the end if I don't get over that wall of water. The wave is upon me just as it looks ready to collapse and I push as hard as I can on my paddle, screaming in rage and fear. My kayak climbs up the vertical face of the wave and I can see the crest foaming above my head. I'm sure that I am done for and I close my eyes, expecting the worst as I hear the deafening sound of the tube collapsing on the stern of my kayak.

I feel the boat go airborne and when I open my eyes, only my rudder is still touching water. The crest has passed rapidly under me and I'm falling off the steep backside with an immense splashing sound. I manage to come down and stay upright and, for a moment, I sit frozen in disbelief. But there are two more coming and they look like they could even be larger and thus break sooner, so I paddle hard to get out to deeper water, and barely clear the two massive walls of water.

At this point, I wonder if I will be able to land at all. My timing will have to be perfect. The problem is that now the breaking zone is much longer with waves of different sizes forming and breaking in different places. Luke got lucky with a predictable calm set. I decide to hedge my bets and paddle in on the back of the next big set. A couple of minutes later, it comes. I stroke hard and follow what I think is the last one of the set. Once up to speed, I look back and, to my horror, I realize that it wasn't the last. I'm in the middle of another large set. The first gigantic wave catches up to me and jets me down its face. When its speed dies, it leaves me broadside and I only have a few seconds to straighten my kayak. A look back over my left shoulder reveals a worst-case scenario: two waves coming in at different angles, converging just behind me. The smaller one undercuts the larger one, which rears up into a curl. It catches me just as it begins to collapse. I lean in to brace with all my body weight on the paddle, but it closes on me. There is nothing I can do to prevent capsizing.

Inside the washing machine ride, I focus on keeping a grip on my paddle. Just as I am being ripped from my cockpit, I feel something snap in my left shoulder. I am so pumped with adrenaline that I don't feel any pain. Wave after wave passes over my head; they catch the paddle each time, dragging me by the arm closer to the beach. After one more violent yank, my body suddenly locks up. I can't swim, I can't move and I can barely breathe. I don't understand what is happening to me. I can't even scream. When Luke sees that I am motionless, he runs down the beach. In waist-deep water, he holds on to my kayak and pulls me up, but I can't stand. I collapse over the deck of the half-submerged kayak and ride on it while Luke tows it in. At the water's edge, I roll off onto the sand and lie there in the wave wash.

Luke drags me higher onto the beach and we assess my injuries. There is sharp pain in my left wrist, biceps, shoulder, chest, neck and lower back. My entire upper body is a mess: I am alive but this is serious. We are on a beach in the middle of the Osa Peninsula with no road access and I can't paddle or even move, perhaps for weeks.

Our rescue options look bleak. We have no communication equipment, our emergency marine radios have long melted with salt and, even if we could summon a rescue boat, it wouldn't be able to land through this insane shore break. Fortunately, we have enough painkillers to tranquilize an elephant for a month, because unless we abandon our gear and walk, it may take us that long before we can get out of here.

The Corcovado National Park here on the Osa Peninsula is the most remote and inaccessible stretch of coast in Costa Rica; it's completely wild. According to our map, the closest dirt road is twenty nautical miles away as the crow flies, through pure jungle. There is a small symbol on the map five miles southeast of our location that looks like it could be a cabana, but it is too late in the day to attempt anything. I swallow eight ibuprofen tablets, strap my left arm to my body and lie back to rest while Luke sets up camp.

Once enclosed in our tent to escape the bugs, I am in too much pain to sleep. I toss and turn all night. For hours on end, I listen to the sound of large crabs digging holes around the tent. I can hear the soft clicking and clanking of dozens of hermit crabs crawling through our unwashed cooking gear looking for scraps. In the morning, I'm red-eyed, exhausted and so stiff and sore that I can't even pull my shirt on by myself. I'm totally incapacitated.

While Luke prepares oatmeal, I study the map. We could walk out, but not with two kayaks fully loaded with 300 pounds of gear. And I'm not about to abandon more than $40,000 worth of equipment. Our best option is to try to reach the structure marked on the map five miles away. Out in the middle of the national park, it might be a ranger station.

We wait for low tide and try to pull our kayaks down the beach by walking through the wave wash by shore. In thigh-deep water, it's frustratingly slow. The waves flip the boats numerous times and, with only one arm, it's hopeless for me. I am suffering so much that the pain nauseates me. In an hour, we cover less than a mile so, waterlogged and exhausted, we stop and brainstorm for an alternative. It looks like we will have to leave the boats for a while and take our chances.

Luke anchors the kayaks to coconut trees high on the shore above the high-tide line. I mark our position on the GPS and, with our water bottles and a little food, we set off. We are already tired and the heat of the midday sun takes its toll on us.

After two hours of walking on the scorching sand, we come to a small estuary. There are two canoes tied to mangrove roots. Behind them is a narrow path leading into the thick forest. Ten minutes later we emerge into a clearing to find a big wooden building set at the back of a short plane runway hacked out of the bush. The station turns out to be a jungle lodge run by the national park. We inquire about evacuation options with one of the park rangers and he gives us bad news:

"The only way out is by plane or by foot," he says. "Sometimes boats come into the estuary but we never know when. Most boats have passengers though. And they're too small to carry your kayaks anyway. Doesn't look like they'll fit in a Cessna. So, the only solution would be to charter a helicopter."

I ask Luke what he thinks. But we both know that it's too expensive. Luke says that he will go get the boats and bring them here, paddling one first then walking back to get the second. But after that, who knows?

The park ranger interrupts our conversation. He seems to think that it is not possible to kayak any of this coast. People have come here with kayaks before, he says, but they couldn't get out through the waves. They are too big. The foreigners who tried before had to charter a special boat to evacuate them with their gear. "You won't be able to paddle out to sea from this estuary." I turn to Luke and ask again, "You're confident you can do it alone?" He nods. He looks scared but he knows that we have no other choice.

The walk back to our kayaks is miserable. My cheap sandals have begun to disintegrate and they rub my heels raw. Any skin we leave exposed to the sun burns in the angular light of the afternoon, and the pain in my shoulder is excruciating.

"Are you having fun?" I ask Luke.

"No, I'm fed up."

"So am I," I reply.

I imagine our friends thinking that we are in a tropical paradise, kayaking and enjoying life. The truth is, at the moment, a nine-to-five office job, a hot shower and a good bed would be a dream vacation. Overall, our expedition has been very positive. With the exception of our hellish month in Nicaragua, we are happy to have paddled Central America. But as time passes, our patience for the daily inconveniences and hardships wanes. Month after month, for over two years now, we have endured. And then, when things like this go seriously wrong, it really makes us wonder, *Does it still make sense for us to be out here? Are we just going through the motions to finish it?*

When we arrive back at our campsite, an unwelcome visitor interrupts our conversation. There is a seven-foot crocodile sunbathing on the beach just in front of our boats. I throw a piece of driftwood in his direction and he dashes into the waves. I was so hoping that we wouldn't have to deal with salt-water crocs; they will make Luke's paddle into the estuary even more risky.

After dinner, I lie in bed thinking about our situation. We could leave everything and walk out of here but that's a $40,000 decision that I can't bring myself to make. In the morning, the waves will make it for us.

↑

Jean-Philippe, 21 November 2000

We wake up to the roar of the ocean. At 5:00 a.m., the tide is at its highest point. Out where the waves are breaking, the explosion of the collapsing curls is astonishing. I watch as three shore breaks in a row pile up on the beach creating a sandy wall of foam five feet high that surges up the steep slope almost to our camp. Luke tries to go for a swim but he can't even get close to the water's edge. It is impossible to get out now.

We wait until 8:30 a.m., load Luke's boat and sit on the beach for thirty minutes to evaluate the wave patterns. Huge sets of waves are separated by occasional sets that are slightly smaller. The longest period of calm between the sets lasts for less than thirty seconds. It is not enough time to paddle through the 600-yard wide breaking zone. Again I ask Luke if he is sure about this. He is staring off into space as if meditating, and he repeats over and over, "If I time it right, I can do it." I'm worried. This is by far the biggest shore break that we have ever attempted to launch through. This reminds me of an occasion in Honduras when I was waiting behind the large breakers as Luke was unable to get out—only the waves here are even taller and faster.

Luke sits down in his kayak, closes his spray skirt and gives me the ready signal. I push him out and watch as he punches through the first six waves. He then reaches the middle section of the breaking zone where they are rolling through much stronger. He takes his time, alternately back-paddling to avoid being pulled and crushed into breaking surf and building up speed to pass one monster after another. I see him lose balance on one side, brace quickly and paddle forward out of it. It happens numerous times from one side to the other. Surprisingly, he doesn't flip over.

One wave picks him up and surfs him backward but, with skill and power, he is able to reinitiate some forward momentum while half of his boat is still engulfed in foam. The waves are relentless. Any progress he makes is soon lost as a new set throws him backward.

I stand on the beach screaming encouragement that I know he can't hear, occasionally swearing at the ocean for not giving him any break. Where are the calm zones between sets that we had seen before? He is getting none. He is in a constant struggle. Finally, there is a brief gap and he gets in a dozen hard strokes before a huge rogue set rises up. The first vertical face launches him so high in the air that only the tip of his rudder remains in the water. If he doesn't capsize now, it looks like he has enough momentum to make it. I lose sight of him in the troughs and fear the worst, but two minutes later, I see him bouncing along over the tops of the big swell out in deeper water. He's out.

I realize how much his kayaking skills have improved over the last two years. What I just witnessed is mastery. Few if any would attempt, let alone succeed, in launching through these conditions. As he disappears down the coast, I feel a rush of pride in my expedition partner. Words do little justice to that accomplishment.

I am even more impressed when I see him jogging toward me less than two and a half hours later. He has paddled five miles at an average rate of three knots, pulled his boat up into the bushes and run the full distance back on the beach.

Now the plan is for him to paddle the other kayak to the estuary. From there, we will try to arrange an evacuation on a boat. If not, Luke will have to solo paddle one kayak twenty more miles to the road access at the edge of the park and then hike back and do the same with the other.

With only the use of one arm and in spite of the throbbing pain, I have packed camp, loaded my boat and towed it down the bank. The tide is much lower and the waves are breaking in a much wider zone. It's going to be even more difficult now.

As Luke takes a quick break, we see a man riding a bicycle toward us on the beach. When he is still a few hundred yards off, he finally spots us. Oddly, he stops, dismounts, and pulls on a pair of shorts. We look at each other laughing. He's been riding naked! We're stranded in the middle of nowhere and a nude stranger rides up on a bike?

The man turns out to be the head ranger of the Sirena Ranger Station Lodge that we scoped out yesterday. He was worried and came to see if we were all right.

He looks at the waves and says, "It's impossible." He doesn't understand how Luke was able to get out through such surf. He's more doubtful about his doing it twice but, after trying to lift one end of my kayak, he understands that there is no other option. We can't carry it. He tells us that there is a motorboat docked in the estuary, and that we might be able to catch a ride. We assure him that we'll arrive around 1:00 p.m. and be ready to go. He rides off to notify the boat captain.

A few minutes later, I push Luke into the water for his second launch. His struggle is a replay of this morning. Large waves launch him in the air. He braces from side to side as walls of foam slam him in the face and pass over him. And very slowly he gains ground. However, it is heartbreaking to see a large set surf him in reverse all the way back to shore every couple of minutes. I can see him crumbling with exhaustion. I can sense his frustration. His anger makes him more determined, and he won't give up.

At one point, Luke looks so small that I assume he must be out of the breaking zone but, yet again, a set much larger than any other rears up and takes him out. He capsizes and is ripped out of the cockpit. He has no chance this time. This battle will go to the ocean. Five minutes later he floats back into shore and we drag my flooded kayak out of the shore wash.

Our next idea is for Luke to paddle through the wash in the middle of the smallest breaking zone just next to shore. Luke launches and manages to make decent progress but he is bracing and rolling constantly to stay upright.

We progress a couple of miles but the rising tide is making the conditions worse. The beach becomes steeper and waves begin to dump right on shore. Luke can no longer keep the kayak upright and, after numerous capsizes in shallow water, we pull the boat back on shore.

Fortunately, from here, I spot a mangrove canal that runs parallel to the beach, 150 yards away on the other side of the dune. On the map, it seems to go as far as the Sirena River estuary. With the rope around my one good shoulder, I pull the kayak while Luke pushes from the rear. From the top of the dune, we have to plow through a field of shoulder-high elephant grass and we are sweating and spent when we reach the canal. I leave Luke with the kayak and return to the beach to walk toward the river mouth.

When I arrive at the estuary, I look around and Luke isn't there. I start wading up the brackish river bordered with mangrove. I can't understand why he didn't beat me here; he should have been moving much faster. I continue up through the swamp to look for the canal. When I am waist-deep in the black water, I notice a log moving toward me. It seems strange that it's going against the current. I'm so out of it that it takes me a moment to realize that it is a salt-water crocodile. This one is bigger than the one on the beach yesterday, maybe eight feet or longer. All I can see now are crocs swimming toward me from every direction. I instantly turn around and get out of the water as quickly as I can. From the shore, I see more than a dozen salt-water crocodiles.

Back on the relative safety of the dune, I start to worry and create scenarios. I envision Luke getting the kayak stuck on a log and climbing out and into the river to dislodge it, whereupon he encounters a large angry beast. Where is Luke? What has happened to him?

I walk back over the dune toward the canal. When I see mangroves give way to fields of elephant grass, I realize that the canal doesn't connect to the river. Then I spot him 200 meters off walking toward me. We have to return a mile back to get the kayak out of the river and pull it through the elephant grass back to the ocean side of the dune. Luckily, at that spot the beach is flatter and partially protected by the upcoming point. The waves aren't as powerful. Luke is able to paddle the kayak parallel to the beach, through the wash just a few feet offshore, all the way up to the river mouth.

As he is stroking into the estuary, I see him look down at the small rapids in the river mouth and nearly jump out of his seat. "Holy shit! There are bull sharks and crocs in this river!"

By the time we get to the landing, the motorboat is gone. The head ranger tells us that it was full of tourists. We'd have been out of luck anyway. We are hesitant to leave the kayaks out here unguarded but the ranger says that we shouldn't camp among the crocs. So, we hide the kayaks in the woods and spend an hour ferrying all our important gear the half-mile through the woods to the lodge. For six dollars, the bunk bed and showers suddenly seem like affordable luxuries. Besides, the boat evacuation is no longer an option and we need at least one day of rest in the lodge to work on our alternative exit plan.

Luck smiles on us during dinner. We meet a group of four couples traveling together. Two in the group, Morten and his girlfriend, Tatum, from South Africa, are both whitewater rafting and kayaking guides. Morten has had a lot of experience paddling in the surf of South Africa. I ask him if he would be willing to paddle my kayak out to the park entrance with Luke. He seems pleased to switch places with me, especially when he gestures to his huge backpack that I will have to carry.

In the morning I numb myself with a handful of ibuprofen, shoulder his pack and join the group trekking out to the road access. Morten seems eager to tackle the waves with Luke. I wish them both the best of luck. As with many of the most beautiful, remote places in the world, there's only one way out of paradise, and it's rough.

Fortunately, there was no sign of the seven bull sharks we had spotted the evening before and the waves were smaller and manageable. For a day, Morten figuratively put himself into my shoes while I literally put myself into his. My sandals broken, I had to borrow his hiking boots to make the twenty-kilometer walk through soft sandy beach and thickly forested trail.

Thanks to Luke and Morten, my gear and I made it out of the Osa Peninsula, thus finishing our paddle of Costa Rica. Resting our bodies will allow us to catch up on computer, writing and photo-editing work.

This last section of Costa Rica was a humbling experience for me. I realized how much I've come to depend on Luke's partnership and friendship for an expedition that I had originally planned as a solo adventure. Over time, Luke and I have had our highs and lows with conflicting personalities, but every time it came down to it, one of us was there to save the other one's life. Our trust in each other was unconditional and so is our friendship. With only Panama left to paddle, we knew that no more bandits, storms or injuries could stop us. We had made it too far not to be able to finish it. But a forced few months of rest I spent in Panama among native Embera and Wounaan people made me realize that the end of this expedition would only be the beginning for me. My goal was not to paddle from Mexico to Panama—this was only the means to achieve my true goal. My mission is to make people aware of the beauty of Indigenous cultures and to inspire people as much as Jacques Cousteau inspired me as a child. My goal is to make a difference.

For days I wondered, *Have we really made a difference so far? Will reaching Panama advance the cause I believe in?* Probably not. Our website has become popular amongst kayakers and adventure seekers, but we could capitalize on our adventure to accomplish much more. I spent the next months designing a new website that would no longer focus on the expedition, but rather use it as a vehicle to promote the preservation of Indigenous cultures. I realized I could not stop there. Panama couldn't possibly be the end. Luke and I agreed to rename our project Native Planet, and to continue to run it as a non-profit organization even after we returned to our respective lives. Luke would continue to write our journal entries in Panama, while I would focus on the development of our new site and on promoting local efforts to help Indigenous communities. I was certain that our cultural documentaries would appeal to a broad audience and entice people to extend a hand and help in their own way. Before it ended, CASKE2000 became the project that launched Native Planet. When I felt ready to paddle again, I sat in my kayak with a new vision. After nearly three years, paddling and camping on tropical beaches had long ago lost its original exotic attraction—now it had become a meditative state in which I could plan the future of Native Planet. The expedition was no longer about Panama; this journey had already taken us far beyond that.

CHAPTER 7

PANAMA

Introduction

Jean-Philippe, 30 January 2001

IT TOOK A couple of months for my shoulder to heal, time that I used to design a new website for Native Planet. I knew when planning CASKE2000 that unknown people receive no help—they vanish as silently as they have lived. It seemed then that this kayak expedition would shed sufficient light on native peoples' lives to introduce them to the rest of the world; now it is obvious that a lifetime probably won't be enough to do it. My skills and experience, accrued over the last twenty years, will facilitate my becoming an ambassador for traditional people: Native Planet will strive to educate people, making them more conscious of the plight of Indigenous peoples, their cultures and their lands.

We have been paddling both the coasts and jungles of Central America for the last three years but we still haven't found exactly what we were looking for. Each country presented its own challenge while offering us new cultural insights, but what I had wanted most was to spend time with and document the lifestyles of Indigenous peoples, especially those who had preserved their culture and could still survive in the jungle as their ancestors did. I was hoping to find people who had not yet been entirely assimilated by Latino culture and Christianity. In that respect, Belize, Honduras, Nicaragua and Costa Rica were disappointing. Guatemala has kept some of its colorful culture, but the Maya people, in contrast to all the other communities we have visited, now live and farm in the mountains instead of hunting and gathering in the jungle as their ancestors did. Panama was our last remaining hope. We had heard of the "primitive" Kuna, Embera and Wounaan peoples who lived south of the capital and planned to spend our last months visiting isolated villages in search of people still close to their roots.

Luke and I rejoined each other at the end of January, anxious to resume our paddling, but we could not wander off too far for weeks as we were on call to join a trip led by Scott Muller. A dual citizen of Panama and the United Sates, Scott is an Olympic whitewater paddler, an environmental policy maker/lobbyist and a guide for Mountain Travel Sobek. When he's not guiding, he works closely with a Kuna non-profit organization called Osiskun; together they are creating a marine preserve in the Kuna Yala that will host various research facilities and serve as an ecotourism attraction. He has spent years cultivating a relationship with the notoriously wary Kuna congress and the tour that he runs for Mountain Travel Sobek is the only authorized kayaking trip in the entire Kuna archipelago, better known as the San Blas Islands.

The Kuna are fiercely independent and proud people; in the 1920s, they gained autonomous control of their homeland, a long string of 350 gorgeous islands along the Caribbean Coast. They are very strict with visitors. A few islands run official lodges endorsed by the Kuna congress and several others allow only day visits from cruise ships and sailboats. Tourists may enter villages during daylight hours but overnight stays are not permitted (except for guests in official lodges). After spending the first two weeks on Scott's tour, we hoped to continue paddling the Kuna islands on our own, led by his best native guide. I am now officially desperate to leave modernization far behind.

War body paintings and loincloths were the first things I learned about the inhabitants of the Darien jungle of Panama. Further research revealed that the Embera and Wounaan people in the jungle live primarily from their traditional fishing, fruit collection and hunting with blowpipes and poisonous darts. Despite the fact that research on this destination provided very little information, it promised to be one of the expedition's highlights. Of course the very dearth of facts raised my curiosity even more. Numerous books are available on the Kuna people but the Wounaan and Embera, who lived a semi-nomadic lifestyle until late this century, have managed to escape much of the influence of the modern world.

We would go to the Darien later when we had more time, but for now, Embera Drua, a traditional Embera settlement not far from the capital, seemed a perfect opportunity for us to escape the metropolis.

↑

Embera Drua, Jewel of the Upper Rio Chagres

Jean-Philippe, 2 – 9 February 2001

Panama is best known for the canal and the fast-growing, cosmopolitan Panama City. Most people, including nationals, remain unaware that less than two hours from the booming city, people still live in houses made of logs or bamboo. Embera Drua, located on the Upper Chagres River, the main source of water for the canal, is less than an hour's drive from Panama City. A large lake providing the main reserve for the canal marks the limits of the adjoining national park. There, we unload our old foldable kayaks for the last time and start paddling toward the river's mouth.

Wild ducks and white egrets abound and fish jump all around our boats. The entrance into the river is graced with the first Embera community. Children playing in the water wave to us. We paddle close by to return their greetings and notice that their bodies are covered with black, tattoo-like designs. The dark ink is made with the extracted juice of the *jagua* fruit and then boiled before the Embera and Wounaan use it to paint their bodies. Although *jagua* painting is inky black initially, it completely disappears in less than three weeks, allowing people of all ages to regularly change the designs on their faces and bodies; each design has a cultural or spiritual meaning, specific ones for each age category.

We paddle up the river, snaking its way through the dense jungle as the muddy shores slowly give way to granite cliffs covered with dense vegetation. Small beaches appear, large stones sprinkle the river offering good diving platforms and the water becomes incredibly clear. After a couple of hours, we have to fight strong currents and wonder how a motorboat could travel on such a shallow river. Thinking there could be no villages upstream of some of the rapids we had just dragged our kayaks through, we almost decide to turn back but suddenly hear the roaring of an engine. A long *piragua*, a local canoe dug out of a single tree, makes its way downstream, its eight local passengers wave at us, beaming with large smiles. We resume our paddling upstream for another hour and land on a beach from which we can see houses hanging more than 100 feet up the riverbank. Their location in a turn of the river is idyllic with a large, deep, crystal pool between two rapids that host numerous fish.

Walking up the steps dug into the riverbanks, we hear the drums and flutes and wonder if we are dreaming. After a brief walk through the center of the village, made of elevated stilt houses, we follow the music up to the large communal house. The women dance, wearing only fabric loincloths beneath vibrant *paloma* skirts and thick necklaces of beads and coins. Their ebony hair gleams in the sunshine as they clap and sway and stomp and dip, faces intense with concentration. They are surrounded by a half-circle of men dressed in loincloths, dyed all the vivid colors of the tropics, a riot of oranges, yellows and blues. The men are playing bamboo flutes and various percussion instruments including a turtle shell. A half-dozen tourists were taking photos and listening to village history tales and about the plants used to make the *canastas*, splendid baskets woven so tightly they can hold water. A man greets us and tells us the village chief will be with us shortly. We stroll around while waiting, in awe of the more than 180-degree view overlooking the river and surrounding jungle. The only concrete building is a school constructed by the government.

First, we meet with Emerildo Amagara, the second to the *noko* or village chief. Emerildo, the village jeweler born in the Darien of Colombia, had lost a leg in an accident during the construction of a large boat. He shows us how to melt coins such as quarters and dimes, and forge them into various shapes to make the necklaces so prized by Embera people. We then meet the *noko* and Johnson and Harris, the two people coordinating the small cultural ecotourism program that provides the only possible revenue for the village. The two men, both in their late twenties, go out of their way to make us feel welcome in their community. I explain that we want to make a documentary on their village, culture and daily lives that could promote their tourism efforts in the process.

Embera Drua, like other communities within the boundaries of the Chagres National Park, was founded before the park even existed. The Panamanian government has proven to be one of the best and most sensitive to the needs of its Indigenous citizens and has rarely relocated people. Nevertheless, when establishing the Chagres National Park, they applied new rules that choked the life out of the village. Villagers are no longer allowed to cut trees or produce any food for sale to outsiders and their usage of all-natural resources is limited to village needs. The government doesn't provide the higher education many Indigenous people seek or even basic medical assistance. In addition, their proximity to Panama City and regular visits from outsiders drives a desire for city products including soap, sugar, salt, rice and flashlights.

Johnson explained that the village had been struggling for a long time; many young people have left for the capital hoping to find work but most end up jobless and living in ghettos, instead. The villagers have revived their culture and use it to attract tourists: for a small fee, they perform their songs and dances hoping to sell their *canasta* weavings or intricate carvings made from wood and nuts. A few ecotour companies, lured by the beauty of the site and culture, the friendliness of the people and the ease of access from the capital, have seized the opportunity and make the two-hour trip to the village when they can gather a group of tourists.

The tourism profit is shared between all families participating in the project as well as being used for communal needs such as building a large boat or a house and buying motors. The craft revenues go directly to the artists. There are a handful of church followers who, influenced by the priests' ban on traditional clothing and opposition to reviving traditional songs and dances, choose to not participate.

Luke and I are impressed by Embera Drua's plans, organization and by how harmoniously the villagers work together toward their common goal. It is completely unlike what we had seen in Las Marias, where some families were left out of the ecotourism projects. Here, we had finally found real ecotourism: a project initiated by the village itself that serves the entire community in one way or another. People who do not entertain the tourists sell sodas or other goods in their small shops and the village is cleaned daily and well kept. This is a project that, having revived the old ways, now protects the culture, a project that reinforces the cultural pride of children and teenagers. We like it, we like the village and we like the people.

One day, we go downriver with a large motorized dugout, a small *piragua* and two expert fishermen, Harris and Melesio, who demonstrate their skills with a fixed line baited with *espave*, a type of nut that fish mistake for a sardine. Then, standing on the tippy *piragua* or walking knee-deep in the current of the river, they fish with a long spear. They tell us that today's young people prefer to dive, especially at night, with a pole spear as it often yields more fish in less time. Emberas' skills as boatmen are best seen when a man paddles down or poles up a rapid while standing on a dugout *piragua*.

Then we walk in the jungle in search of *chungas*, the palm fronds whose fibers are used to weave their *canastas*. Twenty-year old Hannibal is a climbing expert but a thick layer of ten-inch long thorns protects the *chungas* trees. To get to them, the climber must cut a narrow tree, set one end on top of the palm, climb on that tree and cut palms with a machete. Sometimes, without warning, the bees and wasps nesting in the trees also deny access to them. When we return, Gerardina, the leader of the women's community here, sticks one palm leaf between her toes and trims off both razor-sharp edges. Not careful enough, I cut my hand as I move some of the palm around to take a better photo. Gerardina dries some of the fibers and dyes others with various natural colors. Naturally a yellowish white, boiling fibers with *achiote* fruit colors them orange, pieces of *cocobolo* bark dye turn the fiber brown and *yukiya* roots make them yellow.

Achiote is also used to dye the skin and ancestral tribes from the Amazon covered their body with it to protect themselves against insect bites. The Yagua people (some of whom I'd met while on one of the expedition's breaks) were the most famous users of achiote; notorious for smearing thick layers all over their faces, they were nicknamed "redskins" by surrounding tribes.

Another day, we take a short walk in the jungle with Celenio, a botanist and one of the oldest men who had escaped from the guerilla-laden Darien of Colombia, to find this peaceful place to found a village. He looks like a fierce warrior with his full body covered with black *jagua* dye up to his upper lip. He teaches us trapping techniques, points out the vines we can drink water from and some of the fruits we can eat.

He tells me that you can't die of hunger if you get lost in the Darien. Pointing at a palm tree, he explains, "This tree grows everywhere and you can easily cut it down to eat its heart." After a few machete strokes, we eat the tender, sweet center; the couple of layers directly around it are also edible, though bitter. After drinking from a vine, our survival master teaches us how to catch a deer or kill a *gibnut*, a small rodent that makes a delicious dinner. Learning how to set up a temporary camp, we lay wide leaves between the roots of a giant tree and roof it with palm fronds. Celenio has already warned us that you never really sleep in the jungle because you have to keep an eye out for *el tigre*, the local name for jaguars. On our way back to the village, Celenio also tells us that people in Panama no longer use blowpipes because rifles are more efficient.

After a week together, sharing numerous stories, we knew that the Embera had a lot more potential: we wanted to help them dig deeper into their culture. It seemed that the elders could teach the younger generation skills from their past to turn their ecotourism project from a half-day of activities to several days. Forced to return to Panama for now, Johnson and I plan my return to Embera Drua before the end of the expedition.

↑

Landing in the Kuna Yala: El Tigre Island

Luke, 10 March 2001

The plane wobbles and then punches out of the bank of clouds. Below us, dozens of tiny islands lie sprinkled off the mainland shore. From my perspective at 6,000 feet, it looks as if I could use them as stepping-stones and walk all the way to Colombia without getting my feet wet. Our four-passenger Cessna is stuffed with equipment: the two disassembled Feathercraft kayaks, tent, sleeping mats, tarps, cooking gear, medical kit, five Pelican cases full of photo and computer gear and a mountain of food. We have reached the cargo weight limit for the plane so I'm worried about a short-field landing.

Wind currents and updrafts toss the plane around as we fly. Although neither the pilot nor Jean-Philippe, also a small aircraft pilot, seem worried, it feels to me as if we have no more control over our direction than dandelion fluff in a gale. And, when we swing down and approach the islands, I worry even more. They're all too tiny to land a plane on.

El Tigre appears in front of us and we circle around the far side to line up with the runway. Unfortunately, the community built the asphalt strip without considering the prevailing wind patterns. It blows at such an angle to the runway that we have to glide in at minimal airspeed, facing into the wind, and then perform a "crab landing." At the last instant, the pilot straightens out the plane and we touch down. I am amazed that the Cessna needs less than 200 yards to land.

A small patch of palm trees and three thatched cabanas just off the runway are the base camp for Scott and his tour group. We are eager to explore the island but habit takes over and we unload and set up before doing anything else. After nearly three years, our routine is automatic: we set up the boats, sort and repack the gear in dry bags, divide it all into two equal loads, erect the tent and organize the cooking station. It is early afternoon by the time we get a tour of the village.

In Kuna communities, visitors must follow rigid protocols. We are all *waga*, outsiders, but still subject to all local laws. Our first priority is an audience with the *sayla*, the senior chief, in the communal meeting-house. He lies in a hammock strung from the rafters in a central clearing; lesser chiefs sit on benches surrounding him and we all crowd onto a single open bench directly across from him. Scott and Nemessio, his best Kuna guide, explain the purpose of our tour. Individually, we introduce ourselves to the chief, shake his hand and receive a slight nod of recognition. He's old, frail and as stoic as a statue. We can't tell if he is overwhelmed or unimpressed. Neither his eyes nor his shriveled, elfin features give anything away, yet there is a very powerful energy in the room that makes us feel self-conscious and uncomfortable. We don't know if we should smile or remain serious.

The lesser chiefs explain to us that the Kuna were once feared warriors who dominated the Embera and other Indigenous tribes in the area. Even the strong-arm tactics of the Spanish, and later the Panamanian government, failed to subdue them. In a quick and bloody strike in February of 1925, the Kuna gained their independence from the young Panamanian government and they have just celebrated the seventy-sixth anniversary of the Kuna revolution. Ever since then, the Kuna Yala has been an autonomous province, with representation in the national congress. Once again, the *sayla* nods wisely and says nothing.

I marvel at the organization and strategic thinking that the Kuna have put into the establishment of their nation and the preservation of their way of life. Most people know this area as the San Blas Archipelago and are familiar with the beautiful *molas* (brightly colored, reverse-appliqué textiles) made by the Kuna women, but that's about it.

There are no roads into the Kuna Yala (the land of the Kuna) and there is very little police or military presence. Visitors must fly or sail in and they do so only on the Kunas' terms. Independent of the Panamanian government, they control all the tangible resources including land, fish, coconuts, water and food. They also regulate the intangible resources; they are well aware of the value of their culture as a tourist attraction and even charge visitors who want to take photos of their faces. It's only fair—the Kuna are consummate business people.

Scott and Nemessio add to the information we have read in books. For the past 500 years, the Kuna Yala, as the San Blas Islands are now officially known, has been the homeland of the Kuna people. They migrated from the Darien jungle area of eastern Panama and western Colombia at about the same time as the arrival of the first Spanish conquistadors. Among other Indigenous groups in Panama, they have a reputation as strong warriors, intelligent strategists and fiercely proud, independent people. During the eighteenth and nineteenth centuries, the island archipelago was a stopping place for trading ships and pirates, all of whom bartered for fish and coconuts from the Kuna. The Spanish trade routes bringing gold from the Peruvian Andes on the Pacific side crossed mainland Panama just east of the Kuna Yala, thus bringing more and more traffic—and attention—to the area. In turn, this regular military presence in the Kuna Yala generated more and more resentment among the Kuna.

When Panama gained its independence from Colombia, the Panamanian government tried to maintain control of the Kuna Yala. Additional missionaries and military police were sent to Kuna communities, agitating the Kuna political, cultural and spiritual leaders and setting the stage for insurgency. The Kuna congress secretly contacted the American government to request that the American military act as a watchdog over their independence movement. The Americans agreed and parked a destroyer off of the archipelago. The Kuna congress planned the revolution to coincide with *carnaval*, knowing that the resident soldiers would be incapacitated by drink. In swift attacks beginning in El Tigre and continuing along the archipelago, they killed or captured all the Panamanian soldiers and declared their independence. Since then, the Kuna Yala has been an autonomous *comarca*, a department, of the Republic of Panama.

As we retire for the night, we are overcome by a very powerful feeling that we are outsiders, privileged visitors here on their terms and not welcome any deeper. It's the Kuna Yala, the land of the Kuna. Nobody tells them what to do with it and it's going to stay that way.

↑

Out of This World: Nubesibudup Island

Luke, 19 March 2001

Nubesibudup. The name sounds like a big hiccup and a burp. The language of the Kuna is full of p´s, b´s, o´s and u´s, like nothing I have ever heard. In the past few days we have paddled around and camped on islands with names like Ogopsibudup, Esnatupile and Chichirtupu. Luckily, many Kunas speak Spanish and by now we're nearly fluent.

It's much hotter here than I imagined; if not for the wind, we would fry. Sunrise forces us out of bed in the morning and by 7:00 a.m., the tents are saunas. By 9:30, we are looking for shady spots out of the heat and by noon, we are sitting in the shade on the windward side of the island to take advantage of the cooling Caribbean trade winds.

Our week's paddling with the members of Scott's tour has been very relaxed; with only a couple of exceptions, they aren't fit, experienced kayakers. A motorized wooden skiff, the gear boat, follows the group, so

Jean-Philippe and I are paddling empty boats, something we haven't done in the three years since our training in Thailand.

So far, we have met only a few Kuna families and we're anxious to get started with our documentary work. The folks on the tour came to paddle a tropical island paradise and get a little dose of culture. It's quite the opposite for us. It's sad to realize that we've had more than enough of the beautiful turquoise waters, coconut palms and secluded, breezy isles. What we want is to spend time with the people.

Most of the islands we pass are uninhabited and the Kuna use them as coconut farms. The caretakers spend a few days each month out on these islands, gathering coconuts and fishing. If they see us land, they come out to say hello, collect a "user's fee" of one dollar per person and try to sell us *molas*. They are friendly but there is no mistaking that they are smart and aggressive business people.

In the afternoon we have a very lucky encounter with two fishermen. They see our kayaks on the beach and head toward us in their typical wooden sailing canoe: the hull is carved from a solid length of tree trunk and the sail is a triangle of cloth spread between two long sticks. Even though the boat seems heavily loaded, it moves with surprising ease. They have been diving along the reef most of the day and have a boat full of treasures. We drool as we look in and Scott and Nemessio begin negotiations to purchase our dinner. Five minutes later, we are carrying a trio of king crabs and a large barracuda back to our campsite. The legs of the crabs are nearly two feet long.

One of the young sons of the caretaker family climbs a palm to get coconuts. Much to the surprise of the guests on the tour, Jean-Philippe matches him on the neighboring tree. We cook rice in pure coconut juice and boil the crabs in seawater and then sit down for a feast with our hosts as the sun sets over the mainland. Dinner is a frenzy of self-indulgence: people are ripping open shells, pulling out the meat and splattering themselves with the juices. The *wagas* are happy.

Nemessio ends the evening with a story from Kuna mythology about the celestial origins of the traditional *mola* art. In many Kuna tales, there are references to extraterrestrial visits; this story tells of one of the most important.

Four women from the stars visit the Kuna Yala and are taken captive by four brothers. The three eldest women escape, but the youngest and most beautiful one can't get away. After a while, she and the youngest brother fall in love and marry. Because of her alien origin, she possesses great skills and artistry with textiles and embroidery and becomes the creator and the original teacher of *mola* textile art.

Our buddy Eric, the CEO of Panama City Bank whom we met in Embera Drua, acts as interpreter for the group and brings the whole story to life. In his New York accent he spins a masterful tale, loosely translating and embellishing Nemessio's words. We head to our tents, full of good food and laughter.

↑

Headwinds, High Cheek Bones and Hammocks: Mulatupu Island

Luke, 26 March 2001

All our paddling in the Kuna Yala has been very easy. UNTIL TODAY! We said goodbye to the tour group a few days ago and continued moving west through the archipelago. The wind comes from the east this time of year and, for the past two weeks, it has provided a nice tailwind. Now that we are against it, though, we truly feel its power. We have made promises to Nemessio and Vicente and to their families, so we must return eastward to their villages of Carti and Mulatupu. Plus, those might prove to be our only opportunities to do any documentary work. So far, most of the Kuna communities have been completely uncooperative. No money, no photos; one photo, one dollar. They don't see the value in what we're trying to do with our website.

We stroke away from the protected backside of the island in the late morning. Our tardy departure is our first mistake. The wind is softer around dawn; we should have left then. At 11:00 a.m. it is honking, right in our faces. I turn toward Jean-Philippe, "Can't we just stay here today?" Little whitecaps break over the bows of our kayaks and the spray coats our faces. In the opposite direction, fishermen in their *cayucos* under full sail head home after a full morning of work. They nod and give us a look of pity as if to say, *Poor dumb* wagas. Hours later we arrive in Mulatupu.

Vicente's family is ready for us. Vicente's mom, his two aunts, four sisters and grandmother are all lean and long-limbed with high cheek-bones and angular features. They are a fiesta of colors in their best *mola* blouses, red and yellow bandanas and leg wrappings of woven beads. Over a period of an hour and a half, we take ten rolls of film of them at work carrying water, pressing juice from sugar cane, sewing *molas* and cooking. The picture of the day is of Vicente's eighty-five-year-old great-grandmother. Wearing the brightest, most delicately sewn *mola* of them all, she sits on a stump peeling yucca root and smoking a pipe. Her leathery face is creased with deep lines. She looks up at us and shakes her head, incredulous that anyone would want to take photos of her.

We will sleep in the house of Nemessio's sister on Carti, the neighboring island, so we leave Mulatupu in the late afternoon. From afar, Carti looks densely packed with houses. When we arrive, we realize that it is beyond crowded: nearly 4,000 people live on an island less than 300 yards long! They have extended the shoreline outward with mounds of dead coral and dirt brought from the mainland. And, with the exception of narrow paths for walking and a couple of small gathering areas, there isn't a spot without a structure.

Family and community are very important to the Kuna and they sacrifice a lot of comfort for them. The average household is eight to ten people and they all sleep in hammocks strung up next to each other, so there is very little privacy. Jean-Philippe and I are fortunate to have our own room (something that I have to remind myself of as we get ready for bed, for it is not a comfortable accommodation). We suspend our hammocks from the rafters, leave our sandals down on the dirt floor and wriggle around trying to get situated. Just then, a rainsquall hammers the tin roof and little rivers of water seep in through the gaps in the bamboo wall. I need sleep badly but it looks like it's going to be a long night.

↑

Leaving the Land of the Kuna: Carti

Luke, 31 March 2001

For the past few days, we have slept in hammocks in Nemessio's sister's house. My entire body hurts and I am exhausted. The one night in the past week that we paddled out to an island to visit a family and camp, I slept like a baby on my inflated mat. Anyone over six feet tall will sleep better sitting up in a chair than in one of the tiny Kuna hammocks. It's impossible to find a position where your body lies flat. I sag, toss, turn and my lower back stiffens up so badly that I can barely move in the morning. Each morning I roll out of the hammock and whine to Jean-Philippe to open the bottle of ibuprofen. I take four with my morning coffee.

Every day I am more impressed with the pride and independence of these people. Things that I have read in histories and anthropological accounts now resonate strongly. We have a chance for a conversation with a Kuna spiritual leader about religion. Missionaries from various Christian denominations have been here for a long time. Most Kuna have tried various churches yet few have remained converts. Currently popular is a hybrid faith, a big spiritual compromise: a combination of Kuna mythology and some Catholic traditions. The Kuna have their own saints, their own spirits and a God they call the Great Father Spirit. They even have their own Bible.

We sit on the balcony listening for hours to a ninety-year-old man's thoughts on the world and the Kunas' place in it. He has been all over the States, Europe and Asia as a deck hand on merchant ships. He has studied Islam, Buddhism, Judaism and all facets of Christianity. He speaks flawless English in addition to Kuna and Spanish and he is currently studying French. And although he speaks wistfully about his many journeys, both physical and spiritual, there is no place he'd rather be than the Kuna Yala.

In the afternoon, we paddle around the island to take a break from the stifling heat. Life is harder than we thought it would be in these villages; we never imagined that they would be so densely packed. No breezes blow through the interior and we sweat and accumulate a patina of dust on our skin just from walking on the dirt paths. Unlike the community offshore of the graveyard that we visited the other day, there is no running water here in Carti. They bring it over in big barrels from the mainland. There is not enough for people to wash themselves every day and many have skin rashes and small lingering infections.

There are no gardens on the island, so all the food must be brought in as well. As a result, the cuisine lacks diversity. The occasional bits of fish are nice but I am nearing insanity on this diet of rice, beans and plantain. Yet for me, waste disposal is an even bigger issue. There is no such thing as a septic system here. In our twenty-minute trip around the island, we count over 200 latrines built on docks out over the water. Where can all that waste possibly go? The fish can only eat so much. I have to hold my tongue when I see kids frolicking in the water by the docks. Needless to say, when we want to swim we go out to the deserted islands a couple of miles away.

Generally the Kuna are friendly and curious but their suspicion of outsiders underlies everything in their society. A week ago, on the island of Maquina, home of one of the most traditional communities in the area, we made a proposal to the *sayla* to do a photo shoot in the village. We explained the purpose of our documentaries and how we intended to promote Kuna culture and local ecotourism. With very little deliberation he denied our request. His response was, "Kuna culture is not for outsiders to take and teach to other outsiders. It is ours."

Part of me respects that attitude. They live as they want to live and are economically independent. It's patronizing of us to think that we are here to help them. The other part of me wonders why they don't see the value of sending a message to a much broader audience, why it wouldn't appeal to their sense of cultural pride. Jean-Philippe echoes my sentiment. So, without expending any more effort, we pack up the foldable boats and reserve two spots on tomorrow's flight.

We have some paddling to do and our hard-shell Kevlar kayaks await us. From the western border of Panama we will continue where we left off after the Costa Rica leg: the big waves of the Pacific await us.

↑

Watch Your Step in a Banana Republic: Puerto Armuelles

Luke, 18 April 2001

After spending a couple of weeks compiling the stories of our Kuna trip at Eric's place, a beautiful apartment in the highest luxury building overlooking the beaches lining the capital, we return north close to the border of Costa Rica.

"We've just pulled into a banana republic and the waters are surprisingly calm."

A civil engineer may have made the same comment 100 years ago upon arriving in Panama to assist in the design and digging of the "Big Ditch." He steps off the steamer and—expecting endless malarial jungle—makes that remark while strolling through the colonial charm of the Casco Viejo sector of Panama City. However, this time it's coming out of my mouth as I stand on the beach by the docks in Puerto Armuelles on Panama's far western border. And this time it's not a metaphor, it's based on personal observation. Here in Armuelles a geographical quirk, a long arcing cape, protects a busy harbor from the angry Pacific surf and the docks are awash in bananas. In these parts, there is no other economy.

The needle-thin cape juts out from the coastline just at the point where Costa Rica and Panama meet. On the map it looks as if a cartographer extended the demarcation line out into the ocean. The difference in water conditions from the Costa Rica side to the Panama side is remarkable. Most days you could water-ski here in the bay of Puerto Armuelles.

Banana prices are down these days so the area is experiencing a depression. So are we as we scout around for a decent place to sleep. For many miles, the beach is developed. There are no quiet, out-of-the-way spots for us to camp. It doesn't feel safe to be in a tent while unemployed and unhappy youth wander about but we have little luck finding a cheap hotel.

Fortunately, we are mobile: my aging Montero SUV is still with us. When I drove it down to deliver the new kayaks last fall, I looked at the car as yet another lost investment. Already burning oil and haunted by poltergeists in the electrical system, it was on its last legs. Miraculously though, we've been able to keep it going although at this point, the car is a liability. This morning we will have to befriend some local and find a place to leave it for a few weeks. If it is stolen or damaged, there is no insurance to cover it. Any arrangements we can make will be based on little more than good faith.

Eventually we spy a white-walled compound that turns out to be a love hotel. By the hour or by the night, it's the same price. Business is slow and the evening caretaker cuts us a deal. For the price of one room plus a little tip, we each get our own. I am so tired that I don't pay attention to the layout of the room. It's only upon waking up in the morning that I look around. The bed is a thin mattress set upon a three-foot-high concrete island in the center of the room—Fantasy Island. Thinking about the uncountable trysts that have occurred in this room makes me cringe. The shower stall is constructed of painted cinder blocks. A pipe protrudes from one of the walls and from it dribbles an anemic stream of tepid water. I get up, shower and step outside at almost the same instant as Jean-Philippe next door. We look at each other and laugh. *"Que romantico, no?"*

We find the nearest beach access in a poor residential neighborhood. It's 7:00 a.m. and already a large matronly woman and her young daughter are out working in the yard. Their house of concrete block and corrugated tin is modest but immaculate. They gesture to a narrow turn off across the street where I can park my car. *"Muy tranquilo aqui,"* a very peaceful place, they assure me.

As we unload, they begin to sweep up leaves and brush into a great pile and burn it. The wind shifts often and plumes of acrid smoke, smelling like burning hair and rubber, drift over to our spot on the beach. They watch us pack the kayaks and smile encouragingly, but the smoke is nauseating. I want to ask them to wait until we've departed to continue burning but I hold my tongue and work as quickly as possible. After an hour-long eternity, we drag the boats to the water's edge. The thought of food makes my stomach churn; I stow what we brought in the deck bags in hopes that my appetite will return later. I am lightheaded as we shove off into the lapping swell.

In the breezy hot weather, my condition improves over the first hour. We leave the busy shoreline of Puerto Armuelles behind and head toward the opposite side of the bay. Rows of houses give way to open stretches of dunes and cultivated fields. After another hour, all we see is empty beach and fallow farmland, wild and overgrown with head-high grasses. We are completely alone.

The water conditions change drastically as we paddle further, putting us more and more on edge. We are no longer in the lee of the cape. Now, seven-foot swell passes underneath us, thrusting us skyward. The size of the waves and the shape of the beach worry us; the shore drops steeply away from the edge of the dune into deep water. The waves, with no shallows to slow them down, come in at full speed and rear up abruptly before pounding the beach. Thick masses of foam rush part way up the steep slope, hover briefly and then retreat, sucking driftwood logs and great quantities of sand back down into the water. It's a clear day and for miles we can see two-story high clouds of mist hovering above the shore, glinting in the sun. By now we've paddled seventeen or eighteen miles and we are tired, frustrated and afraid. Jean-Philippe looks at me and I make the decision to land. I can't go much further.

To land in these conditions is insane. There is no more difficult technical maneuver in all of sea kayaking than landing on a steep beach with a huge shore break. We wait offshore for twenty minutes to study the wave sets and judge the timing of our move. After a set passes, there is a fifteen-second window before the next one arrives. In that amount of time, we have to make it through the breaking zone, hit the shore and pull our boats up high enough to avoid the crush and foamy vacuum of the next set. I was fatigued and dead in the water fifteen minutes ago but now, as I count the waves to time my entry, I am twitching with adrenaline.

A massive set passes and Jean-Philippe makes the move; I follow instantly. Due to the deep water, the breaking zone is mercifully short. We paddle madly toward the foaming beach to overcome the powerful undertow from the receding waves. Jean-Philippe is slightly ahead of me and to my right, separated by what appears to be a safe distance. I have no concept of time and have not looked behind me; my eyes are glued to the beach. Jean-Philippe hits the shore and in a smooth motion rips off the spray skirt and hops out, an impeccable and masterful landing. I am less than two seconds behind him, but I make the mistake of stealing a glance backward. A nine-foot vertical wall of water is about to pounce but I still have a chance to make it. I tear off the spray skirt and dive out of my cockpit. My foot gets caught on the coaming and I fall over backwards. The wave thunders onto the stern of my kayak and I yell as it envelops me, "Shiiiiiiiiiit!" Jean-Philippe is already pulling his boat up and, when he hears me, he whips around. He's too late. The wave wash tosses my kayak up the beach like a driftwood twig, right toward him. The eighteen-foot boat filled with gear, sand and water must weigh over 500 pounds. I see it career into the back of his legs just as I am enveloped in foam.

I am shocked to see him pop back up. We both recover quickly and, pumped with adrenaline and fear, we haul the boats up as high as we can and collapse at the edge of the dune. It is only then that we pause to assess the damage. From high on the dune looking out, our perspective of the waves leaves us agape. We'd have continued paddling all night if we had known it was this bad; we had never landed through anything like this, and might not be able to launch from here for days. It would be impossible to punch through this two-story high wall and suicidal to even try. We're extremely lucky to have come out with our gear and bodies intact. And as we sit staring, frozen, the adrenaline rush wears off. Jean-Philippe stands up and, screaming in pain, drops back down to his knees. There is something wrong with his ankle.

The joint looks as if it has been inflated with air and above it, the skin is gone leaving ragged and bloody flesh. It's too swollen to determine if it is bruised, sprained or broken. We are in the middle of nowhere, eighteen miles from town and who knows how many miles from the road and unable to escape via the sea.

With no other alternatives immediately obvious, we reluctantly set up camp. It's the middle of the day and the sun is blazing so we flatten out a spot on the top of the dune, dig holes for driftwood posts and string up the tarp to create some shade. By this time, Jean-Philippe is in extreme pain. He immobilizes himself and props his leg up to try to reduce the swelling.

According to the map, evacuation looks nearly impossible. Twelve miles of farmland and a maze of tractor trails separate us from the main road and civilization. We debate our options. I could conceivably walk out to the main road to get help but chances are that I would get hopelessly lost on the farm roads. We could wait until tomorrow and see if Jean-Philippe's leg allows him to paddle. Or, to ensure that I don't get lost, I could walk back on the beach twenty-five miles to Puerto Armuelles and summon help from there. As we weigh the pros and cons of each, something way off in one of the fields catches our attention.

A flock of gulls and smaller birds hover in the sky above a cloud of dust that is moving slowly in our direction. I wade through the head-high bramble of grasses separating the dune from the farm field to check it out. Eventually, a large tractor pulling a mulcher and a plow comes into view. I jog toward it and the driver nearly falls out of his seat when he sees me.

I explain our situation and, although he's curious, I don't think he believes me. He puts the tractor into low gear and points it straight through the high grasses and up the steep dune. He nearly runs over the stern of my kayak before he sees the campsite. Shaking his head in bemused disbelief, he gestures toward the trailer. In fifteen minutes we break down camp, pile the kayaks and bags on top of the plow and lash everything down. The only space for us to sit is on top of the wheel wells on either side of the cab. So situated, we head off, bumping and clawing our way through the half-plowed field. It takes us an hour and a half before we arrive at the first sign of civilization: a cluster of houses and a well-traveled dirt road. After compensating our local savior with thirty dollars and sending him home with a huge smile on his face, I'm optimistic that we'll be in a motel in a couple hours and at the clinic to get Jean-Philippe's ankle examined in the morning.

I leave Jean-Philippe and the gear in the shade of a crumbling bus shelter and hitch a ride from the first passing car. I plan to return with the truck to pick him up. As I climb in, my mind wanders, looking for a way to justify such a random sequence of events.

In the remote frontiers of developing countries, life is filled with endless inconveniences and mishaps. Yet many of them, through a string of minor miracles, are somehow resolved. Daily, we witness the balanced push and pull of luck and fate. When the calm waters reared up and smote us, leaving us broken on the sandy margins of abandoned cropland, a helpful farmer ended up as our hero. Although I feel bad about being the cause of this accident, I have to laugh about it. Two kayakers slip and fall in banana land and are rescued by a tractor. It's okay to make light of our situation. We've had our quotient of trouble for the day. What else could possibly go awry?

↑

Bumping into the Legacy of Noriega: Dusty Back Roads, Western Panama

Luke, 19 April 2001

I'm stuffed into the back seat of an ancient Toyota Corolla with two young boys; a young farmer and his wife are up front. Somehow this car has survived since the 1970s. On the exterior, it's impossible to discern where bondo ends and sheet metal begins; the entire thing has been frosted like a cake with a thick layer of white house paint. The suspension is non-existent. In place of the original cushioning, the seats have been stuffed with old rags and chunks of mattress foam and someone has tried to re-upholster them by hand. What's left of the cloth ceiling hangs down in tattered streamers from raw metal. The two boys next to me pick at it, ripping off little pieces of rotting fabric and throwing it at each other like confetti. The farmer must be somewhat of a mechanical magician, for the engine is purring but his disregard for the rest of the car is evident in his driving style. The chassis feels as if it is going to disintegrate as he blasts along the rutted country road. Initially grateful for the ride, I am now extremely uncomfortable. As it turns out, the bus stop from which I started is in the middle of nowhere. It takes us forty-five minutes to get out to the main road.

It's just after dusk when I unfold my cramped legs and crawl out of the back seat. I offer profuse thanks and a few moist dollars to the family. They gesture to a concrete shelter on the opposite side of the road and tell me I can wait there for a bus.

Twenty minutes later I slump down into a seat next to a pretty local girl who, surprisingly, offers me a smile. I smile back. The joke is on her: she hasn't smelled me yet. In the dim light, she can't see the grime on my face or the salt and sweat encrusted on my clothes. Fortunately the windows are open. As the bus rumbles along at sixty miles an hour, the howling wind kills both my stench and any possibility for embarrassing conversation.

It's a twenty-five-mile ride to the border, a transfer and another twenty-mile ride out onto the cape to Puerto Armuelles, where our vehicle is parked. I am dehydrated and starving and my night is far from over. Yet, compared to what Jean-Philippe is up against at that very moment, my ordeal is a joyride.

After I hop in the Toyota, Jean-Philippe lounges among the dry bags on the side of the road with his injured foot propped up on his kayak. He hopes to take a nap and while away the hours in peace but he is rudely interrupted.

If there is anything that Latin America has demonstrated in the last 100 years, it is that it is not possible to make a clean break from the violent legacy of dictatorships. The power mongers who embezzled the country's soul and savings have mostly vanished but the poor brutes they hired as enforcers are still lurking. Idle, disenfranchised and struggling with the anonymity of peasant-hood, many can be found in the most out-of-the-way places—including the isolated roadside where Jean-Philippe meets a pair of Noriega's former henchmen.

A faded red sedan with blown-out windows and knock-kneed alignment rattles past, stops and backs up. Two men eye the kayaks and the mounds of gear. Seeing that Jean-Philippe is alone, they decide to get out. One is massive, a real-life caricature straight out of a comic book or a Rambo movie. They can see that Jean-Philippe is not a small guy either. Fortunately, as it's now dusk and he's lying down, they can't see that he's badly injured. They start asking suggestive questions, as if probing for soft spots.

"What are you doing out here by yourself? Aren't you afraid something might happen to you? What's in all the bags? How much is that stuff worth? Where are you from?"

Jean-Philippe senses that it would not be wise to let on that he is an American citizen. "I'm French," he says. He then explains about the kayaking expedition and how we are well-known adventurers. To avoid the subject of monetary value, he tells them that we have received all the equipment from sponsors so we don't know its worth.

They downplay their current careers as part-time fishermen and farmers; they are clearly not happy with their lot in life. They had been soldiers, henchmen with regular salaries and fearsome identities. Now they have nothing. Out of nowhere they glare at Jean-Philippe and ask him a question that condenses the clammy tension he has felt all along, "How do you feel about Noriega?" Unconsciously, Jean-Philippe flexes his muscles and readies himself for potential confrontation.

From an early age as a new kid in the schoolyard, Jean-Philippe had learned that the best defense is a strong offense. Training in the French Special Forces reinforced that idea. Fortunately, his world travels in adulthood have tempered that philosophy with more sensitivity and sensibility. He now relies almost entirely on smiles and powerful rhetoric to solve potential conflicts; however, if a situation escalates, he has the confidence that he can back it up with physical strength.

"There are some bad people out here," they say. "For example, what would you do if a couple of guys attacked you and tried to take your gear?" Jean-Philippe launches into an explanation of the hand-to-hand, vital-points combat training he received in the Special Forces. With extreme effort, he pushes himself up and, trying not to grimace in pain, demonstrates a few techniques: a deft jab of the thumb toward the eye, a thrust toward the jugular and a short flurry of backhanded punches toward the groin and face. The expressions on their faces immediately shift and soften. The tight creases in the corners of their eyes are replaced by wide-eyed respect and curiosity and the situation is defused. Jean-Philippe uncoils and they spend the next hour talking.

The two men secretly hope for another military uprising or the emergence of a police state. The peaceful democracy that has come to Panama in the past decade since the dissolution of the Noriega regime has not brought prosperity to all. The economy has become regionalized. Banking and shipping fuel Panama City. Large-scale agriculture bolsters some of the western towns. And fishing drives many coastal communities. But for those in the outlying regions, there is little to smile about. As soldiers for Noriega, their daily necessities were taken care of and they received regular, albeit small, pay. And perhaps most importantly they tasted power and notoriety. As fishermen and farmers, they feel emasculated.

By the time I return, the men are long gone. Jean-Philippe has been sitting alone in complete darkness for four hours. It's after 10:30 p.m. and he has passed through the worry stage. No longer expecting me, he is rummaging through the gear to set up camp when I arrive. When he sees me, he tips his head back and sighs, "Ooooh, yeah." The look of relief on his face makes me laugh. Without care or concern, we indiscriminately throw bags of gear into the back of the SUV. You know you are exhausted when thousands of dollars' worth of gear becomes of no more concern to you than a sack of potatoes. I think to myself that I now know what it is like to be an airport baggage handler.

Jean-Philippe's ankle is so stiff he can barely put his foot down and it is a struggle to lift the boats onto the roof. Every shift and loss of balance makes him wince. I tie the boats down while he collapses in the front seat, tilts it back, puts his foot up on the dash and begins to moan.

I am so exhausted that all my senses seem to be processing information in slow motion. The soft roar of the tires on the gravelly dirt road, the occasional muffled ping of a stone bouncing off the undercarriage, the trilled "chee, chee, chee" of crickets and the moans of my injured partner all reach my ears with a liquid sibilance. Dust billowing up from the dry road coats the headlights and creates distorted halos. I don't know what guides me, but we pull into a hotel at midnight without further incident.

The night clerk doesn't know what to say when he sees us. I see his mouth start to form questions but he hesitates, says nothing and hands over the keys. "*Es una historia muy larga,*" I say and indeed it is a very long story. I'd have to go back nearly three years and 3,000 miles to give the guy enough perspective to truly understand. We must look like bedraggled prisoners of war. "*Es la culpa de Noriega,*" I say, half sarcastically. He nods as if he agrees that it must be Noriega's fault.

†

Jean-Philippe, 20 – 27 April 2001

After a long day's drive, we finally reach Panama and head straight to the hospital for X-rays. My leg is not broken, just badly sprained and I am told that I will have to stay on crutches for two months. It's impossible; I have to be able to walk within two weeks, I tell them. After patching the missing pieces of skin, one of the doctors puts me into a brace and says, "This is the best stuff, new technology from the U.S. and you will be able to put your foot down in a couple of weeks and walk with this. But you have to wait two weeks before you do that." Unable to walk, and stuck in the capital, I decide to use this time to extend my political circle. Marianella, an anthropologist, Minister of Indigenous Affairs, friend of the republic's president and an acquaintance of Eric's, introduces me to various anthropologists and Indigenous congress leaders.

We have been waiting for weeks for an authorization from the Kuna government to document a puberty ceremony, the most powerful symbol of the Kuna's strong hold on their culture. Back in town, I meet the Kuna political leader in a restaurant but leave at the end of the meal with no hope of being able to do further work with the Kuna people. I greatly respect their pride, their power to retain their political autonomy and their strong battles for their rights and I understand that they probably do not need much outside help. I am only disappointed because I believe that a good documentary of their culture could be used as a model to inspire other ethnic groups around the world. Their neighbors, Embera and Wounaan people, have recently unified and organized themselves politically in an attempt to receive more government assistance and better defend their human and land title rights.

The next day, I meet Arsenio, one of their most esteemed shamans, who had also been the *cacique nacional*, first supreme chief of the unified Embera and Wounaan people. Arsenio needs to return to Darien; a few people from his natal village have called for his healing powers. It's only been a week since my accident but I can no longer bear sitting around. I decide to throw my crutches away and offer Arsenio a ride to the Darien. Luke will drive and Arsenio will take us to Embera Puru and the nearby villages of Arimae and Puerto Lara. I quickly organize the full trip and return to Eric's place to tell Luke we're leaving the next day at 5:00 a.m. To my great surprise, my girlfriend Yumi, who has been traveling on her own in neighboring countries, arrives just in time to join us.

↑

Jean-Philippe, 28 April – 12 May 2001

We pick Arsenio up at 5:30 a.m. and in less than half an hour, we are cutting through the forest on the only road going south. An hour drive brings us to the end of the asphalt road where it gives way to dust, bumps and potholes.

We have heard horror stories about the danger of Darien. The danger is real, especially a few hours from the Colombian border where guerrillas often escape from Colombian regular armies. Killings and kidnappings of Panamanians and foreigners sometimes happen in frontier villages, but most places in Darien are still relatively safe. We were also warned of the very thorough paper and vehicle checks by the police but find most control points to be painless. Driving on the Pan-American dirt road, we are shocked to see that the lush jungle we heard so much about has been replaced with cattle pasture, the prime forest has disappeared and trucks blast by us hauling giant tropical tree logs.

When we arrive in Embera Puru, we discover a poor village with people struggling to survive on what is left of their rainforest. Arsenio tells us, "When I was a boy, people ate primarily from hunting and fruit picking. Thirty years ago, wild boars and deer were coming into the village every day. Today we have nothing to hunt, so we survive from our *fincas*, small subsistence farms. The problem is that, like most jungle land, once burned and exploited for a couple of years, it becomes useless. The road brought my people closer to modernization. Now they have easy access to the capital, but are no longer able to live from the forest and it has forced them into farming. The road also provides access to our lands for poor *campesinos* from other regions who also come and burn large parts of the rainforest to plant their own crops and raise cattle. Even though we are now politically organized, the road is already here and, apart from a small school, we receive no subsidies from Panama."

Embera Puru doesn't have the charm of Embera Drua and, realistically, no tourism potential but the few families living here touch our hearts. Living from nothing with nothing, they host us and refuse our money. They welcome us to stay with them even while we go to the surrounding villages to document more of the culture and, on our last day, they prepare a ceremony for us: after painting their children's bodies with *jagua*, the youngsters dance to the rhythm of snakeskin drums.

When we arrive in the neighboring village of Arimae, we are welcomed with one of these interminable meetings during which Luke often almost falls asleep. Coming with Arsenio, we are important guests. Everyone introduces himself and states his position in the village, then I introduce myself as the president of our NGO and explain the whys and hows of our desire to document their culture and daily lives. The gathering lasts six hours and Yumi is forced to elbow Luke repeatedly to keep him awake. With the protocol attended to, the entire population of 400 people works hard to accommodate our needs. They understand that with a permanent page on the Internet, they will have greater media exposure and a better chance to receive help from other NGOs, governments or individuals.

They might even be able to sell more crafts and receive more tourists; we hope to be able to accomplish at least that with Native Planet.

A small part of the population of Arimae is Wounaan. The Embera and Wounaan had unified into a single Indigenous group, but they separated a few years ago because the Wounaan people, not as numerous, felt that their Embera neighbors were assimilating them. In reality, the cultures are very similar and, to us, the people look the same but they still speak distinctive languages. An anthropologist in Panama later told me that *canasta* weaving was originally a Wounaan art. Embera people were warriors while the Wounaan were crafters. Today, both tribes practice the same craftsmanship and the Wounaan community of Puerto Lara is one of the best villages to experience their art. Arsenio guides us there. He has healed members of every family of this village and is highly respected. Arsenio starts explaining what we can offer to the village. After a couple of hours of discussion, I am finally called upon to speak. Quickly able to show them that our intentions aren't to violate their lands or culture, people applaud and all the volunteers who want to participate in our documentary project suddenly overwhelm us. We learn that the village is well organized: there is a specific manager for positions as diverse as education, agriculture, fishing, crafting, women's activities, housing, etc. Each manager will be responsible for organizing our photo shoots and replying to our questions.

Throughout the next few days, we immerse ourselves in the local culture. People extract the juice of sugar cane with a press they call a *trapiche*. We drink some of the juice and the rest is used to make *miel* by slow cooking over a fire until the juice transforms into a type of honey. This *miel* is served on top of our fish, rice and *patacones* (fried slices of plantain). People show us the construction of a dugout canoe and women introduce us to their amazing woven art. We admire the most beautiful basket weavings we have ever seen; some pieces take up to a year to complete and the village is sometimes able to sell one to a museum for more than $1,000.

Puerto Lara is far enough from the road that it retains some of its charm and the rainforest around it is still intact. Like many other Indigenous groups around the world, Wounaan villagers plant one tree for each tree they use. Here, they have also planted many species such as the tropical *cocobolo*, which they use for sculpting and building houses.

People in the village tell us about their ecotourism plan and we agree that the village, its surroundings and especially the culture it has retained have good potential for an ecotour project. Michel, a Franco-Panamanian man, is already helping the villagers develop a small but sound ecotourism program that benefits all of the families.

In Puerto Lara, *jagua* is not painted on people's bodies just to please tourists; it is still an art and the intricacy of the designs is amazing. So amazing that after two weeks in the Darien, they are talking us into being painted. Yumi is the first subject. She sits half-naked as Ernestina Valencia, a young expert in jagua design, applies the black dye with a bamboo stick. The native design does not spare her breasts. Luke is next, painted by two women. When my turn comes, Valencia spends nearly an hour covering my body with geometric designs. Although now we look almost native to the village, it is our last day and we're taking the road back to Panama tomorrow.

After naming me the godfather of the community, leaders ask when we will return to visit. It's hard to promise when there are still so many villages to visit and document, but Puerto Lara was our fourth village from the Embera and Wounaan communities and each time we left one, we felt we were leaving family.

Back to the city we return to Eric's suite wearing short-sleeve shirts exposing our body paintings. Judging from the looks we receive by the luxury hotel staff, we must look like a gang of Japanese *yakuza* (gangsters). We shock the rich crowd even more when we enter the pool. Eric, for his part, is envious not to have been able to be part of this cultural journey.

✝

Jean-Philippe, 13 – 15 May 2001

Back in town, I meet with Blas Quintaro, a close friend of Marianella's. Blas, an anthropologist, manages an NGO that works on various agriculture projects to help the Ngobe people in Chiriki, north of Panama. Blas makes a few phone calls; we'll meet a man from his NGO not far from the Costa Rican border in three days.

I spend the last day in town and call Michel, the French guide. We use the day together to discuss the needs the Pan-American logging road has created for the people of Puerto Lara and the potential of their eco-tourism program. A few weeks later, it is with great sadness that we learn from Michel that, a week after our visit, some *campesinos* moved in close to Puerto Lara. To gain land to grow new crops, they cleared the land by burning the existing forest, destroying the *cocobolo* trees and medicinal plants planted by the Wounaan villagers. Since most Indigenous villagers have no title to the land of their ancestors, they have no rights and anyone can utilize those unprotected "government" lands at will. Here as almost everywhere else, they have no means of recourse.

✝

Jean-Philippe, 16 – 27 May 2001

We are spending ten days with two Ngobe communities. In the mountain village of Soloy, we visit the small coffee plantations where people sell the beans they raise for a tenth of the price paid at the town cooperative. In Playa Zapote, on the ocean side, a few Ngobe families have set up a semi-permanent camp to extract salt from the ocean the way their ancestors have for centuries. We watch the process: filtration through nets filled with layers of sand, evaporation done by boiling the seawater in large half-cut oil drums and then the drying process that can take several weeks more. Unable to afford salt, Ngobe people produce it primarily for their own consumption but sometimes sell or trade their surplus for other basic supplies.

↑

Panama: Puerto Armuelles to Cambutal

Luke, 29 May 2001

We are returning to Palo Verde, where six weeks ago I could have died in the shore-break capsize that nearly broke Jean-Philippe's leg. I'm apprehensive: we took a long break and haven't paddled rough oceans in months. Apart from paddling short distances in the protected waters of San Blas and the river to Embera Drua and, with the exception of our last accident here, the last time we paddled through rough seas was back in southern Costa Rica six months ago. There, Jean-Philippe dislocated his shoulder and ripped muscles in his chest in the waves. Today he is not his usual chatty, exuberant self either; he must also be worried.

↑

Jean-Philippe, 1 June 2001

After paddling on both coasts of most of Central America, including the beautiful San Blas archipelago, we have very low expectations for the rest of the Panamanian Pacific Coast. It just feels like it will be a boring stretch we need to get through somehow, but we are pleasantly surprised when we reach Isla Parida. Small beaches covered in sun-bleached sand are lined with coconut trees and separated by miniature rock formations. Turquoise water runs between them, and the crystalline surf offers excellent snorkeling. Seduced by nature's beauty, we decide to stay an extra day. We spend most of it in the water.

↑

Jean-Philippe, 10 June 2001

It takes us a week to paddle from Isla Parida to Santa Catalina. Except for the strong surf we find in places, this itinerary is boring me. It is not so much the paddling that I resent because it helps me think; it is a form of meditation for me. It is the daily routine that I have grown tired of: getting up in the dark and swallowing the same crunchy, sand-coated breakfast for the last three years. Packing stinky clothes into dry bags and loading and unloading kayaks. Sleeping on a thin mat and sharing a tiny tent with Luke, smelling each other's stench and being devoured by bugs anyway. Our frustration builds up and bubbles over, resulting in daily quarrels over ridiculous things. Luke can't help but think that if we had only paddled continuously, the expedition would have been finished over a year ago. I, on the other hand, now enjoy the time we spend in Indigenous communities much more than what we spend camping on each beach. Without the kayaking and beach-camping elements, I could do this for years.

Since Baja, kayaking had been more than a means of transportation to reach Indigenous villages, it had been our life. But today, with only a few miles left to finish, I feel it is now hindering the real mission of the expedition. We have spent a lot of time with the Kuna, Embera-Wounaan and Ngobe people but haven't yet taken the time to document any of it. We must do it without delay or else we'll lose both precious memories and the ability to convey them as they should be communicated.

↑

Luke, 21 June 2001

Our strokes are back to their metronomic rhythms. I slip so deeply into a meditative state that I often don't notice Jean-Philippe signaling me. He gets exasperated; I am ambivalent about his complaints. We are back to our old roles, still helpless to change them. Jean-Philippe is preoccupied with the website and presentation of our documentary work on the Embera, Wounaan and Ngobe villages. He's worried that we have all this raw material on hold and that the longer we delay its organization and writing, the more we will lose. When we reach Cambutal, we have only three weeks of paddling left to finish the expedition. But we both agree that not only do we need to consolidate our notes into real documentaries and update our new Native Planet site, we both need our own space and a change of landscape. I return to the States for a much-needed break, while Jean-Philippe stays in Latin America to compile all the documentaries.

↑

Jean-Philippe, 1 September 2001

After more than two months off the water, Luke and I meet back in Panama City; we drive from there to the east coast to retrieve our kayaks and equipment that have been stored in the garage of Michel's beach house. We drive back to Playa Cambutal to launch from where we last paddled our kayaks. Luke arrives from the U.S., while I have just returned from South America. I had completed our web pages after returning to Embera Drua for a week. Afterward, Yumi and I traveled through Columbia, Ecuador, Peru and down the Amazon to Brazil and Venezuela. I am now convinced that simply paddling into Panama City won't fulfill my thirst for accomplishment. We need to paddle the last stretch to fulfill this expedition, but for me the real journey of documenting everything to help Indigenous people will begin only after we reach the capital and send all our gear back to the U.S.

↑

Back in Action: Playa Cambutal, Azuero Peninsula

Luke, 14 September 2001

It is a long haul out to this town at the end of the Azuero Peninsula. The road to the beach is cracked, parched and dusty. By the end of the day, my throat feels the same. In the midday heat, when I breathe through my nose to avoid choking on the dust, my nostrils sear as if in a sauna. During the dry season, the Azuero Peninsula becomes a semi-arid desert. Over the last few miles of driving, before the beach comes into sight, my pulse quickens. Black vultures wheel in the sky over the desiccated carcass of a cow. Wispy reeds and thigh-high grasses, burnt and bleached by the sun, rattle in a stiff wind. Crumpled brown leaves scurry like rats across the road.

I distract myself with these observations on purpose: I'm apprehensive. We took a long break and haven't paddled in months. We arrive mid-morning and I look out to check the tide and I see that we already face a dilemma. Unfortunately, low tide is between 10:00 and 10:30 a.m., about the same time that the morning winds pick up. We'd hoped to be finishing our paddling about now yet what greets our eyes is a 300-yard portage from the water line to the high tide mark. Scattered throughout are clusters of large rocks, like teeth, waiting to chew up our kayaks. I look at Jean-Philippe. "Plan B?" "Departure just after first light so that we can see to clear the surf break, then three to three and a half hours paddling, max. We don't make that carry each day," Jean-Philippe says.

We watch the winds and currents increase throughout the day; an early departure and short paddle are the only option. There will be no more ten-hour days, no more marathon sessions, battling through malnourishment and dehydration. We watched our bodies melt away in

Nicaragua and we won't do that again. We'll assess the conditions and climate and adapt rather than struggle on.

For now, there is no rain and, mercifully, no insects. Our adversaries are the wind, surf and heat. As we did in Baja, we'll move in the cool margins of the day, find shade to escape the heat and progress steadily. This is the home stretch—in three weeks we will be at the "finish line" in Panama City.

⇡

Pastoral by Day, but by Night the City Beckons: Nueva Gorgona

Luke, 1 October 2001

In many ways the tiny protected cove and fish camp of Nueva Gorgona is an oasis, one we're delighted to reach after paddling ten days from Candlemas. Space at the west end has been carved out of mangrove swamp for a few huts and cabanas, a small parking area and a beach for launching the boats. For many miles east and west of Nueva Gorgona, the beachfront is developed. Houses, exclusive day resorts and restaurants, are interspersed among open stretches of lightly forested field. In contrast to their neighbors, the few families here in Nueva Gorgona make a living the way Panamanians used to, from the sea.

For the two days prior to arrival in Nueva Gorgona, we moved through an evolving landscape. Playa Blanca, Playa Santa Clara and Playa Rio Mar were new, clean little developments built along manicured access roads off the Pan-Am Highway. Most beachfront was taken up by private houses and the only semi-public access points were the day resorts, complete with loud stereos and beach umbrellas. Visitors to those places must pay to park and camping is usually not permitted. We stopped for meals in a few of those places, but made a point to continue on elsewhere.

In the heat of mid-morning, against the pull of the ebb tide, we stroke into the tiny inlet to see a vision from Panama's past. The name "*panama*" means "plenty of fish." Although the fisheries aren't what they used to be, apparently this community still believes in the ideal: its entire existence is based on fish. Narrow wooden *lanchas*—their paint peeling and faded, gunwales gouged and pitted—bounce in slight chop. Some of them lie keeled over, beached by the low tide. Huge mounds of fishing nets, buoys and lines lie in the shade of trees higher on shore and pickup trucks, parked adjacent to the trees, smell of their cargo. Up close, I can see them dripping bloody brine onto the hot sand. A couple of dozen fishermen and their families sit on benches in open-air huts, drinking sodas and listening to the tinny wail of merengue on old radios. A pack of young kids, naked but for tattered undergarments, frolic in the water, jumping and diving from the idle boats.

Except for a few children, nobody even blinks when we pull up. It's not that we feel unwelcome, but they seem oblivious to or ambivalent about our arrival. I sense that they must feel the same way about progress, modern development and the passage of years. Time stands still in this little cove; I can't imagine that much has changed in the last four decades.

Jean-Philippe and I are not used to this kind of blasé reaction. The oddity of our expedition and our fully outfitted kayaks usually make us instant celebrities upon arrival in a small village. Everybody wants to try the boats; everybody wants to look at the equipment. We spend at least a couple hours explaining who we are, what we do, where we came from, what all the gear is and so forth and so on. Here in Nueva Gorgona, nobody asks us a thing. I go to buy a *pargo rojo* (red snapper) for dinner and I steel myself for the onslaught of curious questioning. Nothing happens. It is just a matter-of-fact transaction to them. We set up camp, cook dinner and go to sleep with little more interaction.

Dulled by the inactivity of the day before, my senses are unprepared for what we encounter after our pre-dawn launch. We are on our way before 5:00 a.m. and we paddle out of the cove in total darkness. For an hour we move along the coast then a dull glow appears off to the east; we assume it's the sun. I check my watch and it's too early to be the sunrise. As we approach a low stretch of land, off in the distance, the skyline of Panama City appears out of nowhere. Along the waterfront, there are a dozen buildings of more than forty stories. Lit up, they form an electric bar graph that pushes upward to various heights from the flat axis of the shoreline. Having spent the previous day in a wrinkle of time decades in the past, it takes our breath away. We stop paddling for a few minutes to just stare.

I imagine this wave of surprise is the first of a large set that will wash over us during the four days it will take us to actually reach the Bay of Panama and the Canal Zone. It's hard to reconcile passing through a pastoral fishing village one day and surfing the wake of a supertanker under the Bridge of the Americas the next.

†

Into the Canal Zone: Arrival in Panama City

Luke, 5 October 2001

The Bay of Panama is a grand sight. Paddling toward Balboa and the outskirts of the city, the view changes with the time of day. During daylight hours, we can't see the city until we're within fifteen miles as a soft haze makes it impossible to see that far. What we do see are the islands. The biggest and most historically important is Taboga and its hills and towering forest canopy draw our eyes to it immediately. Pizarro, the Spanish conquistador, used the bountiful hardwoods from its forest to build ships and the island became the base from which he sailed south to conquer the Inca Empire of Peru.

Thoughts of history and nature fade with the sunset as the sparkling skyline of the most modern city in Central America dominates the night sky. The waterfront is the most developed zone of the city. Compared to the small coastal towns and villages that we have seen in the past three years, it is both surprising and beautiful.

The ten-square-mile area around the mouth of the Canal Zone is full of cargo ships, all waiting their turn. From near the shore looking out, it looks like a naval blockade. Our destination is Playa Veracruz, on the western side of the canal over the bridge from Panama City. It's a surprise to find a clean, white sand beach so close to the city. We have the good fortune to arrive on a quiet weekday. This beach is the hotspot on the weekend for the young crowd: thousands of cars pack the parking lots, and the endless strip of eateries and bars hums with activity and thumps to the cacophonous beat of competing car stereos. It is mercifully calm this morning.

We're ready for a soft bed and cold drinks. Viva Panama!

↑

Turbulence and Resolution

As I joined Jean-Philippe in the planning of CASKE 2000, one of my most preoccupying concerns was enlisting the moral support of my family and friends. Once they grasped the full scope of the trip and gauged our determination to go through with it, many grappled with conflicted notions about what it means to be loving and supportive. Following Jean-Philippe's example, I made it clear to all that I was not asking for approval; I was going regardless. What I needed was for everyone to stand by me and to join us in spirit. Even if their support was lip service only, I needed it.

Most kept their reservations to themselves. Some veiled their concerns in humor. Some grilled us about our preparation, wanting to make sure that we had all angles covered before lending their support. A few, namely our respective grandparents, had no qualms about expressing their dissent.

Generally though, the support overwhelmed us. Jean-Philippe's father, Alain, and his girlfriend Viviane, were excited at the prospect of meeting us at various points along the way. My parents and my sister proudly told everyone they met about our grand adventure. And all of Jean-Philippe's friends from Seattle were enthusiastic about his permanent quest for adventure. His French soul brother, Gilles, with whom we stayed for a few days while in Seattle trying to line up sponsorships, toasted us with exaltation over dinner one night: "What you guys do is incredible and I am proud to know you." All that feedback was wind at my back urging me forward.

However, any opposition, no matter how small, created painful turbulence. And for me, although I tried to ignore it, it tossed around in my subconscious and proved to be a disruption that threatened to dog the expedition throughout its entirety. In the months leading up to our departure I became keenly aware that I was leveraging everything in my life: my skills, endurance, meager fortune, reputation and relationships. I hoped that by completing the expedition with Jean-Philippe and by producing critically acclaimed documentaries I would ensure my success, and that success would be my vindication.

Now that the expedition is complete, it is difficult for me to be objective when I think about the worth of our photos and stories. It's hard to assign a financial value to an image or word that cost not only money to produce, but blood, pain and time. And when presenting our material to people, I am always tempted to proselytize, to deluge them and try to make them truly feel and understand what we went through to bring it back. So, I make a conscious effort to prod viewers gently and only go deeper when asked. I don't want our message to become dogma; I want it to be an epiphany. And when people walk out after one of our slideshows, I can see it on their faces. That, for me, is vindication.

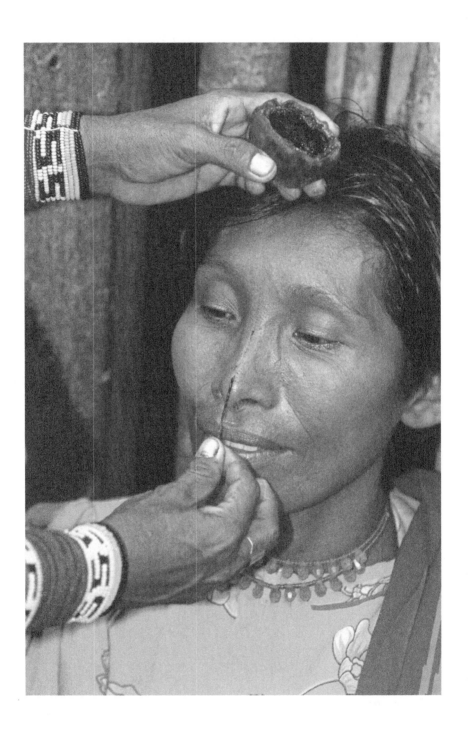

CHAPTER 8

NOMADS DON'T STOP

Jean-Philippe

REACHING PANAMA CITY brought about a mixture of joy, satisfaction and accomplishment, tempered by the same antagonistic feelings that had haunted us for days. While the journey had shaped me in significant ways, there had been no grand finale when we reached Panama. We weren't explorers reaching an unknown land. We already knew the city. We'd already met with all the country's Indigenous groups. There was no real finish line to cross or welcoming party to greet us because nobody knew when and where we'd end our kayaking in Panama, not even us. After three years of intensity and survival, in that final week of paddling, there was no genuine sense of adventure, no incredible encounters, no real physical challenge. Not even any real danger. Our last week of the big adventure was just an anticlimactic formality.

After two and a half years of preparation, three years of expedition, 3,000 miles of coastal paddling, hundreds of miles of jungle and dozens of villages visited in seven countries, CASKE2000 had reached its end. Through countless nights spent camping, twenty-four hours a day of feeling sticky wet during monsoons and a multitude of memorable encounters establishing cherished friendships that we would remember forever, we had finally done it. Together, Luke and I had paddled from Mexico to Panama and managed to document much of it online.

Upon reaching our final destination, we celebrated with our friend Eric in a good Panama City restaurant. A couple days later, Yumi flew from South America to celebrate once more. Through the following months, we toasted the success of our expedition every time we would meet with other friends and family. But why didn't I share Luke's deep satisfaction and sense of accomplishment?

I think there were a few reasons.

The first one is that the kayak expedition had been a greater success than I'd ever imagined. We had survived, which we knew from the start wasn't a certainty. We'd done what no other adventurers had done before. We'd pushed our physical and mental limits beyond anything we could have possibly envisioned. Plus, we had written materials to teach and inspire thousands of children and even more online visitors. We'd far overreached our original goals. But as the journey unfolded, so had my vision of what we could accomplish. Reaching Panama no longer seemed the final destination.

From 1999, in the midst of the expedition, our expanding vision had given rise to Native Planet, a globally active non-profit organization dedicated to building a bridge between traditional cultures and the rest of the world by inspiring "modern" people from the outside and helping Indigenous communities from the inside. With our Native Planet work, we had sensitized a few thousand people while offering positive exposure to the communities we'd met. But why did my soul crave more?

Although Luke and I had forged an incredibly close friendship during the expedition, after more than three years of rich, intense and sometimes dramatic experiences, we understood that our life goals were different. I was hoping we'd do more expeditions together, something Luke also wanted on a smaller scale. But more than anything, he wanted to return to the States to live a more settled lifestyle. I could not envision myself doing so: I was a nomad at heart, and I still had an unquenchable thirst for adventure.

Although I longed for a few weeks of rest in a comfortable bed after a warm shower, I couldn't imagine settling into sedentary living for long. While still in Panama, less than a couple of days after we'd packed our kayaks, I was already missing the feeling of not knowing where and how we'd spend the next night.

Now that our mission was complete, where was I to go? As a world citizen, I'd look to the horizon and imagine all the cultures out there from which to learn, all the friends waiting to be met. I felt neither French nor American—but solely human—as my life had been enriched by my immersion in each new culture I'd visited. I needed to continue my journey to learn more about the beauty and cultural diversity of our planet and to bring it alive for others.

I wished that I could continue this with Luke, but I understood it would soon be time for us to take different paths. We were still celebrating together in Panama, yet I was already missing my friend. Although Luke was committed to continuing our work together on Native Planet and to co-writing our book, I knew that our lifestyles would no longer be the same. And that filled me with great sadness. Yes, CASKE2000 was over, and this phase of our lives had come to an end, too.

It took us a couple of weeks to finish our daily journals, update our website and ship our gear back to the States. Luke then returned to live with his parents in Vermont, where his fiancée joined him.

For me, the journey that had begun with a few paddle strokes into the past and an eye to the future would continue on to new continents: perhaps the mode of travel and partners would change, but the path would remain filled with the adventures, joys and challenges of forging new links to old cultures.

CHAPTER 9
TYING THE KNOT

Jean-Philippe

OF ALL THE cultures in which I've lived, Japan seemed the least likely to produce another adventure-traveler with a passion for Indigenous people like me, but sometime during a short paddling break, in a small Indigenous village in the remote mountains of Guatemala, I met one like-minded soul. Yumi had already spent time living in Guatemala and was ready to move on. As Luke and I continued paddling, she went on to explore all of Latin America on her own. During our short expedition breaks, she assisted Luke and me with our last documentaries of Panama and Guatemala, and together we ran the Amazon down from Peru to Brazil.

After shipping all my gear to Eddie's place in San Diego, Yumi and I flew there to spend a few days with him. It was her first visit to the States, and after Eddie gave us a pleasant tour of his neighborhood, we rented a car to visit the Grand Canyon and other Southwestern highlights. By this time, Yumi had lived in Latin America for more than four years and longed to visit her family. In November 2001, we left all the gear stored at Eddie's home and flew to Japan, where I proposed.

All her family wanted to attend our wedding and convinced us to celebrate our marriage in Japan before moving back to the States. After seeking counsel from an astrologer, as it is customary in Japan, the best date was determined to be December 16th, Yumi's birthday. Her family went out of their way to organize the most amazing wedding. Following tradition, Yumi wore a splendid white kimono, and I looked like a real-life samurai warrior in mine. It was a beautiful and very emotional ceremony for the entire family and for my dad, who had flown from France on very short notice.

I never imagined that the expedition I'd started to plan while living in Japan would take me back to Japan to get married to a woman I'd met in a small Guatemala Indigenous village. Life surprises us, sometimes in the best of ways.

Our honeymoon had to wait though, as Luke and I still had much work to do. Yumi and I stayed in Japan throughout January 2002, with the plan to reunite with Luke in the U.S. to expand our work with Native Planet and to write the book about our adventures.

CHAPTER 10

ON A DIFFERENT PATH

Jean-Philippe

WITH THE EXPEDITION finished, I wanted to move back to Seattle, where I'd lived until the early 1990s while working at Microsoft. Apart from Luke, most of my closest friends lived there, and it was the place I called home in the U.S.

However, in February 2002, upon Luke's request, Yumi and I agreed to move near his hometown in Vermont, where he now lived with his fiancée. There were still online journals to finish; hundreds of slides that needed editing and scanning; two websites that needed new galleries and documentaries; and, last but not least, a book to write. It made sense for us to live near each other in order to tackle all these tasks.

The book's aim was to highlight our adventures and to bring readers to the Native Planet website, where they would learn more about the Indigenous cultures we were documenting online. Our hopes were to expand global awareness about the various cultural, humanitarian, and self-empowerment projects we were planning. It would be key to our fundraising efforts and the anchor that would connect all our goals.

The challenges were many. I had not known a word of English until age twenty, and although I had mastered speech fluency through my four years as a Microsoft International Program Manager in the States, unlike Luke, apart from my photography being featured in publications during the expedition, I had only published one article in a survival magazine. Writing a book together would mean relying on Luke to do some heavy lifting. Assembling the manuscript from our daily journals and stories, he corrected my grammar while I focused on the content editing.

While Luke took on the role of the book's narrator and focused most of his time on fundraising, I stepped up as the driving force of the Native Planet projects, including all Indigenous-related matters, public speaking and the tech-based tasks such as web design, programming and search engine optimization.

Reunited with Luke, we returned to the CASKE2000 pre-launch conditions: looking for funds and publishing options during the day, and computing through both day and night. It soon became clear that we were better paired as expedition partners than as work associates. We enjoyed each other's company on the cross-country ski track, in the pool, at the gym, and in restaurants—anywhere but in our temporary office—but after three years of paddling together, these last few thousand strokes (this time on computer keyboards) were proving the most difficult of all.

By 2002, I had poured more than $70,000 of my own money into CASKE2000 and the launch of Native Planet, and both Luke and I were in the red. The future of our NGO was uncertain, and we hoped that the success of this book would help give it a much-needed financial boost. In spite of putting in long hours and striving whole-heartedly toward our goals, we were struggling to secure fundraising, especially when venture capitalists slowed their investments in light of the September 11th terrorist events.

Aside from fundraising issues, we were facing challenges with the manuscript as well. We had created more than 1,500 pages of written material during the expedition, and progress on the book was proving slow. But good things were happening. Our website had grown from a small collection of pages with a few dozen fans to a well-curated and informative site that attracted more than 50,000 visitors per month. Through the website, we were able to give positive exposure to many of the communities we had documented in Central America, and we received many supportive emails from those who had been inspired to try new adventures from the information they had received through Native Planet. The villages of Blue Creek in Belize and Embera Drua in Panama thanked us for the donations and visits they received from our readers, and these productive results fueled our desire to grow Native Planet in hopes of providing further support to Indigenous villages.

After three months, money was running out. Luke told me he was planning to switch his focus to finding a job and would only play a small role in Native Planet once the book was finished. I understood his financial decision, but I was disheartened. He'd been my partner for more than three years, and navigating the next steps without him didn't feel right.

We put our focus on finishing the book, and within six months we had a completed manuscript. Luke began pitching the book to literary agents and publishers. With the scale of our adventure, the important message it sent and the increasingly solid engagement on the Native Planet website, we felt confident that publishers would want to offer our story to readers who craved adventurous tales like those penned by author Jon Krakauer. Unfortunately, they didn't share our enthusiasm.

Shortly after receiving our first few rejection letters, Luke officially quit Native Planet, withdrew from the book and shifted his focus on finding a new job. While I certainly understood his shift, I was now solely responsible for producing future projects, documenting them online, raising funds, and managing the NGO. Despite the challenges though, I wasn't ready to give up.

CHAPTER 11

THE FUTURE OF NATIVE PLANET

Jean-Philippe

IN THE EARLY summer of 2002, Yumi and I moved to Seattle, where she took a job in the educational field. I was happy to be back among friends in a city I loved, and together we focused on launching a new phase of life on the west coast.

Through the years I had come to appreciate both the comforts of modernity and the more traditional lifestyles of Indigenous peoples. I felt like I spent most of my time caught between these worlds, thinking about what each represents and wondering how I could best help bridge the gap of understanding between the two. In an age when the world seemed to be shrinking quickly, with cultures assimilating more than ever, I felt inspired to continue documenting the irreplaceable knowledge that Indigenous people have been passing down for generations.

I had more ideas than could fit inside a computer. I also had valuable photos and stories already on the website. I knew I could use these tools to make a difference. But I couldn't do it alone. If I stood any chance of making Native Planet a viable source for promoting diverse cultures and encouraging the protection of our valuable resources, I'd need two things: a team of volunteers and some funds.

As so many non-profit organizations quickly discover, volunteers proved unreliable, often abandoning their commitments before training was complete. After a few months of frustrations with volunteers who had committed for a full year and yet quit within weeks or even days, Liz came on board. It was clear from the start that she was different. She wasn't another kid out of college, bursting with enthusiasm only to vanish as soon as real work was involved. Liz also couldn't have been more different from me. Twenty-five years my elder, she was an academic and sedentary introvert who loved her horses and cats more than any human being. She rarely left her Oregon farm, her only neighbor lived a ten-minute drive from her, and the Internet was her only steady connection to the outside world. Everything opposed us, and we would have probably never met were it not for our shared interest in Indigenous people and their culture and wisdom.

Liz immediately replaced Luke as the vice-president of Native Planet. Suffering from a terminal disease, she received a small medical pension that allowed her to survive without a job, and with true passion she dedicated all her time to the NGO. An English major, Liz loved the power of words and possessed an incredible mastery of grammar. She shaped my stories into a clean format for the page, and she also helped to balance my extrovert energy. Liz and I were completely connected, and together we made a magical pair.

With Liz at the helm, we were able to ignite dozens of volunteers and produce the largest and most complete database of traditional Indigenous communities from all over the world. Soon, hundreds of schools and universities began linking to our website as a reliable academic resource.

Although we had a ninety percent attrition from volunteers in their first months, a few remained. Most were researchers for the database. We also had a half-dozen grant writers and people who concentrated on fundraising. Liz managed them all while I focused on the tech issues and leading the ongoing and new projects with Indigenous communities, particularly the Mentawai, whom I'd last lived with on the island of

Siberut for four months in 1993. I did all this as a full-time volunteer for many years while my wife, Yumi, supported us financially.

Before the end of 2002, I was able to return to Siberut, not only as a visiting clan member of the Mentawai but also as a project leader, helping them with essential health and cultural preservation programs. After ten years, it was a very powerful and emotional reunion.

In 2003, Luke granted me the rights to all his writings and said I could do whatever I wanted with them. He'd moved on to focus on his career and no longer had the time to worry about publishing. Liz suggested we had enough material for three or four books, but no reader would choose a *War and Peace*–sized saga from unknown authors. She loved some of the journal entries and stories, and she agreed to help prune and polish, insisting that I cut the manuscript in half if I had any hopes of publishing. Luke and I had already spent months trimming it from the original 1,500 pages of material to what we felt was a reasonable 700-page manuscript. How could I possibly cut it in half?

Liz argued that since I had served as the driving force behind both CASKE2000 and Native Planet, I should let my words guide the flow of the book. She believed we should keep Luke's best stories, but that I should write both the introduction and conclusion and provide the primary narrative voice throughout the manuscript.

Liz and I had already spent six months writing documentary materials for the website together, and like Luke, she had confidence in my storytelling. I had none. Especially since English was not my native tongue. I felt confident giving presentations in front of an audience, but I had never studied writing and the task seemed daunting. I wasn't sure this was where I wanted to focus my time, but rewriting the introduction, the conclusion, and trimming the book to a maximum of 400 pages were Liz's conditions in exchange for help, and I hated to abandon the book project after all the work we'd poured into it so far. That's how I started the long, slow process of revising the entire manuscript from scratch—a grueling but tremendously rewarding learning process.

By 2003, we had made progress with the website and projects, but we still needed to secure significant funding. After spending long days and nights working at the computer, my only sanity was when I was on my bike. As a competitive cyclist, I founded a cycling club and began to rely on that stress outlet to keep me moving forward with the Native Planet work.

From 2004 on, Yumi and I organized a couple of annual cycling fundraising events, with the help of key club members. For each race we gathered a few hundred participants, with most contributing a fee to enter the events. However, because administrative costs were eating up most of these funds, we still needed to find another solution for funding Native Planet.

To keep Native Planet alive, I founded Around the World in a Viewfinder, a travel stock-photo agency through which I sold my original photographs. Among my first customers were the National Geographic Society and the United Nations. Along with other magazines and book publishers, they motivated me to embrace travel photography as our main source of income.

This new opportunity allowed Yumi and me to travel together for months at a time, producing intercontinental photography documentaries. Our photos sold through nine photo agencies around the world, and their proceeds helped us to make a living and continue financing Native Planet projects. Indonesia, China, India, Vietnam, Laos, Cambodia, Japan—each photoshoot focused on one or two countries. We loved these travel times together and enjoyed the many cultures we learned from and all the people we met. Through it all, we continued to work with the Mentawai people.

Between 2002 and 2005, I returned numerous times to Siberut to ensure the success of the Mentawai projects. I kept hoping that one day we'd find a few institutions to back us, but Native Planet never raised enough money to fund all the projects we'd hoped to launch. We mostly survived from the income of travel photography, and against all financial advice, we'd begun to dip into my 401k.

Over the years, Yumi and I self-financed the reconstruction of the Mentawai clan's large communal house. This allowed the entire clan to move out of the government village, where they had been forbidden to practice any of their tribal rituals. We were honored to help them return to live on their ancestral land in a pristine part of the jungle. In addition to funding the construction project, we financed malaria control and other hygiene and education projects for the Mentawai children.

By this time, my adoptive brother, Teureun, had become a well-respected shaman and leader. More than just a bridge between the spiritual and terrestrial world, he was now also a bridge between traditional Mentawai culture and the modern world. Teureun and the Mentawai had an important message to share, and it was upon their request that I returned to Siberut in June 2006 to help them reach a broad international audience.

This time, a French TV team accompanied me. They were traveling to produce a unique documentary titled *Rendez-vous en Terre Inconnue*, with the participation of renowned journalist Frederic Lopez and French celebrity and humanitarian Patrick Timsit. Lopez said that in all his travels he had neither felt so welcome nor witnessed such egalitarianism, and Timsit noted that every aspect of the Mentawai lifestyle was a true model of success for our modern societies. The documentary received record viewing on the French national TV and was highly acclaimed.

These were probably my biggest accomplishments with Native Planet. After years of hard work and personal sacrifice, I felt proud to have shared the beauty and wisdom of the Mentawai culture and to have helped sensitize people about the importance of preserving it.

Nearly four years after Luke left Native Planet, I had finally written a worthy story that I believed publishers couldn't turn down. I'm forever grateful to Liz, for she taught me not to try to emulate Faulkner, or even Luke. She not only taught me much about grammar and patiently edited my never-ending rewrites, but she always found the right words to encourage me when I hit a dead end or had a block. At times she was also devastatingly blunt, slashing a piece I had spent hours or days to write. But she was the best teacher I ever had, and she helped me gain confidence with my writing. Although we only met twice, we were corresponding numerous times every day, and we had become best friends.

I spent the following year submitting my manuscript to publishers and agents. In 2006, after more than twenty rejections, and even more unanswered queries, it was time to focus on other things.

In 2007, big changes were also happening in the photo industry. Digital cameras slowly replaced the old slide equipment. Bill Gates created the Corbis Photo agency to compete against fast-growing Getty Images. The two largest photo companies quickly purchased most of the small agencies. Those who refused the mergers perished rapidly as prices dove ten- to twenty-fold. Only agencies with millions of images could survive. A couple of excellent small agencies I was selling photos through were purchased by Getty, others were pushed out of business. Magazines who'd been paying $1,500 for a double spread or cover suddenly offered less than $100 for the same image usage. I embraced digital photography for the amazing revolution it brought, but combined with global Internet sales these changes killed the documentary photography market.

The price collapse made our travel and documentary photography business no longer viable. I had no interest in switching to the more sustainable niches of commercial, fashion and wedding photography because what I loved most about photography was my communion with the people we met during our global travels. To capture their culture and lifestyle, to immortalize a moment that had been a magical encounter . . . that's what fueled my fire.

In 2007, as Yumi and I were still organizing cycling fundraisers, I designed and guided a bike tour for my American friends, introducing them to the Pyrenees. I ran this first tour at a loss, but cycling was another true passion and one I saw as a potentially profitable endeavor. I loved the challenging terrain, and I particularly loved my native mountains. I understood that this could be a way for us to organize cycling tours half the year while continuing to work on Native Planet projects the other half of the year. All early indicators suggested this new income stream would replace the loss of the travel photography business. So, the following year, I designed many new Pyrenees cycling tours. But then the subprime crisis took the United States by storm, and our first full tour season didn't meet the success I had hoped for.

At the same time, our volunteer pool was waning and Native Planet had dried up nearly all of my 401k. After years of pouring all our resources into this mission, we were broke; and without being able to pay for the notoriously expensive medical insurance in the States, we moved to France. With a solid footing in the mountains I loved, we pivoted our efforts to plan and design cycling tours of the Pyrenees with the highest standard of services. This meant that we had to put all Native Planet projects on pause, at least until we could secure financial sustainability.

Over the years, we rose up from the ashes and turned our cycling business into a reputable and profitable venture that allowed us to make a good living while doing something we loved. I enjoyed sharing my passions with others and contributing to the dreams people had to conquer the majestic French mountains. In time, we expanded our cycling tours to include all the major mountain ranges of France, Spain and Italy. And Yumi also rose to become an incredible cyclist, standing on the podium of every long-distance mountain road race she entered.

Making the cycling business into a success story required years of around-the-clock work and physical training, during which I wasn't able to dedicate any time to Native Planet.

During these first years in France, when we were struggling financially, my friend Liz passed away. She'd outlived her disease many years past what the doctors had predicted, and it was only after she was gone that I realized how dear she was to me and how much I owed her. Native Planet died with Liz. And with it, all my desires to revive it. I realized that I wasn't a businessman. I wasn't a fundraiser. And maybe I could never be.

I continued to maintain the Native Planet website until 2012 because it was filled with valuable information and provided an incredible database of Indigenous knowledge. The website still received thousands of visitors, and I wanted to offer access to that resource as long as possible.

By 2012, the Internet had changed so much that the Native Planet website required a complete overhaul, which would have meant months of intensive work. At that time, I made the painful decision to abandon it online. Since the CASKE2000 Expedition, Native Planet had accomplished all that we had originally set out to do, and much more. Even though I hadn't developed the NGO into a viable large-scale non-profit organization that would help make global changes for the long term, I'd learned a great deal from the experience. All those years when Yumi and I had worked directly in the field with Indigenous people and when Liz and I had developed this database and tried to turn it into a global NGO, I'd been growing at every turn and appreciated every moment.

Before wrapping up the Native Planet chapter, I want to express a few words on cultural tourism. Throughout the expedition, I praised the benefits of ecotourism. (The term *cultural tourism* wasn't yet in vogue in the late twentieth century.) In the early millennium, I genuinely thought it could be a key to cultural preservation.

Indigenous communities, even and particularly the most remote ones, aren't insulated from the world. It's not like we can build an invisible wall around them so they can continue their lives undisturbed. They are being displaced, their rainforest cleared, and new diseases from around the globe continue to ravage vulnerable communities. There is no escape from their inevitable interaction with the rest of the world. I always thought that it would be better for communities to interact with the world on their own terms rather than being imposed upon to change or adapt to a threatening outside influence.

I thought cultural tourism could be a good way to help empower these communities, preserve their culture, and for them to benefit from it. It certainly is better for a kid to become a cultural guide on his ancestral land than go live in a city slum because he's ashamed of his own culture and wants to live a modern life—often without any chance to ever thrive in a society that will always denigrate him.

Dedicating twelve years of my life to try to make a difference in helping indigenous communities with health, educational, and self-empowerment projects, and with documenting their lifestyle, I followed my heart, doing what I thought was good. I received much praise for my efforts but also a fair amount of harsh criticism. I'm open to constructive criticism but never understood the badgering from people who had never accomplished much, or never donated time nor money toward a cause.

It was easy for them to criticize, hiding behind their phone or computer screen, for they never put themselves in the spotlight. As Theodore Roosevelt wrote:

> *"The only man who never makes a mistake is the man who never does anything."*

I've made many mistakes and will continue to do so, and it's something I'm not ashamed of because I always followed my heart and gave everything I had to any cause I believed in. Jack London inspired me as a kid, so it's natural that I quote him here too (from an August 21, 1903, letter to Charles Warren Stoddard):

> *"I do not live for what the world thinks of me, but for what I think of myself."*

Really, the concept of cultural tourism made sense, and there are examples of very well-done projects. Over the years though, I witnessed more cultural tourism projects that had gone wrong. Corruption among local guides and government officials, along with outsiders only interested in financial rewards, seemed to be more frequent than real success stories.

It took many years for me to understand that the concept was excellent, but that its implementation could sometimes cause more harm than good, and that maybe I was naive and even wrong to believe that it was a solution that could be implemented by most communities.

I still believe that cultural ecotourism may be beneficial, but it's not always the best solution. I don't know what the best solution is. I guess it's like everything else. Love, respect, and understanding are what allows us to live in society as human beings. But love, respect, and understanding come from knowledge.

We can't appreciate another culture we know nothing about. We can't care for people we don't know exist. The most traditional indigenous communities are so remote from our daily world that most people will never be aware they have even existed.

Unknown indigenous people receive no help—they vanish as silently as they have lived.

If I hadn't succeeded in making Native Planet the NGO I envisioned it could become, at least I hoped that my photos, writing, and life could inspire people to understand, respect, and appreciate the beauty of cultural diversity, whether it is that of people living in the remotest jungles or that of your neighbor down the street. In the end, human beings are all the same. We want to love, be loved, be respected, and provide and care for our family and loved ones. In that respect, the most traditional people aren't any different from us. That's something I learned all along from the Mentawai and each community I met during the expedition and my years doing photographic documentaries.

Today, Yumi and I continue to live and work in the beautiful French Pyrenees. We share our passion for sports and the outdoors, and we aim to inspire people who long to explore the best mountain regions of France, Spain and Italy. We still travel across all continents. And I remain a nomad at heart, longing for wild expeditions, extreme endurance challenges, exotic adventures, cultural discoveries and wonderful encounters with people from all walks of life.

EPILOGUE

IT WAS ONLY in 2018, a full decade after returning to France and once our cycling tours were well established, that I felt compelled again to see this story published. Publishing it would be the final true achievement of all the sweat and tears Luke and I had put into the expedition. It would also be an homage to Liz for all her dedication to Native Planet and to this book. And it would be an acknowledgment to the Indigenous communities who welcomed us and to all the people we met along the way. After years of pushing this project to the back of my mind, I suddenly knew I had to publish it. With renewed passion, I rewrote the manuscript again, toiling every night for six months while hiding the project from my family. In the past I'd spent years talking about my book that never appeared in print. This time, I didn't want anybody to know until I could put a physical copy in their hands.

Revisiting my own story seventeen years after the expedition and twelve years after writing the last draft proved to be an emotional experience. More than ever, I was convinced that the lessons we'd learned on that journey would have more value if shared. Finally, nearly two decades after the end of CASKE2000, I held the first printed copy in

2019. The published book in my hand was the closure I'd been seeking for decades, bringing the experience full circle and delivering the finality I'd long needed.

I'm publishing this revised version twenty years after the end of the expedition, and it's important for me not to alter the feelings and thoughts I had then. I was in my early thirties when I embarked on this life journey, and it is these feelings, emotions, and thoughts that I kept as they were from my journals.

Today, I would likely write about this experience in a different light, and might have even done things differently, but one thing is certain: I wouldn't venture on such an epic and long challenge anymore, but I wanted it to be true and unaltered by the wisdom I may have gained over my recent years.

As I wove the story together and rewrote this ending, I looked back on the young man I was at that time, honoring him for the physical and mental limits he reached. Together, Luke and I often thought that kayaking a giant swell in a storm was like dancing to the rhythm of the ocean. When storms proved to be more than we could safely handle, we were Dancing with Death, and there were countless times we thought we wouldn't survive.

I will forever hold vivid memories of my near-drowning experience between Nicaragua and Costa Rica, when I was dragged underwater by monster breakers in the estuary of Rio San Juan. I remember how Luke fought for his life when surfing huge waves as he wasn't able to reach the sandbank on the mouth of the Rio Colorado. I recall dislocating my shoulder in giant surf. My body was stunned, and I almost drowned in less than a meter of water. Or when Luke fought his way out of the Osa Peninsula, capsizing in a place filled with bull sharks and salt-water crocodiles.

We flirted with death numerous times and not only in our kayaks. Many people believe that my shark attack in Belize was the most frightening experience I faced during those years. It wasn't. The shark attack was entirely my fault, and something I could have avoided. Maybe the most dangerous situations of all had been the bandits' attack in Nicaragua and our bouts with malaria. In Honduras, I thought Luke was going to die when I covered his malaria-ridden body with ice to control his fever, only to watch him lose his sight and then consciousness. It happened again when we reached the port of Bluefields, Nicaragua. I was pulling a zombie in a kayak, landing in the filthiest harbor we'd ever seen.

We had been Dancing with Death for three years, and there's no doubt I would have died if I had done this as a solo expedition. Luke and I saved each other's life more times than we could even mention in this book. Most people have never saved a life or had anyone save theirs. By sharing such soul-shaping experiences, we both became indebted to each other.

After reading segments of our early expeditions, some readers reacted to the conflict Luke and I had shared during the expedition, criticizing us for not being more enlightened by one another throughout this journey. Some friends even cautioned us to only write about the positive experiences, suggesting that we were heroes for what we had accomplished and that we should polish that hero image with a Hollywoodesque script and ending.

We both felt that only writing about the positive wouldn't reflect the true experiences we'd lived and shared. Luke and I had our differences. Our opposite personalities were both a gift and a curse. Yes, we often bickered; and yes, we occasionally had some fights. Who wouldn't argue through such an expedition? We'd pushed ourselves to the limits physically, mentally, spiritually and emotionally, and it was only natural to take that stress out on one another at times, no matter how much we loved each other.

Luke and I also had different goals from the beginning. We particularly felt our differences in the final few months, during the last dull stretch of paddling through Panama. We were physically tired and emotionally drained, and we may have lost patience with each other more often—something we understood to be normal in these circumstances.

I'm overdriven, while Luke is extraordinarily laid-back. Apart from the disproportionate dedication and amount of work we'd invested, it played out to be a beautiful balance for the success of the expedition.

Together, we'd lived the most physically and emotionally intense experiences of our lives. Married couples rarely spend half the time we spent together. We shared every moment of every day, all the joys and discoveries, all the pain and fear, twenty-four hours a day, day after day, for three years—not counting the two additional years spent planning and working on follow-up projects. We also shared the tiniest of tents, and we chose not to hide any part of our experiences from readers.

Those intense years allowed us to get to know each other like very few human beings ever do. We learned all of each other's strengths and weaknesses, and we learned to accept and appreciate them. Together, each day, we learned who we really were through our quarrels, our victories and by saving each other's lives.

Still today, we have the greatest respect for each other and we've built a friendship that transcends anything imaginable. We've felt like brothers since we first met in Japan, and the expedition brought our brotherhood to another dimension.

For over a decade now, Luke and I have been living on separate continents; and in spite of life taking us in different directions, we've remained, and will forever remain, brothers. A bond forged through our strongest and weakest moments, before and during one of the greatest adventures—the adventure of a lifetime.

Twenty years after the expedition, Luke and I met with our families in Spain and he told me, "It's nice to be with someone who knows me better than anybody else on Earth. Even our wives will never know us like we know each other." Yes, Luke and I are bound for life. And after twenty years, now in our fifties, we still look at the future and dream of the next adventure we'll share.

When people hear of our expedition, they often ask me what I learned about myself during that time. They're eager to be told of a single highlight that changed my life, a pivotal revelation that made it all worth it.

The truth is much more complex than that.

My enlightenment started when I was four years old, inspired by Jacques Cousteau. I fought my way through a difficult childhood and early manhood, joined the French Special Forces and worked in mountain rescue. At twenty, I moved to the U.S. with no money and without speaking a word of English. After landing a high-tech job many people would have longed for, I ended up living the American Dream, but that was never *my* dream. My dream had never been centered around wealth or career. I longed for adventure, and I wasn't ready to surrender my real dreams for one that didn't feel right to me. My first twenty-six years had already been filled with more drama, danger and hardship than one could imagine. A real-life story so epic it would read like a novel. And I wanted more.

So, at age twenty-six, I quit my high-paying corporate job to fulfill my childhood dreams of world adventures, expeditions and jungle living with Indigenous peoples. My life with the Mentawai was one of the greatest revealing experiences and paths to enlightenment a young man could have, and for that I will always be grateful.

CASKE2000 was the logical continuation of a life already filled with magical encounters. Throughout the expedition, we were enriched by millions of smiles. Smiles from the youngest Latino kids to the oldest Indigenous elders. All the small moments we couldn't possibly write about, for they were not adrenaline-packed action scenes; yet each moment of hospitality, communication, shared laughter and international love and understanding was as important as all of the more physically exciting moments highlighted in this book.

This expedition helped us better understand who we are as human beings and to better appreciate the beauty of nature. Indeed, there was no single enlightening moment. My epiphany was and is the miracle of everyday life. It's all the people I meet, the experiences we share and how far I can push my own limits to accomplish what at first seems impossible.

Living a full life every day is my greatest epiphany.

Looking back, I'm glad we were able to inspire people, bring some help to various communities and help the Mentawai in concrete ways. And although my desire to help the Indigenous community at large was genuine, even if I only achieved a fraction of what I would have liked to, I now realize that I may also have failed with Native Planet because I'd made the project too much about me. At that time in my life, the grand vision of what I wanted to accomplish was driven by my ego.

Now I realize that I've received much more from that experience than I could ever give back. I wanted to and genuinely tried to help Indigenous peoples, but as it turns out, they are the ones who helped me.

My greatest forte proved to be my biggest weakness. I've always been driven by an incredible will and an equally fiery ego. My formidable drive was the fruit of an insatiable desire to be recognized for my accomplishments. Something that was anchored inside my deepest being from early childhood, as I was denied any form of recognition from my parents. My drive to accomplish things was a blind quest to appease the ego I had cultivated through childhood—a necessary evil to survive my first twenty years. In some ways, even until I was in my thirties, during the expedition, I was still that insecure kid who felt like he had to pick a street fight just to feel alive.

I can't say I've toned down my ego to nothing, not even to the level I've wished for, but through the wisdom of the Mentawai, the expedition with Luke, our work with Native Planet, the love I've received from my wife and friends, and the support of so many people around the world, I've learned to better understand my ego and to soften it. They've all helped me in fighting my demons and in thriving to be a better human being.

It took fifty years for me to understand that I didn't realize my life dreams. Instead, I've lived my dream life because the people I met offered it to me. Luke did it by joining me on this expedition and becoming my brother. The Mentawai people did it by adopting me as one of their own and making me a part of the clan. All the Indigenous people I met did it by sharing with me parts of their life and teaching me to give more than I take. Yumi and all my friends did it by encouraging me and supporting me when I doubted myself. Thanks to all these people, I've lived my dreams. Impossible dreams that parents, society and endless adversity repeatedly tried to destroy in my early years. When I look back at the weak, abused, frightened child I once was, I'm proud of that little boy. He's faced a path of tough events, emotional moments and hard lessons that could fill an entire shelf of books. And he's still here, stronger, braver and wiser from having survived it all.

Inspired by all these people, I am now able to reflect on how far I've traveled on the path of life. And with any luck, I'll have another fifty years to keep traveling, learning and sharing the beauties and wonders of this world.

Jacques Cousteau, my greatest inspiration as a child, wrote: "When one man, for whatever reason, has the opportunity to lead an extraordinary life, he has no right to keep it to himself."

I finally understand that, like Jacques Cousteau, I too could use my experiences to inspire other people to live a better life. I visualized the kid I was, following every Cousteau expedition and reading about the world's greatest explorers, and after finishing *Dancing with Death*, I felt compelled to write more—certain there were other souls out there (young and old) longing to make the most of this journey. I'd learned a great deal while penning this book, and I've now put all that experience into authoring *I, Tarzan: Against All Odds*, a story that dives deep into my earlier years, exploring the childhood and young adult experiences that led me to embark on CASKE2000 in the first place.

As Jacques Cousteau suggested, I hope that *Dancing with Death* and *I, Tarzan* will inspire you to believe in your dreams, reach for your goals, embrace cultural and social diversity, learn from all people and find joy in everyday life.

Jean-Philippe and Martina, Siberut 1993

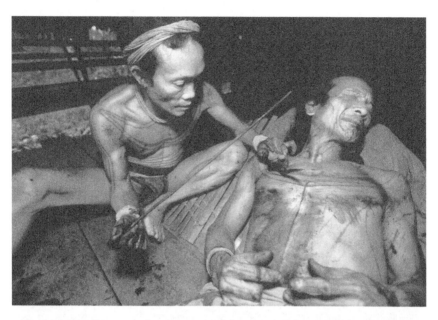

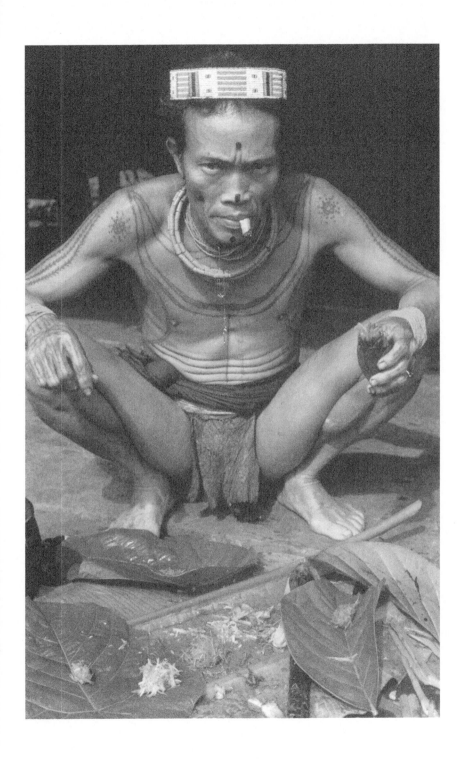

Jean-Philippe and Teureun, Siberut 2005

Jean-Philippe and Teureun, Siberut 2008

AUTHOR'S NOTES

I'd like to invite you to view photos illustrating *Dancing with Death* and many other adventures at www.jpsoule.com, where you can join my mailing list and tell me about your own adventures.

The fascinating Mentawai and their culture and lifestyle are the subject of my future travel memoir *My Life with the Mentawai* and its companion coffee-table photo book, *Mentawai: Healers and Jungle Dwellers*, illustrated with twenty years of original photographic work, profound cultural insights, and epic tales of my experience living with them as an adopted clan member. Before the book publication, I invite you to peruse a sample of these photos at: www.jpsoule.com.

If you've enjoyed this story, your honest review can help me continue to write new books. I can't express how grateful I would be if you followed this link to leave a review:

https://geni.us/reviewdancingprint

Thank you,
Jean-Philippe

MORE BOOKS BY THE AUTHOR

I, Tarzan: Against All Odds

From the award-winning author of *Dancing with Death* comes an epic memoir that will delight fans of *The Glass Castle*, *Wild*, and *Unbroken*, as well as *Educated* and *Can't Hurt Me*. The thrilling *I, Tarzan* is a deep journey into the author's innermost secrets that will have you questioning your own self-understanding and life goals.

From the back cover:

By age thirteen, I was an alcoholic—anything to numb myself from my world of emotional abuse.

That wasn't who I wanted to be.

My dreams of adventure and exploration were so far out of reach. I'd never become Tarzan. I'd never become Jacques Cousteau.

But I was wrong.

This is my story . . .

Celebrity endorsements for *I, Tarzan*:

> *"Jean-Philippe's life is like the ultimate ultra-marathon, where hope, perseverance, and grit determine the outcome. I, Tarzan: Against All Odds is his story of redemption and remembrance that inspires and energizes the reader to believe that far-reaching dreams can come true. Jean-Philippe proves that your attitude determines your altitude — and high he climbs in this must-read memoir!"*
>
> — Dean Karnazes, ultramarathoner and *NY Times* best-selling author

> *"Marco Polo meets Tom Sawyer, I, Tarzan is the roller-coaster chronicle of Jean-Philippe Soule's early life of challenge and adventure. . . . This is a story of success, wrought in the fires of despair and wrapped up in good old-fashioned storytelling."*
>
> — Ian Adamson, author and world's most celebrated adventure racer

> *"I, Tarzan tears at the heartstrings and brings to remembrance every unfulfilled childhood dream. Jean-Philippe's story lends us the courage to see them as future possibilities. His grit and determination inspire and electrify. An emotional journey of enduring accomplishment. I highly recommend it."*
>
> — C. J. Anaya, *USA Today* bestselling and multi-award-winning author of *The Healer* series

Jean-Philippe is currently working on new books. Find out more about Jean-Philippe and all his books and view his award-winning photos at www.jpsoule.com.

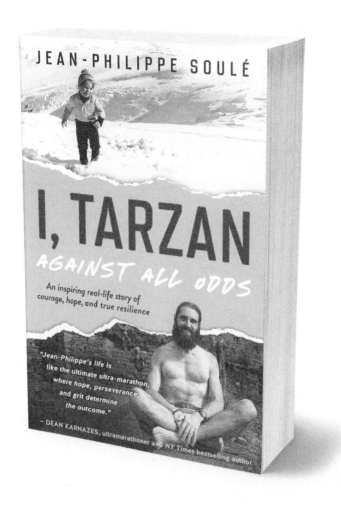

"*Any reader who believes that early adversity sets a life's course in stone should read* I, Tarzan: Against All Odds.*"*

— D. Donovan, Senior Reviewer, *Midwest Book Reviews*

ACKNOWLEDGMENTS

We cannot begin to list all the people who have helped us during CASKE2000 and the creation of Native Planet, but I'd like to give special thanks:

To my wife, Yumi Soulé, who has stood by me and supported me during the years it has taken to finish this book and launch Native Planet, and who has personally founded much of the NGO initial projects;

To my late close friend and Native Planet VP Liz Farr, for her dedication and support with all the projects and the earlier version of this manuscript;

To my close friend Dominique Blachon for the hundreds of hours he spent editing the entire book;

To the many who read and gave editorial support;

To Randal Irwin for his years of technical support with all our website needs;

To Eddie Dinkins for all his logistical support and assistance;

To Richard A. James and his family for their extensive logistical support in Honduras;

To John "Caveman" Gray, Dave Williams and Ed Gillet for teaching us the necessary kayaking skills; and

To the Mentawai people, who inspired the mission of this expedition and the creation of Native Planet.

I would also like to extend my gratitude to all the people we met in every country and to all the Native Planet volunteers for their invaluable support. Without all of you, our dream could not have come true.

#

Thanks to the generous corporations who sponsored CASKE2000: REI, Lowepro, Pelican Products, Lightning Paddles, Fujifilm, The Japan Group, HIBA & Voicenet, Garmin, Five Ten, ClifBar, Princeton, TDK, TeleAdapt, Gerber Blades, Boulter of Earth, Lighthouse Diving Center, Kyocera, JBL, Darazone, Seaward Kayaks, Feathercraft.

Printed in Great Britain
by Amazon